The Baby Decision

The Baby Decision

How to Make the Most Important
Choice of Your Life

MERLE BOMBARDIERI

❦

Rawson, Wade Publishers, Inc.
New York

Library of Congress Cataloging in Publication Data

Bombardieri, Merle.
   The baby decision.

   Includes bibliographies and index.
   1. Parenthood. I. Title.
HQ755.8.B65   308.8'7   80-51246
ISBN 0-89256-138-6
0-89256-175-0 (pbk.)

Published simultaneously in Canada by McClelland and Stewart, Ltd
Manufactured in the United States of America
Composition by American–Stratford Graphic Services, Inc.,
Brattleboro, Vermont
Printed and bound by R. R. Donnelley & Sons Co.,
Crawfordsville, Indiana

Designed by Jacques Chazaud
First Edition

To Rocco

ACKNOWLEDGMENTS

So many people have contributed to this book that it is impossible to thank everyone personally. I especially want to express my appreciation to the individuals and couples who shared so much of themselves during workshops or interviews.

Thanks to all the people whose enthusiasm and expertise added so much to the book:

To the psychotherapists who trained me: Elsie Herman, Nancy Leffert, Teresa Boles Reinhardt, and Ron Reneau.

To Elizabeth Bunce-Nichols and the Nashville YWCA for helping the project get started.

To the following people for sharing their professional knowledge: psychoanalysts Jean Baker Miller and Carol Nadelson; psychologist Glenn Larson; COPE workshop facilitators Ginny DeLuca and Randy Wolfson; gynecologist Kenneth Blotner; Miriam Ruben of the Association for Voluntary Sterilization; and Preterm staff members Pat Lurie, Mag Miller, Maxine Ravech, and Billie Rosoff.

To Nina Finkelstein, Sherrye Henry, Erica Jong, and Letty Cottin Pogrebin for their insights on feminism and motherhood.

A special thank you to author and television commentator Betty Rollin, whose explanation of her decision was both inspired and inspiring. This book is also easier to read thanks to Ms. Rollin's no-nonsense approach to writing. Imagining her reading over my shoulder and circling every bit of jargon has helped me behave myself at the typewriter.

To the National Alliance for Optional Parenthood (NAOP),

especially Gail McKirdy of the National Resource Center, for helping me track down all kinds of information.

To the staffs of the Boston Public Library—Copley Reference Library and Roslindale Branch; of the Divinity, Psychology, Social Relations and Widener Libraries of Harvard University; and to Irene Laursen and Debbie Smith of the Wellesley College Science Library.

To the following people for reading all or part of the manuscript: Rocco Bombardieri, Steve Cohn, Carol Conner, Judy Eron, William Farago, David Holzman, Glenn Larson, Sadie and Sol Malkoff, Marianne Perrone, Teresa Boles Reinhardt, and Martha and Steven Richmond.

To Judith Appelbaum and Nancy Evans for their skills and support, first in *How to Get Happily Published,* and later through correspondence.

To Ginger Downing, who typed the manuscript, for her speed, patience, flexibility, and sense of humor.

To the women who provided loving care to my daughters while I wrote: Kathy King and Catherine Zirpollo in the early stages; high school students Dorothy Staffier, Jeannie and Joanne Varano on occasional weekends. A very special thank you to Alice Staffier, who took care of my children during most of my working hours. Without her intense dedication, this book would have taken twice as long to write.

To the following people for their enthusiastic support, which included resisting the temptation to say, "You've got to be crazy to write your first book the same year you have your second baby!" It was crazy, but it was also possible, thanks to Sandy and Tom Anderson, the members of the Arlington Street Church, John Baeder, Barbara Berger, Steve and Edie Cohn, Carol Conner, Emily Dunn, Zelda Fischer, Mimi Goss, Kathy Hearne, Susan Jordan, Marianne and Fred Perrone, Arthur and Betsy Purcell, Caryl Rivers, Beth Rotondo, Susan Schein, Barbara Sheedy, Barbara Sher, and Claire Willis.

To Judy Eron, for serving as a model of a woman who balances beautifully her two vocations: writing and psychotherapy.

To Glenn Larson, who helped me understand the meaning of self-actualization. The growth orientation of this book owes much to him.

To Marianne Perrone for her loving encouragement, and for her artistic and conceptual fireworks which never failed to make my own imagination skyrocket.

To Rawson, Wade editors Eleanor Rawson and Sharon Morgan:

To Eleanor for her expertise and interest.

To Sharon for her dedication and skill. Thanks to Sharon, this is a stronger book.

To my agent Anita Diamant, for her support and commitment.

To my parents, Sadie and Sol Malkoff for their enthusiasm, and to Sadie for her editorial suggestions.

To my daughters, Marcella and Vanessa, for giving me firsthand knowledge of motherhood, contributing to the realism of the book, and also providing comic relief when the going got rough.

To my husband, Rocco, for believing in this book from start to finish and for making the enormous sacrifices it required. Without his loving support, *The Baby Decision* could not have been written.

CONTENTS

The only right is what is after my constitution; the only wrong is what is against it.
—RALPH WALDO EMERSON

Freedom is the will to be responsible to ourselves.
—FRIEDRICH NIETZSCHE

Step One

Defining
the Problem

❧ 1 ❧

The Great Cradle Debate

Laura and Michael Rose have everything they could possibly want—or have they?

She's thirty-two, a successful painter. He's thirty-five, an exuberant philosophy professor. After eight years of marriage, Laura and Michael enjoy each other more than ever. They seem to have the perfect balance of independence and relatedness. Apart she does yoga; he plays guitar. Together they meditate, jog, and give gourmet dinner parties. They ski in Vermont and snorkel in the Bahamas. What more could they possibly want?

Possibly, they want a baby. But they don't know. And the question is driving them crazy.

"Why can't we decide?" asks Michael. "Are we neurotic? Selfish? Immature? Why don't we just chuck Laura's pills and let nature take its course? Maybe things were better in the old days when contraceptives weren't around. Sometimes I almost wish an 'accident' would take us off the hook."

"To make matters worse," says Laura, "we're not even consistent in our conflict. It isn't as if one of us wants a baby and the other doesn't. One minute I'll say to Michael, 'I'm just chicken. Let's throw away the pills,' and he'll say, 'But what about your work? Will you still be able to paint?' A few minutes later, Michael will say, 'I'm nuts about kids. I want to be a father.' Then I ask, 'But what about our relationship?' "

Michael wonders, "Will life still be exciting if the closest we get to Vermont is our pancake syrup? We think of our best friends, who love being parents and who still practice law together. Then we think of my brother and his wife, who have a sick infant and a spoiled toddler. My sister-in-law wishes she'd never quit her executive job. One child-free friend sends us quotes about how children wreck your life. We've read books and articles about this decision, but we still don't know what to do."

Does this story strike a familiar chord? Are you and your spouse, like Laura and Michael, caught up in an endless cycle of conflicting emotions and doubts? Do you spend too much time discussing and worrying about the issue without ever reaching any firm conclusions? If so, take heart. The baby decision need not drive you crazy or drive you and your spouse apart. The question that tugs at you like a lead weight is actually a golden opportunity for you and your spouse to grow as individuals and as a couple; to deepen your marital relationship; to *choose* the kind of life that will bring you both the most happiness. In fact, if you dig deeply enough, you'll find buried treasure at your feet. But you aren't likely to come across this bonanza unless someone offers you a treasure map.

The Baby Decision is such a map. It will not only help you make a decision that's right for you but also show you how to use that decision as a springboard to greater fulfillment. It will guide you, step by step, through the five stages of uncharted, sometimes rocky, territory to a decision you can live with happily ever after.

By now, you may be thinking, But I've read other books and articles on the subject and I *still* can't make up my mind. In most cases, couples are long on talk because they're short on information. The available literature on the subject has focused primarily on weighing the pros and cons of parenting or measuring an individual's potential skills as a parent. Although these issues are useful and necessary, they add up to only two pieces of a larger puzzle. And because they overemphasize logic to the detriment of emotion, they're often less than help-ful. This book, however, is much more comprehensive because it will fill in these five, important missing pieces:

1. *How to discover secret resources for decision-making—feelings about children and life goals.* Exercises designed especially for this book use fantasy, visual imagery, and other techniques to stimulate new insights.

2. *How to make allies of emotion and logic.* Often mistaken for enemies, emotion and logic form an amiable partnership in the best of all possible decisions. *The Baby Decision* offers steps to a rational choice based on emotional awareness.

3. *How to use the new emotional awareness as a guidepost to growth.* This book offers many examples of how couples have grown from their decisions. It shows you how to reap similar benefits from your decision.

4. *How to focus on potential happiness.* I help you ask yourself, "Which choice offers me (and us) the most satisfaction?" I examine the ways that each life-style both helps and hinders personal and marital fulfillment.

5. *How to overcome a dangerous blind spot.* The "children are heaven" illusion has been replaced, in the swing of a pendulum, by a "children are hell" illusion. But who can base a wise decision on a foolish distortion? *The Baby Decision* splashes a bucket of cold reality over the new soap-opera fantasy. It also challenges other illusions that prevent good decision-making.

Once you've learned how to tap into the *right* information, those seemingly fruitless discussions will yield a surprising number of insights. You'll know how to direct your conversations to extract the kind of knowledge necessary for a decision.

SAFETY OR GROWTH—IT'S YOUR CHOICE

The word "decide" comes from a Latin root meaning "to cut away from." Thus, decision-making, by its very nature, involves loss; we have to give up one or more options while at the same time grasping another. When we decide to have a child, we cut ourselves off from the freedom and other satisfactions of child-free living. Similarly, the decision to remain child-free means that we must give up the intimacy and joys of parenting. By *not* deciding, we hold onto the illusion that we can have it both ways—that we don't have to give up anything. Nor do we have to face the risk of discovering that we've made the wrong decision. But we pay a price when we try to hang onto this illusion—in emotional turmoil and feelings of frustration and ambivalence. And in many instances, that price is too high. Our fears notwithstanding, when we face the issues of loss and risk squarely, we force ourselves to come to terms with our ambivalence and, in the process, we grow.

The late humanistic psychologist Abraham Maslow distinguished between two kinds of motivation—growth motivation and deficiency motivation. When a person is motivated by deficiency or safety needs, he or she acts out of a desire to decrease anxiety. Any kind of change seems too risky, and therefore frightening, to undertake. On the other hand, when a person is motivated by growth needs, his or her actions reflect a desire for greater fulfillment. The risks seem less important than the possibility of improving one's life.

This distinction between growth and safety needs applies equally well to the decision-making process in general, and to the baby decision in particular. There are, in fact, six possible baby decisions, three of which are growth decisions and three of which are safety decisions.

The three growth decisions are:

1. The decision to become a parent.
2. The decision to remain child-free.
3. The decision to postpone the decision, but with definite goals for the postponement period and a target date for re-evaluation.

Why are these "growth decisions"? Because when you make them you:

- Take responsibility for yourself.
- Take a risk.
- Make a commitment.
- Learn something about yourself.
- Have an opportunity to use all four of the above actions to develop and grow.

The three safety decisions are:

1. The nondecision to have a baby (also known as the "nonaccidental accident"). After perhaps five years of marriage with no previous "accidents," a couple struggling with the baby decision suddenly have an "accident." It may be unconscious (such as forgetting to take the pill), or conscious ("Let's not bother to put more jelly in with the diaphragm"); it may be a joint accident or the result of one spouse's actions. However it happens, the result of such a nondecision (besides the baby) is that the couple are taken off the hook. They declare themselves victims and avoid having to answer to anybody—including themselves—for their "decision."

2. The nondecision to remain child-free. In this situation, a couple tell themselves and others that they don't know whether they want children. Maybe later on, they say. So they simply drift without ever making a conscious commitment to the child-free life-style. And, in the process, they don't have to admit their desire to remain child-free, or deal with disapproval from others or their own fear of regrets.

3. The nondecision to agonize. This is the antithesis of the growth decision to postpone. In the latter case, a couple postpone the decision for specified reasons and a finite period of time, in order to meet specified goals. However, in this type of nondecision, a couple set no goals; rather, they circle the issue frantically, full of doubt and confusion. Although they claim they would love nothing better than a resolution, they actually get a payoff—in the form of unhealthy satisfaction generated by their painful soul-searching.

Although all three of the safety decisions appear to be emo-

tionally cheaper in the short run, they are more costly in the long run. Nondecision-makers are bound to feel like victims rather than masters of their own fate. While they may avoid the momentary agony of making difficult choices, they are actually condemning themselves to chronic pain. By clinging to a safety decision, they miss an opportunity to take stock and use what they learn about themselves. In fact, safety decisions really are danger decisions because they are detrimental to development. If you make a nondecision, you won't have to deal with your pain directly, but you'll never really get rid of it, either.

In direct contrast, the three growth decisions offer you the opportunity of getting to know yourself and all your strengths and weaknesses. You may not like everything you find, but if you know what's there, at least you can make the best of it. And with the help of this book you'll be able to make one of these three growth decisions—if you're willing to take the risks involved.

Hard as this decision may seem, it is undoubtedly one of the most important you'll make in your life. And it should not be made lightly, by default, or by blind adherence to custom. In fact, you're extremely lucky to be able to make a real decision about childbearing, although in the midst of grappling with the issue you may feel less than fortunate. Twenty years ago, however, the kind of questions you're asking yourself were all but unthinkable. Men and women married and had children without ever making a conscious decision. It was, after all, the natural order of life, what their parents, grandparents, and great-grandparents had done. And many discovered, too late, that parenting was not as easy, natural, or rewarding as they had expected.

Recently, on a Nashville talk show, I was asked whether it was a sign of sickness in our society that couples like Laura and Michael were questioning whether or not to have children. "Absolutely not," I replied. "It's very healthy for couples to decide carefully, rather than simply having children because 'that's what people do.' "

Certainly, not everyone is suited, by temperament, circumstance, or desire, to become a parent. And when couples have children without considering the issue carefully, they may find themselves trapped in a situation they did not anticipate and may not want. The result is a great deal of unhappiness for the parents, the child, and for society. The child, sensing that he or she was unwanted, may become a troubled, unhappy adult, burdening society in some way. And the parents, because of their own frustrations and resentment, may be unable to lead productive or fulfilling lives. It has always been assumed that society benefits from the birth of a child. But surely two happy, productive child-free persons can contribute more than two unwilling parents with one unwanted child.

John Stuart Mill said: "He who does anything because it is the custom makes no choice." Choice is the foundation of happiness and mental health. When we make a *conscious* decision about parenthood we can, if we so choose, embrace parenting wholeheartedly and joyfully, fully aware of all its responsibilities and ramifications. Similarly, if we *choose* to remain child-free, we can enjoy rich, productive lives without guilt or self-doubt. Only if we consider the child-free life-style a valid option can we be certain that a parenthood decision really is a decision.

Whether you are in the midst of agonizing indecision right now, or anticipating the issue in the future, it is vitally important to realize that *the decision-making process is both healthy and necessary,* and that *there is no universal right decision.* Whether you ultimately choose to become a parent or remain child-free depends entirely on the unique qualities of your personality and your marriage.

THE DECISION-MAKER'S BILL OF RIGHTS

You are entitled to:

- Make the decision that is right for you and your spouse.
- Take into consideration your needs, values, goals, and personality before making a decision.
- Base your decision on your potential happiness rather than a sense of obligation.
- Take time if you need it before making the decision.
- Be an active partner in choice rather than a passive victim of your spouse's bulldozing.
- Make the decision that is right for you even if others disapprove.
- Put a stop to others' attempts to shame or intimidate you into making either choice.
- Be your own judge of your reasons for choosing your lifestyle: to be child-free without being accused of selfishness, immaturity, or neurosis; to be a parent without being accused of selfishness, immaturity, or neurosis.
- Be a mother even if you're a feminist.
- Be a parent without being married.
- Change your mind under certain circumstances: You originally planned to have a child but now realize you don't want one; you once made a commitment to child-free living but now want to have a child.

HOW TO USE THIS BOOK

Even if you think you've already made your decision, do all five steps. If you don't, you'll never know whether your first decision really was your best decision. The process won't sway you—unless your decision was built on shoddy foundations. In fact, even if you're confident that your decision is the right one, following the steps will give you a clearer understanding of your choice and how you can make the most of it.

Similarly, if you and your spouse are in conflict over the decision, you may be tempted to go straight to the "Tug-of-War" chapter (Chapter 8). Please don't. Only if you both carefully examine your own needs and wishes will you be able to separate valid areas of conflict from those that are windmills best left alone.

The inward journey you're about to embark on will be facilitated by a number of exercises. Please study the following guidelines before beginning any of them.

Put yourself into the exercises. Bear in mind that there are no right or wrong answers. They do not test your parenting skills or your mental health. Nor will you score them. They are included solely to help you in the same way that ancient Greeks consulted the Delphic oracle. Existential psychologist Rollo May describes the oracle's work in this way:

> The sayings of the shrine, like dreams, were not to be received passively; the recipients had to live themselves into the message. . . . The counsels of Delphi were not advice in the strictest sense, but rather were stimulants to look inward, to consult their own intuition and wisdom.

So try to *live yourself* into these exercises. If you do, you'll return from your journey with a decision you can live with.

Let yourself go. Don't be afraid to be honest with yourself. You can't stand to hear a baby cry? You can still be a parent if you want to; you can get used to tears and learn to cope with your tension. Do you have a weakness for freckle-faced three-year-olds? You can still be child-free if you want to. You can "borrow" a freckled sprite on Saturday afternoons. What you cannot do, however, is exercise freedom of choice *unless* you consider both options thoroughly. Conflicting feelings don't mean you're hopelessly confused. They mean you're human.

Consider yourself. Do the exercises *alone* first. Later, you can compare notes with your spouse, but there is no point in forcing a joint compromise before you've each had a chance to make an individual appraisal. You might end up with a decision that doesn't please either of you.

Read each exercise all the way through before starting it. Then, close your eyes to help yourself turn inward.

By now, I hope you're ready and eager to begin. Remember, hard as the decision-making process may seem at times, the rewards you'll reap are enormous. And you may even discover that the journey is more fun than you'd ever imagined it could be. You're going to learn a lot about yourself, your spouse, and your relationship and, at the end of the process, you'll have the satisfaction of knowing you've made one of the most important decisions of your life.

A Bird's-Eye View

Even with a map in hand, exploring new territory can be frightening, especially since no map can illustrate every rock and pebble in your path. Therefore, it's helpful to scout out the territory first to get a bird's-eye view of what's to come. And that's what this chapter is all about.

The questions in this chapter are those most frequently asked by couples when they first consider the baby question. And I've discovered that unless these issues are covered immediately, couples are too tense or worried to venture out. It is hard to make a decision if you don't know what to expect or how to proceed. This chapter, therefore, provides some basic and necessary guidelines: who should make the decision; how to get rid of a sense of panic; why a wrong decision won't ruin your life. After all, forewarned is forearmed. So use this chapter to gain some necessary perspective before delving into the decision-making process itself.

Is This a Woman's Decision?

"I don't want Walter to come to your workshop," Martha, a feminist client says to me. "I don't think I could discuss my feelings honestly."

"Sooner or later every *woman* faces the question of whether or not to have a baby" (emphasis mine).

　　　　　　　　　　　　　　　　　—*Publisher's Weekly*

This is not a book for *women*. It's a book for people, male and female, who are contemplating parenthood. Women who feel it's their right to make the baby decision alone cling to the traditional assumption that mothering is more important than fathering—that women are necessarily more involved in parenting. And these same women are often resentful when their husbands don't assume their fair share of the child-care burdens. Yet, how can anyone be expected to participate cheerfully in a decision in which he had no part? This attitude actually invites a man to maintain minimal involvement at best. The wife who offers her husband only a mouse's nibble of decision-making may wind up with the lion's share of the work! "If she decided without me, she can change diapers without me," her husband may conclude. Only if a woman is living alone and considering single parenthood is she entitled to make this decision alone.

Even if a woman chooses to remain child-free and her husband goes along with her wish, a decision made independently still buys into the sexist notion that children "belong" to the female world in the same way that work "belongs" to the male world. In the past, when motherhood was a woman's primary source of identity and prestige, this assumption had some validity. Because most women stayed at home to care for their children while men worked, they *were* more involved in parenting. But now that women are meeting these needs through their careers, they are becoming more aware of the difficulties of mothering, especially if they want to combine motherhood with a career. And the common belief that all women want babies and talk their men into having them is slowly being dispelled. In my experience, in fact, when there is a disagreement, more often than not, the woman wants to remain child-free. While men are pushing for children, women are taking a shrewd look before they leap.

As we struggle to define marriage and family life more equitably, we must begin to let go of such arbitrary and artificial notions about roles and the division of labor within a family. Certainly, it is in a child's best interests to have two fully involved and responsible parents—two parents who participated equally in the decision to bear that child. So if you're a married person considering parenthood, you had better also consider the wishes of the person to whom you're married.

As the pendulum swings the other way, we can expect to see some women pressured into a pregnancy by their husbands. However, a unilateral decision by either spouse does not bode well for the future of a couple's relationship or their ability to be good parents. In fact, it may indicate that the balance of power is out of whack in some way. If either your spouse or you are inclined to make this decision alone, you would be wise to consider other aspects of your relationship. Do either or both of you continue to subscribe to traditional roles? Does sexism, in one form or another, permeate other aspects of your life together? If you want your spouse to take on an equal share of the parenting responsibilities or embrace the child-free life-style as joyfully as you do, then it may be time to rethink some of your attitudes. Do you communicate effectively on other issues? Do you consider each other's needs and wishes in other areas of your relationship? A quick review of these questions may turn up information that can be invaluable *before* you begin to make this vital decision.

How to Get Your Hand Off the Panic Button

Because this issue often generates so much anxiety and tension, many couples decide prematurely simply because a decision—any decision—relieves their sense of panic. But hasty decisions usually are not good decisions. The calmer you are, the better the chance that you will make the right choice. So force yourself to relax. The following guidelines may help.

1. Ask yourself why you're in such a hurry to decide. Taking the time to understand the reasons will slow you down. Here are some possibilities:

- You can't stand not knowing what will happen in the future. Or you can't stand your own inner conflict. In either case, you feel impelled to decide quickly to end your discomfort.
- You have been misled to believe that women must give birth by age thirty-five.
- With encouragement from the media, you tend to see your problems melodramatically.
- Because panic is a communicable disease, you have become infected with your friends' sense of urgency.
- You're leaning toward the child-free choice and you're afraid that if you don't decide now, you'll change your mind and be sorry later.
- You're leaning toward parenthood and you're afraid you'll have trouble getting pregnant. Even though you are not yet sure that a baby is the best choice, you won't relax until you get a positive slip from a lab.
- You know what you want. Your spouse is wavering. If a decision is made immediately, you think that he or she will agree to your choice. But if you wait, you're afraid your spouse will change his or her mind.

2. Jump off the "must-decide-today" treadmill. All these pressures stem from your feelings, not from the facts. It's not a biological time bomb but an emotional time bomb that is threatening to explode within you. Keep reminding yourself that you *don't have to decide now*. Even if you're thirty-five or thirty-six now, you can still have a baby in several years' time.

3. Give yourself permission to be anxious. "Anxiety tells you that something important is about to happen," says Dr.

Glenn Larson, a clinical psychologist in private practice in Nashville, Tennessee. Of course you are anxious. You are making one of the most important decisions of your life. Anxiety indicates that you're taking the process seriously. In fact, moderate anxiety can be useful because it encourages you to work on the decision. It's only extreme anxiety that gets in the way, and you can reduce your anxiety level by following all the guidelines in this chapter.

4. Turn your anxiety into excitement. Excitement is the flip side of anxiety. To change your anxiety into excitement, pay attention to it. Isn't there a part of you that is stirred by the baby question? A part of you that is eager to learn more about yourself and to put these bits of knowledge to work for you? A part that's curious to know what the final decision will be? Try to imagine how good you will feel when you have made the decision. Visualize the joy of having a child or the joy of building a life free of children.

5. Tell yourself it's okay to be uncertain. In the name of no-nonsense decisiveness, a lot of nonsense is committed. You will have to live with the consequences of your decision for the rest of your life, so it's reasonable to take as much time as you need to consider the consequences carefully. It's fine to make a quick decision about buying a car or taking a job. You can always decide just as quickly to sell or quit, but a baby decision can't be reversed. The amount of attention given a decision should be in proportion to the seriousness of its results.

6. Try to keep your sense of humor. A light touch is always helpful when you're facing a heavy question.

Ed and Mary, who collect antique glass, joke about whether they'll be buying old lady's bottles or new baby's bottles next year.

Cathy and Steve laugh at the idea of themselves rocking by the fire in their sixties still debating whether they want a child.

Can you see a humorous side to your situation? If you can, use it for comic relief when the going gets tough.

7. Tell yourself that you will make a good decision. Shut

off that raspy voice that says you are going to blow this decision and regret it for the rest of your life. If you follow the five steps in this book, you will be relatively satisfied with your choice. Rest assured that your intelligence, imagination, and courage will enable you to choose well.

8. Don't compare yourself to other couples who made their decision more quickly. They may have decided prematurely or they may have made a compromise decision. And even if they claim to have decided in a matter of days or even on one special night, if it's a good decision, they probably worked on it for weeks, months, or years. Perhaps they didn't have constant discussions, but in the backs of their minds, they probably had been considering the question for a long time.

DECIDING UNDER EMERGENCY CIRCUMSTANCES

In some cases, of course, a sense of panic is generated by more than emotional pressure. There are two circumstances in which a decision *is* a genuine emergency:

1. You have an unplanned pregnancy and you're considering an abortion.

2. You have an illness or a condition that is worsening and your doctor tells you that with each month you wait, (a) your chance of conceiving lessens; (b) the probability of having surgery that would preclude a future pregnancy increases; (c) the likelihood of serious complications arising from a pregnancy increases.

If either of these situations applies to you, try to keep your wits about you. You'll make a wiser decision if you're calm. Even though you have to decide quickly, *you don't have to decide in the next five minutes.* Don't give in to the temptation to pick a decision, any decision, just to end the crisis. You will have to live with that decision for the rest of your life.

You may not have several months, but you certainly do have a few days or maybe even a week or two to think it over.

You (and your husband) may want to take time off from work to allow yourself time and energy for decision-making. As a preliminary step, fight off feelings of panic by meditating, deep breathing, running, swimming—whatever exercise or activity helps you relax. Then, take the time to do all the exercises in this book. They will help you uncover your real feelings about children, and they'll also help you consider the compatibility of children with your other life goals and values.

In the case of a medical problem:

- Ask your physician to give you a full explanation of your condition, its meaning in terms of your childbearing potential, and the risks involved in delaying motherhood.
- Read lay literature on your condition.
- Consult another doctor. Does he or she consider the decision an emergency, or is it possible that your own doctor has overreacted? Are there other possibilities, contingencies, or treatments your doctor didn't mention that may make the decision to delay parenthood more feasible?

Finally, whether your problem is an unplanned pregnancy or a medical condition, consider counseling to help you make your decision. If the first person you consult is not understanding and unbiased, seek out another counselor. See Chapter 10 for suggestions on finding help.

How Long Is Too Long?

For some couples, however, haste isn't the problem. They've given themselves plenty of time to make a decision, but the right choice continues to elude them. If this problem sounds familiar, you may be wondering if it's possible to spend too much time making a decision. The only way to answer this question is to ask yourself another question: How do I feel? Do you feel that you are using the time constructively, growing and moving slowly but surely toward resolution? Can you and your spouse tell each other, "Even if we don't know or don't agree, at least we're sharing something important with each other." If your feelings are generally positive, stop worrying about time. You're certainly not wasting it. Quality of time, not quantity, is what counts in decision-making.

However, if you feel that you're caught on a treadmill, getting angrier and more frustrated, heading slowly but surely toward the nondecision to agonize, then you're probably not using the time wisely or well. But there are solutions, and you'll find advice about seeking professional help in Chapter 10.

WILL THE WRONG DECISION RUIN YOUR LIFE?

Finally, we come to the question uppermost in many couples' minds, yet a question that often remains unasked because they're afraid of the answer. In fact, the anxiety produced by this issue is often a major obstacle to the decision-making process. But the answer, with rare exceptions, is an unequivocal no. How can I say this? There are two reasons:

1. How you make your decision and how you work it into your life generally indicates more about your future happiness than the decision itself. Let's look at two couples:

Don and Cindy got married because they liked telling each other their troubles. Cindy cries on Don's shoulder about the discrimination she runs up against as the only woman executive at her bank. Don dumps at Cindy's feet all his wrath at the school board for banning his lessons on controversial fiction in his high school classroom.

Everyone needs support. But if you are to be happy, you have to move beyond support in order to find solutions. Don and Cindy, it seems, would rather wallow in the mud than make mud pies. They discuss the baby decision seven nights a week. It invades every aspect of their lives. It has crawled into bed during lovemaking. It has toddled around the restaurant table when they tried to celebrate Cindy's birthday. Now, instead of wailing about the unfairness of their co-workers, they wail about the unfairness of decision-making when the outcome is unknown. They view parenthood as an albatross pulling them down; child-freedom as a free-floating emptiness. If they decide to remain child-free, they will spend an endless amount of time reassuring themselves that they have made the right decision. Then, when Cindy is past childbearing age, they will engage in long breast-beating sessions, bemoaning their supposed selfishness, envying their friends with children, and cursing the antiparenthood proponents who "misled" them. If, on the other hand, they decide to have a child, they will spend nine months worrying about birth defects and their parenting abilities. Will they be relieved when they have a healthy baby and find they can cope with it? No! They will simply find something else to worry about.

No matter what Don and Cindy do, they will not enjoy themselves. The power tools of decision-making will slip right through their fingers. They are so threatened by the question "What do you want?" that they cannot permit themselves the awareness necessary to answer it. Each will try to second-guess the other, coming up with the decision s/he thinks the spouse would want. For Don and Cindy this opportunity to grow merely becomes an opportunity to be unhappy in a new way.

Ruth and Phil are just as uncertain about children but the question excites them. They are having trouble deciding because they anticipate deep pleasure from either choice. They're enjoying the opportunity to learn about themselves and each other in new ways. The closeness they feel as they discuss this intimate issue is enhancing an already good relationship. If Ruth and Phil remain child-free, they will enjoy nurturing the preschoolers in the day care center they own and run. Ruth will have plenty of time to study yoga and ballet. Phil will be able to climb mountains and grow vegetables to his heart's content. If they become parents, they will be thrilled with the thousands of ways children unfold. For a while, they'll have to gear down on work and outside interests, but they will do so willingly, aware that all too soon their child(ren) will be off playing with peers, allowing them to gear up again.

These stories are, of course, exaggerated to emphasize the differences between these couples and their approach to life. As you work on this decision, you will find that you have some of Don and Cindy's destructive fear and some of Ruth and Phil's constructive openness. But you can use Ruth and Phil as an inspiration, realizing that a positive approach to life is crucial to happiness regardless of the decision you make.

2. The very fact that a decision is necessary indicates that both choices have some appeal for you. Therefore, regardless of the decision you make, a part of you will enjoy the outcome. And you can use the opposing part to help you steer clear of possible pitfalls.

Actually, no matter which decision you make, you'll probably have some regrets. But that isn't so terrible. Coming to accept the imperfection of life and making the best of it is a wonderful way to grow. It will help you cope with other issues that you're ambivalent about, too.

By now, you may be wondering why this decision requires so much care, especially since a wrong choice won't ruin your life. Even though you can probably live a good life with or without children, it's definitely to your advantage to make an informed, thoughtful decision. Here's why:

- It offers the opportunity to learn about yourself and your spouse. In order to answer the baby question successfully you must also answer two other questions: "Who am I?" and "Who are we?" And these answers can help you solve other problems.
- It forces you to take responsibility for yourself. By making a conscious decision, you take control of your life.

Even though you risk failure or regret, you earn self-respect. You cannot help but take pride in assuming responsibility for yourself rather than drifting passively, waiting for an accident or your spouse's preferences to take you off the hook.

- It increases the probability that you will enjoy and make the most of your choice. Working on a conscious choice forces you to consider carefully the possibilities offered by each life-style. This gives you a head start in taking advantage of your ultimate choice.

- It provides an opportunity to build skills for future decision-making of all kinds. Technological advances and changing societal mores mean that in the future we'll have to make even more decisions about our lives. Making a good baby decision is good practice for other important decisions.

ANXIETY-PROOF YOURSELF

If you still feel some anxiety about the baby question, try this fantasy exercise before you delve any further into the decision-making process. Ask yourself: What is the worst thing that could happen in this situation? Pinpointing potential problems or disasters and recognizing your ability to cope with them is an effective way to reduce anxiety. And you can put the mental energy previously wasted worrying to more productive use.

1. Imagine that you and your spouse decide to remain child-free. What's the worst thing that could result from this decision? How would you feel about it? What would you do about it?

Susan and Mark tried this exercise. For both, the ultimate horror was the idea of facing a lonely old age full of sadness that they wouldn't live on through their grandchildren. They imagined they would be angry about their choice, but realized they could find comfort in their artistic, athletic, and professional activities and in loving relationships with their nieces and nephews.

2. Imagine you decide to have a child. What's the worst thing that could happen? Try to picture it, as well as your reaction to it. What would you do about it?

In this situation, Susan imagined that her career was ruined, filling her with anger and resentment at the baby and at Mark. Mark imagined that he and Susan wouldn't have any time together any more and that their relationship would go downhill. They agreed that Susan's fantasy wouldn't happen because Mark would take equal responsibility for the baby if they had one. To deal with Mark's fears, they talked about ways in which their friends had managed to maintain good relationships while their children were young.

These fantasies helped Mark and Susan feel a lot freer to explore both possibilities. Now, you try them.

Step Two

Overcoming Obstacles

∾§ 3 §∾

Secret Doors

How well do you know yourself? Are you in touch with the myriad emotions, beliefs, and attitudes that shape your personality, your life, and your choices?

All of us have an inner core—a reservoir of private dreams and goals—that has been building and changing since we were small children. But all too often, this inner core gets locked away in a back closet in our minds, in part because our hectic lives don't permit leisurely introspection. Moreover, many of us bury these thoughts and emotions because they are painful to acknowledge. We might be forced, if we took a good look at them, to accept unpleasant truths, or to give up cherished dreams.

But how can we know what to choose if we don't even know who we are? Because our inner core changes as our lives change, we have to be able to separate old dreams from new ones, letting go of the parts of ourselves that are outdated or unrealistic. Otherwise, these unacknowledged emotions can hopelessly tangle our thinking process.

For example, Joan, a woman in her late twenties, couldn't seem to make a commitment to the child-free life-style and she couldn't understand why. She didn't really like children and she loved her work. She wanted, more than anything else, the time and freedom to pursue her career. On the surface, there seemed little need for her to make a decision, yet she felt conflicted in some way. With the help of self-exploration exercises, the reason came to light. Joan had been raised in the constricting 1950s, when mothering was not an elective but a required course. When she was growing up, a girl's upbringing was synonymous with preparation for motherhood. Joan had learned her lesson so well that despite her total distaste for parenting and her husband's comfort with remaining child-free she could never quite bring herself to make a decision. Through the exercises she came to understand that this long-held image of exalted motherhood was holding her back. Even though she wanted to remain child-free a part of her hung on to the old belief that she would some day find happiness in motherhood. As soon as she held this flawed childhood belief up to the light, she was able to recognize its uselessness and throw it away.

In this chapter, you're going to take the same journey that Joan did. You're going to open the door to your mind's hidden library. The exercises will help you draw out forgotten or hidden feelings and attitudes about yourself, your marriage, children, parenthood, and your life goals. You will be able to discard old emotions that may be blocking you, and track down and study the feelings that will shape your decision. With this knowledge you can begin to lay the foundation for a satisfying life—a life that encompasses the goals and dreams that are still a part of your inner core.

INNER CONFLICT

A. CHAIR DIALOGUE

When you're torn between conflicting desires—wanting a child and wanting to remain child-free—a conversation between these two parts of you can help you better understand the nature of your conflict. You may even discover that one desire is much stronger than the other.

To begin, place two chairs face to face and label one "I want to be a parent" and the other "I want to be child-free." Sit in the parent chair and tell the child-free part of you why you want a baby. Then switch to the child-free chair and tell the parent chair why you don't want one. Continue this dialogue, changing chairs whenever each side is ready to talk. To ensure total honesty, do this exercise alone, otherwise you might feel too inhibited to express all your feelings—both the positive *and* the negative.

Here is an example of one young woman's dialogue. (PC = parent chair; CC = child-free chair)

PC: I think I would miss something if I never had a child.

CC: But I don't think I'm willing to make the sacrifices I'd have to make for a child.

PC: But wouldn't it be worth it for the pleasure of seeing a child grow and change?

CC: It looks to me like 90% pain for 10% pleasure. I don't think it's worth it.

PC: Aren't you just being selfish?

CC: No! I'm looking out for what's best for all of us. My career as a systems analyst doesn't leave much time for a child. I don't want to give up my work, and I don't want to be overburdened, either. I don't think I would enjoy being a mother. I think Tom [her husband] and the baby would suffer as much as I would.

This woman was surprised at the strength of her child-free side. And as she continued the dialogue, her parent side became even weaker. Finally, in desperation, the parent side asked:

PC: I thought you and I were about even. How could you be so much stronger without my knowing it?

CC: Because you haven't been listening to me. Every time I tell you I don't want to be a mother, you ignore me.

PC: Why would I ignore you?

CC: Because Tom and my parents are dying for a baby. Because all my friends tell me what a good mother I'll make and I'm flattered. You pay more attention to what others want than to what I want.

Now, try the dialogue yourself. What happened?

- Was one side stronger than the other?
- Were you surprised by some of the feelings you expressed?
- Did you have different bodily sensations in the different chairs?
- Did you sound or feel different in the different chairs?
- Did you have trouble speaking for both sides of yourself? If so, this does not necessarily mean you have no conflict. It may mean you're afraid to face the other side.

Try this exercise more than once. You may discover that different sides are stronger on different days. You may also find this exercise easier after you've done the others. Coming back to it periodically is somewhat like using a compass—it helps chart your direction and keep you on course.

Moreover, this technique, which is a part of Gestalt therapy, can be used in many other ways. For example:

- You can play yourself in one chair and take someone else's part—your husband, your mother, a friend—in the other chair.
- You can play two other people and leave yourself out entirely. For instance, put your mother in one chair and your father in the other, and have them discuss their hopes for grandchildren.

These two variations can help you understand why family and friends may be pressuring you. And that understanding may improve your ability to cope with the pressures.

- You can bring in another "actor." For instance, if you and your spouse disagree on the issue, play each other's role to see if you're both really listening to each other's arguments. Or, invite your spouse to observe you playing both roles, then ask him or her if the portrayal was accurate. Then, reverse the process, watching and giving feedback to your spouse.

Further application of this technique to the baby decision will be described throughout the book.

LOOKING BACK

The next exercise is designed to help you recall some of the attitudes about children and parenthood that you formed in your childhood, many of which may be affecting and shaping your current dilemma. So sit back, close your eyes and send yourself back into time.

A. YUCKY BABIES

Did you ever see the *Saturday Evening Post* cover by Norman Rockwell called "Home Duty"? It shows a boy wearing a suit and a frown as he pushes his baby sister in her carriage. Two friends in baseball uniforms smirk at him as they go off to play.

Do you remember thinking babies were "yucky"? Why did you develop that attitude? Were you repulsed by smelly diapers, spit-ups, and tears?

- Did you have younger siblings? How did you and your parents respond to the pregnancy and birth? How did the sibling change your life? If you had more than one younger sibling, did you respond differently to each one? How did these experiences color your view of children?
- If you are a male, were you ever called "sissy" for playing with a baby or a doll? How did you react?
- Perhaps you baby-sat for younger siblings or for other

children. Was it fun or frustrating? Did you like children more or less as a result?
- Do you still feel that babies are yucky? If not, what made you change your mind?
- In fantasy, return to your childhood home. Play with the dolls or stuffed animals you find there. Try to re-create the fantasies you had of growing up and becoming a parent.

If you or your parents still have some of these baby toys, in some attic or closet, try to get your hands on them. Actually holding them may call forth some powerful memories and feelings.

The boy in the Rockwell picture bitterly resents watching his sister while his friends play ball. Would you feel the same way if your friends went jogging while you stayed home? Would certain child-free friends scorn you the way the ball-players scorned him? Are you afraid of such a reaction? How might you handle it?

Body Talk

A. Metamorphosis

Women, close your eyes and picture yourself:
- During early, middle, and late pregnancy
- During childbirth
- Nursing (possibly)

Do these changes attract or repel you?

- Does fear of childbirth pain affect your desire to get pregnant?
- Are you held back by thoughts of getting fat and staying fat?

- Do you think pregnancy would make you feel more sexy, less sexy, or the same? How do you think your husband would react to your changed body? Do you worry about whether he'd still be attracted to you?

Men, read the exercises above. Try to imagine these changes in your wife.

- How do you think you would react? Would you find her more attractive, less attractive, or the same? How do you think she would feel about her new body?

How do both of you picture your sex life during pregnancy and postpartum?

- Do you feel positive about some body changes and negative about others? Why?
- Many people who have a lot of sexual experience still have a little puritanical embarrassment about pregnancy. Do you? Pregnant women sometimes complain, "Now the whole world knows I have a sex life. My private life has gone public." Would you feel this way, too?

B. SUCKLING

Women, imagine yourself nursing a baby.

- How does it feel?
- Is it erotic, as some women describe it?
- How does your husband react? How do you react to his reaction? Now open your eyes and consider: Would you breastfeed if you had a baby? Why or why not?

Men, picture your wife nursing your baby. You're sitting beside them. How do you feel? Proud, turned on, jealous? Does she seem to be enjoying nursing? Why or why not?

Now open your eyes and consider: Would you want your wife to nurse if you had a child?

C. MADONNA

It's not always easy for a woman to separate a desire for the experience of pregnancy and birth from a desire for the experience of parenting for its own sake. These different wishes are like intertwined threads of two hard-to-distinguish colors. The exercises below will help you separate the two strands.

Imagine that you could get pregnant, give birth, and nurse a baby, and receive lots of love, attention, and praise for doing so. Then, when you stopped nursing at say, six months, you could just hand the child over to someone else to raise for eighteen years. You could see the child when you wanted to, but would be under no obligation. Sound good?

Rita, like so many other women I've encountered, was in love with the idea of motherhood but would have hated the reality. A lover of novelty, she craved the pregnancy process but not the product. She certainly didn't want to spend two decades being responsible for that product.

In contrast, although Sonya found this fantasy somewhat appealing, especially since she planned to keep her full-time engineering job even if she became a mother, she realized that she really did want the responsibility and the contact that parenthood requires. This fantasy helped her see that she was as interested in child-rearing as she was in childbearing.

If you *are* attracted to this fantasy, consider some of these possible reasons:

- Are you still using a child's view of motherhood as your frame of reference? Are you still, in some sense, a little girl who wants to cuddle with a baby doll that doesn't make any demands on you?
- Do you crave the attention lavished on pregnant women and young mothers? If you could receive that same attention in more convenient ways would you be less inclined to have a baby? If that's true, perhaps you need to work

on feeling better about yourself so you won't have to depend on others for attention.

Of course, most pregnant women take pleasure and pride in carrying the baby and giving birth as well as taking care of it. But if pregnancy is all that appeals to you about motherhood, then motherhood is not for you. Pregnancy is temporary but motherhood is permanent. Eighteen years of heavy-duty parenting is a high price to pay for nine months of pregnancy!

Visions of Baby

The exercises below will help you tune into your feelings about children.

A. Rock-a-bye

Imagine you are picking up a baby. Sit down and rock it. Hold it in your arms, in your lap, and over your shoulder. Sing to it; talk to it. Watch it smile and coo. Suddenly, it starts to cry. How do you comfort it?

Now try this with a real baby. How does the reality differ from the fantasy? Which did you enjoy more?

B. Dream Child

Describe your ideal child:

- Boy or girl?
- Quiet or rambunctious?
- Introvert or extrovert?
- Intellectual or athletic?
- What interests and talents would you want her/him to have?
- Have you fantasized about a career for the child?

How would you feel if you didn't get your ideal child? Would you try to make her/him into your dream child, or would you be able to accept the child on its own terms?

C. PHOTO ALBUM

When you ponder parenthood, do you consider every stage from infancy to young adulthood? Do you exaggerate the joys while ignoring the problems and sorrows of parenthood, or vice versa?

To help you cover all the bases, consider these images:

- A wailing, red-faced newborn.
- A peacefully nursing three-month-old baby.
- A cranky, teething seven-month-old.
- A red-haired eight-month-old eating his first ice cream cone.
- A one-year-old grinning about the bowl of spaghetti she just poured over her head.
- A toddler taking his first steps and falling with an expression of surprise.
- A toddler in a supermarket rolling on the floor, kicking and screaming.
- A three-year-old dancing in the moonlight.
- A six-year-old reading her first book.
- A seven-year-old saying to her mother, "Why don't you stay home like my friends' mothers?"
- A nine-year-old boy serving you breakfast in bed.
- An eleven-year-old girl winning a blue ribbon for her exhibit at the science fair.
- A fourteen-year-old saying, "You can't make me!"
- A sixteen-year-old smoking marijuana in his bedroom.
- A teenage couple with their arms around each other.
- A seventeen-year-old girl asking you for birth-control pills.
- An eighteen-year-old saying, "At last I'm old enough to get out of this joint and be on my own."

- An eighteen-year-old writing to say that the first semester at the university is just great.

How well did you stay with these pictures? Did you find yourself wanting to skip over some? If you're leaning toward parenthood, you may have passed over the bad and focused on the good. If you're leaning toward nonparenthood you may have done just the opposite.

If you become a parent, are you really prepared to accept the bad moments? If you choose not to have children, have you really considered the pleasures you're giving up as well as the freedom you're keeping?

D. Monster

Picture a perfectly healthy newborn with a touch of jaundice. His eyes and skin are slightly yellow, and, like most newborns, he's covered all over with fuzzy hair. His head has been misshapen by the trip through the birth canal.

Now consider the following description:

> I saw the dull yellow eye of the creature open; it breathed hard, and a convulsive motion agitated its limbs. . . . His yellow skin scarcely covered the work of muscles and arteries beneath; his hair was of a lustrous black, and flowing.

Does the quote above refer to a baby? Well, yes and no. It comes from Mary Shelley's *Frankenstein*. While it supposedly describes a monster, literary critic Ellen Moers insists that Shelley was really talking about the horrors of motherhood. She wrote *Frankenstein* during her third pregnancy, at the age of eighteen, after her firstborn child had died.

Pregnant women often dream about monsters. In some dreams, the monster is clearly the dreamer's baby. Other dreams are more ambiguous, but traceable to a woman's negative feelings about her pregnancy. *Such dreams are completely normal.* They do not indicate that a woman is neurotic or that she should not bear children. They simply show a healthy unconscious mind hard at work, adjusting to an uncomfortable body and making way for the baby.

Waking fantasies of baby-as-monster can also be healthy and helpful when applied to the baby decision.

Let your monster appear. What does it look like? What does it do to you? What do you do in return? How do you feel about it? Do you want to abandon it as Dr. Frankenstein abandoned his creation?

The particular monster you imagine may symbolize your particular fears of parenthood. If you fear the baby would drain your energies, you might envision a vampire. If you're a passionate traveler, you might imagine a large-bellied creature chomping on your airplane tickets to Rome. A monster fantasy may also raise the age-old fear that we are somehow being punished for past "sins." The monster we give birth to in our dreams is related to how we feel about the monstrous parts of ourselves.

Women seem to have more monster fantasies than men, and take them more personally. A woman seems to think, "If a monster came out of my body, that makes me a monster, too." Even a normal pregnancy is an invasion of the body that seems monstrous at times. A woman's organs are literally pushed out of place to make way for baby.

At the most basic level, monster fantasies are linked to the normal fear that the impending child will be less than perfect —retarded, handicapped, or deformed in some way. While such babies are entitled to the same dignity and esteem accorded to all human beings, society tends to stigmatize and treat them in much the same way it would a genuine monster.

All prospective parents are prone to this fear at one time or another, and it is a legitimate one. But you can ease the fear by doing everything possible to assure the birth of a healthy baby. Don't hesitate to take advantage of the various sophisticated medical procedures available. If you're thirty-five or older, take an amniocentesis test to check for Down's syndrome and other defects. If there are inherited diseases in your family history, seek genetic counseling.

E. The Wrong Sex

- Phil wants a son with whom he can play football on Saturdays.
- Kathleen, a feminist, wants a daughter to raise as she wishes her mother had raised her.

Do you want a boy or a girl rather than a *child?* If you do, consider why gender is so important to you. What would you do if your child refused to cooperate and turned out to be the "wrong" sex? Or suppose that longed-for son hates sports and wants to spend his Saturdays reading. Suppose that daughter loves to play "house" and begs for frilly dresses and dolls. Would you still love and accept this "wayward" child? If you're considering a child because you want to mold it in your image, you'd better give some serious thought to your motivation.

Values

The following set of exercises is designed to help you identify some of the things you value most in life, and to consider how those priorities relate to parenthood.

A. Epitaph

Whenever we think about birth, on some level we are also thinking about death. We may look to children as a way of assuring our immortality. Could this issue be a factor in your conflict? Use this exercise to consider that question.

Close your eyes and imagine the events immediately following your death:

- What would you like your tombstone to say? Your obituary?
- Who will mourn your death?
- What will you be remembered for?
- What product or contribution do you want to leave behind?

Do the exercise twice, once imagining that you had children; the second time imagining that you remained child-free.

How did the two fantasies differ? Which did you like better? Why?

Don't confuse persons and products. Even if you have a child, you still have a chance to contribute more than your genes to future generations. And if you never have a child, you'll have many chances to enjoy and influence other people's children.

B. SURPRISE!

You have just discovered that you are pregnant (or that your wife is). It is unplanned.

- Will you have the baby or get an abortion? Why?
- Are you at all relieved that the "accident" made the decision for you?
- Are you ever tempted to have an "accident"? Why?

C. KNAPSACK

"What will I have to give up?" This is one of the scariest questions potential parents face. The purpose of this exercise is to help you see what you think you'd have to give up in order to become a parent.

Imagine that you are beginning the long journey that is parenthood. Take your baby and put her in your knapsack. Now imagine that she kicks a hole in the knapsack, and some of the other objects in the sack begin to fall out.

- What do you see falling out?
- How will you feel about losing these things?

- Must you leave them behind or can you carry them with you, however awkwardly?
- If you leave them behind, will you be able to come back and get them later? Why or why not?

Scott saw the following slip away: freedom, peace and quiet, time for his stamp collection and, worst of all, his wife Emily's happiness. He wanted to throw the baby away and go back and get everything else.

Karen saw her independence, her solitude, and a piece of her career slip away. She tried to pick these things up by thinking about child care arrangements, about her husband's co-operation, about what kind of work she could do during the quiet time when the child was in bed. A key question was whether her husband Rich would put in enough child care time to allow her work time and quiet time.

Harry and Leila watched their expensive Bahamas vacations and their spotlessly clean home disappear. But they thought the fat pink leg sticking out was so cute that they realized they probably could adjust to camping vacations and toys in the living room.

If you, like Scott and Emily, feel that you're losing all the things you value, more or less permanently, and you don't find the replacement—a child—very appealing, you're getting some strong indications that parenthood is not for you. If, on the other hand, you're upset about these losses but like what's dropped in, explore ways of rearranging or lightening the load. Remember, you don't have to pick up all the pieces immediately. You can retrieve some later, and you might discover that some aren't as important as you thought they were.

D. PASSED UP

This exercise will help you assess whether you are being realistic about the career sacrifices that parenthood may require.

Imagine that a colleague moves ahead of you in some way

simply because you can't work as hard now that you're involved with your child. Perhaps he or she is promoted first even though you are more qualified. How would you feel about this? How would you react?

- Larry decided that having a child and assuming half the responsibility for its care was more important than being an all-star at work.
- Caroline couldn't stand the thought of falling behind on the career ladder. And fall she would if she became a mother, because her husband wanted a child only if she agreed to take full responsibility for it.

Although parents of young children aren't necessarily confined to baby steps on the career ladder, they probably won't be able to take as many giant steps as their child-free colleagues. If you, like Caroline, can't tolerate the thought of pint-sized obstacles to your advancement, you're not likely to enjoy parenthood.

E. Moment of Truth

- (For women): Imagine that you are at a critical point in your career. Your gynecologist tells you that it's now or never. You have a condition which will make pregnancy impossible by the end of this year. What would you do?
- (For men): What would you want to do? Would you encourage your wife to get pregnant while the getting is good or would you rather take your chances later and urge her to continue working? (If you actually find yourself in such a situation, learn how to handle emergency decisions in Chapter 2.)

F. Bad News

How would you and your spouse feel if you found out that one of you was infertile?

- If you're leaning toward parenthood, do you think you'd adopt?
- If you're leaning toward remaining child-free, do you think you'd regret the loss of this option, even though it's an option you'd probably never exercise?

G. MAKING CONNECTIONS

Imagine that five years from now you lose your spouse through death or divorce. If you were single again, would you rather be a parent or a nonparent?

Some single parents find their children a source of comfort; a means through which they can relate to the outside world. Others find single parenthood a burden that drains their financial resources and cuts into their social life, privacy, and quiet time.

Unless you're on the verge of being divorced or widowed, you should not base the baby decision on this possibility. You should assume that you and your spouse will be together until proven otherwise. However, this fantasy illustrates the real risks involved. More important, it offers you a chance to find out how committed you are to raising a child.

TIMETABLES

A sensible baby decision requires a good sense of time. Wanting a baby now may be incompatible with wanting to start law school next September. Or combining career and motherhood may look easier in women's magazines than it does in a working woman's datebook.

The exercises in this section will give you a time frame for decision-making.

A. COUNTDOWN

How many hours a week do you spend on:

- Work
- Recreation and socializing
- Hobbies
- Goof-off time
- Relaxation, e.g., yoga, meditation
- Sports
- Politics
- Church or temple
- Time alone with spouse
- Sleep

How many hours a week do you think parenthood will require? How would your schedule change if you had a baby?

- Would you still try to do everything, cutting down hours per activity?
- Would you cut out some activities altogether?
- Would you continue doing some of your activities with the baby present?
- Can you think of substitute activities that would accommodate a child more easily? For instance, you can't swim with a baby on your back, but you can jog with a baby in a stroller.

Don't forget that even if you can afford unlimited babysitting, a child still needs a certain amount of "quality time" each day. And a "quality" ten minutes will not do the trick!

- Are you willing to change your schedule?
- If the prospect of any change is repugnant, why are you still considering a baby?

As you plan, keep in mind that parents of young children sacrifice more weekend time than evening time. You can pursue some of your favorite activities while the kids are asleep, but on weekends and during the day, active children often require constant attention.

B. LIFE CYCLE

Where do you want to be

- in five years?
- in ten years?
- in twenty years?
- in fifty years?

How would a child's development coincide with the different stages in your own development?

C. ROCKING CHAIR

This fantasy can help you predict the regrets you may have about either decision when you're older.

You are seventy-five years old. You're half-asleep in a rocking chair by the fire. Your life swims dreamily before you. Long ago, when you were in your early thirties, you chose not to have children. How do you feel about this decision?

Now, visualize the same scenario with one difference—you had children. How do you feel about this decision? Reconstruct both of these fantasies under these varying circumstances:

- Your spouse is still alive.
- Your spouse is dead.
- You are ill and in a nursing home.

The concept of regrets is a touchy subject, particularly to child-free persons who are rightfully angered by the hostile question, "But won't you be sorry later?" That's not a real question because it comes with a built-in answer: "Of course you will!" And no nonparent, even in these relatively enlightened times, seems to be able to escape this question.

A recent example: In 1979, *Time* Magazine interviewed television commentator Betty Rollin for an article entitled "Wondering If Children Are Necessary" because she was one of the first—and most fervent—to attack pronatalism. In 1970, she published an article called "Motherhood—Who Needs It?," and today it is still read, anthologized, and praised as one of the most articulate on the subject.

Wondering what Ms. Rollin had to say nine years later, *Time* proceeded to ask her "the question that isn't really a question," and printed an answer that wasn't really an answer. Instead of quoting her in context, *Time* printed the following: "Something interesting has happened to a few of the N.O.N. believers. They have grown older and changed their minds. Now Rollin says she 'feels like I've missed something' by not having a child." The article then went on to describe myriads of career women jumping into maternity clothes just before their biological alarm clocks went off.

This "I told you so" attitude gives one the feeling that Ms. Rollin was more taken advantage of than listened to. What she actually said was: "Look, I feel that I missed something, which I'm occasionally wistful about. But that doesn't mean that I'm sorry or that I wouldn't make the same decision again. I think people who do have children miss something, too."

Far from saying that she made the *wrong* choice, Ms. Rollin is saying loud and clear that she made the *right* choice. While she missed something by not having a child, she would have missed even more, she feels, by having one. What *Time* presented as a statement of regret was actually a statement of mixed feelings about the right decision, not of remorse about a wrong one.

In a recent conversation with Ms. Rollin she had the following to say about the misquote. "I felt used and I was upset about it. I wrote *Time* a letter and got a letter back, but my letter was not published. I felt bad about it because I thought, in a sense, I had let down the people who chose the way I did and have been made to feel uncomfortable. I think that's really too bad."

While it's an open question whether Ms. Rollin was deliberately misquoted, I believe the distortion of the quote, hand-in-hand with *Time*'s failure to correct it or print her letter about it, indicates society's prejudice toward nonparents. Indeed, even the choice to interview Betty Rollin reflects a bias. "Do you regret your choice?" could have been asked of equally prominent women *with* children. Asking it of Ms. Rollin alone reveals society's poisonous prediction that nonparents—and only nonparents—will regret their decision. Those who ask "the question that isn't really a question" often act as though there would be no greater pleasure than to be an eyewitness at the predicted "moment of truth" when the nonparent lets out an agonized cry, "If only we had had children!" Such people have already rehearsed the scene, and the words, "I told you so!" practically bounce off their tongues.

The rocking-chair question, on the other hand, is real because it assumes that everyone, parent and nonparent alike, will have *some* regrets about their choice. It does not assume that child-free persons are more likely to be sorry than parents.

Because the "will-you-be-sorry" question is so misused, it's tempting to avoid this issue entirely if you're leaning toward the child-free choice. But *please don't run away from it*. It *won't* persuade you to have an unwanted child. If nonparenthood is right for you, you'll be able to answer, "No! When I look back, I'll be glad I lived my life as I did. Children would have kept me from living the kind of life I wanted."

Moreover, in this exercise, you are *not* asking, "Will I regret my decision?" Actually, that's a meaningless question because the baby decision is so momentous, the pros and cons so compelling, that almost everyone will suffer an occasional pang of regret. Rather, you are asking, "Which decision would I regret the *least?*" This question will give you an important clue to your own baby mystery.

Finally, by tracking down your own possible regrets you will be able to make the most of your potential decision. For instance:

- Mary and Nelson knew they wanted to remain child-free. The rocking-chair fantasy showed them that their only regret might be a lack of contact with the younger generation. Nelson decided to become a Big Brother. Mary, a poet, decided to try writing verse for young children.
- Rob and Sandra want children, but their rocking-chair fantasy indicated that they didn't want to give up their career commitments or their freedom to travel. They decided to have only one child and spend the money they would have spent on another child on trips and vacations.

Treat this fantasy as a friend, not an enemy. You won't regret having done so!

LOOKING IN

Many insights that could help you make your decision are locked tightly away in your unconscious mind. In order to reclaim them, you'll have to catch the gatekeeper—your rational mind—off guard. The exercises below will help you steal past the guard and retrieve these precious pearls of wisdom.

A. DIARY

Keep a diary of your feelings about parenthood. Use different colored pens to differentiate your thoughts on the two choices. Don't force yourself to write daily or a lot. Write only when you have something to say. Don't edit or evaluate in your head—just let the words flow out.

- Over time, what changes do you see? Does one ink color begin to predominate?

- How are your diary entries affected by daily events like these:

    Contact with children
    Contact with child-free friends or friends who are parents
    Your relationship with your spouse
    Your progress at work

B. DREAM POWER

Do you dream about pregnancy, birth, or parenting? Before you go to bed, tell yourself that you will remember any such dreams in the morning. Keep a notebook and pencil by your bed so you can jot down some notes while you're still half-asleep.

What messages are you receiving from your unconscious? How would you interpret these dreams?

If you have trouble remembering dreams, try meditation. Both of these states open the gates between the conscious and the unconscious. Therefore, when you dream or meditate you can get insights you would never have discovered in your waking state.

NUTS AND BOLTS OF PARENTING

Are you *really* prepared to meet the demands of parenthood? Even if you're eager for a child, and willing to spend time with it, you may not be willing to do all the work a child requires. The following exercises will help you see whether you're prepared to get down to the nitty-gritty of parenthood.

A. SWEDISH FAMILY HOTEL

Imagine that you have the opportunity to live in a hotel in your own community that is patterned after the ones in Sweden: your family has its own individual living unit with a kitchenette that allows you to cook an occasional private meal. If you're too busy or too tired to cook, you can eat in the cafeteria downstairs. A cleaning service tidies your apartment while you're at work. Your baby is rocked and cuddled in a nursery right in your building, and your six-year-old's school is within walking distance. Best of all, during the years your children are very young, you don't have to be deprived of adult contact. A meaningful grownup conversation is as close as your neighbor's door.

- If you could live in such a setting, would you?
- How would raising a family in a Swedish hotel differ from raising one in an American house?

If this fantasy is too foreign, imagine hiring a live-in housekeeper who would clean, cook, shop, and chauffeur.

Jim and Joanne, who had strong, positive feelings about children, loved the idea. They were practically ready to board a jet to Stockholm. They realized they had been leaning toward nonparenthood simply because the thought of all the work and planning involved seemed too exhausting to contemplate. But once they pinned down their basic worry, they immediately began to explore creative ways of dealing with this issue.

For Connie and Donald, the exercise was even more revealing. Although they had both assumed they didn't want to be parents because of the work involved, they discovered that even if all the work were done for them, they still wouldn't want kids. They realized they had to dig a little deeper to find out why they really wanted to remain child-free.

This issue is a major stumbling block for many people because they either take it too seriously or not seriously enough. People in the former category really believe that the logistics involved are downright impossible. How ironic that people who expertly juggle many complex responsibilities at work are convinced they couldn't possibly make similarly complex arrangements at home. On the other hand, people who don't take the situation seriously enough are guilty of overconfidence. They assume that if they can hire and manage a staff of ten, they'll have no problem finding one good housekeeper. Or, they may assume that because they can afford help, it's there for the asking.

The point is, both attitudes interfere with good decision-making because neither is realistic. Day care and housekeepers *are* available, but not easily available. If your housekeeper goes home to nurse her sick mother, how long will it take you to replace her? If the day care mother on the corner lands a full-time job, what will you do about your job while you're looking for another full-time baby-sitter? The problems are not insoluble, but they can be rough, especially if you aren't prepared for them.

B. HOMEWORK ASSIGNMENT

This exercise will help you explore some of your feelings about child-rearing activities.

Read some magazine articles or books on parenting and picture yourself in some of the problem situations described. Then, follow the advice offered and visualize how you would handle the problem. How do you feel about what you did— pleased, anxious, resentful?

- Yolanda focused on her feelings of pride in successfully helping her child solve problems.
- Ellen thought, *Yecch!* I don't really want to deal with potty training or the terrible twos.
- Peter realized he expected his wife Liz to deal with all the problems because she was "the mother." Liz thought they ought to share both the joys *and* the problems. It turned out that their differing expectations stemmed from the different values and attitudes their parents had about child-rearing—values they had both learned at an early age. They had been leaning toward parenthood but this prob-

lem was holding them back. Understandably, Liz refused to take on 90% of the burden. Peter had to decide whether he could let go of the pattern of distance he'd learned as a child and take the risks involved in being a closer father.

Obviously, no one likes to handle a temper tantrum in the supermarket or a broken arm on the playground. The question is: Does the idea of helping a child to grow emotionally, morally, and intellectually appeal to you? Even if the answer is yes, must that child be your own flesh and blood? Perhaps remaining child-free while working with children will meet your need for both nurturance and freedom.

C. INTERIORS

Look around your house or apartment. What would you have to change if you had a child? Remember, not only do you have to protect the child from the house (selling the glass coffee table), but also the house from the child (reupholstering your white sofa in something darker).

You may find it helpful to visit the homes of friends with young children to see what the physical space is like. This is especially useful if you were ever in the same home before the baby was born. You can then compare the prebaby and postbaby environments. Try to visit a home with a toddler or at least a crawler. Since infants require the least "child-proofing," you may not get the total picture if the only new landmark in the living room is a playpen.

Would you have to move in order to get more space, more playmates, a safer neighborhood, or better schools? Are you willing to move? Are there any parallels between the physical changes parenthood requires in your home and the psychological changes it requires in your life?

- Ed envisioned his house as terribly cramped after a baby's arrival. It was also true that he and his wife felt a baby

would cramp their life-style of eating out and traveling extensively.
- Randy and Carol, in contrast, have always viewed their unfurnished spare room as a future nursery. Picturing that room filled with brightly colored furniture, pictures, and toys felt to them like filling an empty space in their otherwise enjoyable existence.

In doing this exercise it may be helpful, if you're a confirmed city dweller, to realize that parenthood doesn't necessarily mean being sentenced to suburbia. If you were to choose parenthood, perhaps you could convert an attic or den into a nursery. Or you might consider moving to a less glamorous neighborhood that offered more space for your money.

COUPLES EXERCISES

Now that you've taken a good look at yourself, it's time to turn that same discerning eye toward your spouse and your relationship. Do you have a clear understanding of one another's attitudes and feelings about this issue? Are you in total agreement, total disagreement, or somewhere in between? Have your discussions to date brought you closer together or driven you farther apart?

The next few exercises are designed to clear the air between you and set the scene for some meaningful dialogue.

A. RING OF POWER

Every couple establish their own unique style of decision-making. Over the years, that style becomes a habit, and even when it's no longer effective, partners may not be willing or able to examine or change it. If you and your spouse are stymied about the baby question, perhaps it's time to take a good hard look at *your* style.

How do you and your spouse make other important decisions?

- Each spouse has equal weight; couple decide together.
- Whoever feels more strongly about the issue makes the decision.
- Husband makes the decision; wife goes along.
- Wife makes the decision; husband goes along.

Are you both still satisfied with your decision-making style? Will it work for this particular decision? If not, why? Asking the power question may be scary, but answering it may be necessary before you can go on to the baby question.

B. "ARE YOU THE PERSON I MARRIED?"

In view of all the uncertainty in modern life, most of us like to feel that we can count on our spouses to honor their commitments. When we marry, we sincerely believe the promises we make to our intended. But as we grow older and learn more about ourselves, we may change our minds. On minor issues, this generally isn't a problem, but on major issues, like the baby question, a sudden reversal can foster a genuine crisis. Spouses are understandably furious when mates who agreed with them on the baby issue years ago change their minds. And they're quite likely to feel guilty if they're the ones who've changed.

Take a moment now to recall some of the talks you had before you got married. Did you and your spouse discuss children? Did you agree or disagree? Have either of you changed your mind since then?

If there has been a change, try not to be too hard on yourself or your spouse. Although you may be tempted to hurl accusations at one another, bear in mind that life decisions must reflect your situation and frame of mind *at that moment*. A decision made at age twenty-four simply may not be right by the time you're twenty-eight or twenty-nine. Don't waste your time blaming each other. The best thing to do in this situation is to sit down together and try to figure out how the change has come about. Has either of you gotten to know yourself better, discovered your real feelings about children, or come to see alternatives that seemed impossible years ago?

Also, keep in mind that there are varying shades of disagreement. A spouse who agreed to have three children and now won't even consider one is obviously different from the spouse who in the past made the same agreement but now asks, "Have we really considered the child-free option?" In the former situation, the spouse completely rejects the early decision; in the latter, he or she is merely questioning it. And questioning old assumptions is what the baby decision is all about.

Even if your spouse's position has changed drastically, don't panic. Try to get the whole story. Then you won't waste your breath trying to talk your spouse out of something he or she may not even be into yet. And even if your mate's new position is hard to take, you will have to give it a fighting chance as you work on your decision. In Chapter 8, "Tug of War," we'll cover such disagreement in complete detail.

C. FIFTY-FIFTY

Even when couples work on the decision together, women often seem to feel more strongly about it. Maybe this is because a woman suspects that a baby will change her life more than her husband's. Even in marriages in which the couple previously split chores fifty-fifty, the woman usually puts more time and energy into parenthood than her husband does. For instance, a mother more often winds up arranging for child care and tending to a sick child.

Close your eyes and imagine how your workloads might change if you had a baby. Could one or both of you trim some time off your work week? If the wife stayed home, how would that affect your relationship? If neither of you can gear down, how will you hold up against the new workload? Would the wife be more interested in having a child if the husband seemed more willing to care for it?

Don't make the mistake of saying, "We'll deal with this *after* the baby comes," because it's possible that the baby shouldn't come at all. Sometimes couples enthusiastically agree to have a child, only to discover later that they disagree violently about assuming responsibility for it. If a marriage is egalitarian, a wife may expect it to remain so after the baby's arrival while her husband may assume that she will take on the major share of the child care. She thinks the fifty-fifty split is serious and permanent; he thinks it is a temporary game that will end with childbirth. Once his wife becomes a mother, he somehow expects her to become more like *his* mother. And it's no surprise that both spouses wind up angry and resentful.

D. FAMILY SCULPTURE

In this final exercise, you and your spouse will each have a turn at creating a "living" sculpture—your own portrayal of life as nonparents and as parents. It's your chance to be an artist, and the only "material" you'll need are yourself, your spouse, and a doll. When it's your turn, place your spouse, yourself, and the doll anywhere you like in the room to express your view of your family. You can also bring in additional props to complete the sculpture if you wish.

- To depict the child-free choice, Pam placed herself on the sofa with her husband Dale in a relaxed, cuddly embrace. To depict the parenting life-style, she placed herself and Dale in separate chairs with their backs to each other, the doll naked and forlorn on the floor between them.
- To make his child-free sculpture, Stan pushed back all the furniture to create a feeling of emptiness. He placed himself and Gloria in the middle of the empty room, each slouching down. For the parenting sculpture, he led Gloria to a neighbor child's brightly colored bedroom.

Gloria, the doll, and he were all on the floor, grinning as they rolled a ball to each other.

Although you can fantasize the sculpture, actually arranging it is even more effective. Even if you and your spouse are leaning in the same direction, your sculptures are bound to be different and a discussion of these differences may be helpful, especially if you can tell your spouse how it felt to be part of all four sculptures.

Now that you've completed these exercises, you may discover that some of the mountainous obstacles in the baby decision path have turned into molehills or disappeared altogether. By zeroing in on the complex emotions, values, and beliefs that influence this decision you can shrink scary giants down into friendly solutions.

‚ÄîÇ 4 Ç‚Äì

In and Out of
the Pressure Cooker

- Ilene, happily married and child-free, is about ready to quit her job in frustration. Her boss, a dedicated family man, can't understand why she doesn't want kids, and manages to hint, at least once a day, that childless people are selfish.
- When Kenny and Nan told their best friend George about Nan's pregnancy, George was so sure a baby would ruin their lives that he began to talk about the possibility of abortion. Now their friendship is severely strained.
- Barry and Michelle, parents of a seven-year-old, feel that they're too busy to care for another child. But their parents keep telling them that Susie will grow up miserable unless they give her a brother or sister.
- Thirty-six-year-old Diane doesn't plan to have a baby for another three years. Since she announced her decision, her mother has been sending her articles on mongolism and birth defects, and Diane's becoming depressed and angry.

Family and friends. They sweet-talk us and soft-soap us. They are the pushy people in our lives and they are SURE that we should or shouldn't become parents. We may be uncertain, but *they* are not. They believe they've been sent from heaven to save us from a wrong choice, but to us their halos look strangely like horns.

All the people described above are emotionally healthy, independent adults. They don't care if somebody else thinks they should sell their home, apply for a new job, or save more money. So why are they so shaken by baby-related pressures? Because the pressures are internal as well as external. Every time Ilene's boss implies that she's selfish, a small voice in her head asks ominously if perhaps he's right. Even though Barry and Michelle are satisfied to be the parents of an only child, they can't help worrying that they may be depriving Susie by their refusal to have another child. As happy as Nan and Kenny are about Nan's pregnancy, reactions from friends like George are taking their toll. Once the baby arrives, will the gap between their interests and those of their friends be too wide to bridge? And Diane simply can't dismiss her mother's concern, for she too wonders: Will I be able to get pregnant? What if my baby is mongoloid? Could I handle that?

Pressure from family and friends is hard to ignore because it acts like a magnet, bringing our own doubts and fears to the surface. Every time these key people voice an objection, we hear a corresponding echo: Will our lives be ruined? Will we lose our friends? Are we really being selfish? Will our parents forgive us for disappointing them?

Does this mean that you're doomed to suffer in silence, that you'll never feel "right" about your decision unless you banish the meddler from your life? Not at all. This chapter will show you what's behind their pressure tactics, how to handle well-meaning busybodies and manipulative meddlers, and how you can sometimes even turn such pressure to your own advantage.

You Can Go Home Again

You are in your twenties or thirties, you have a good job, a happy marriage, and a home of your own. You are your own boss, an adult, ready, willing, and able to take responsibility for your own life and make your own decisions. Or are you?

Why, then, is it so difficult for you to imagine telling your parents that you've decided not to have a baby? Why are you tempted to avoid the discussion altogether, even to the point of visiting them less often? Why, if you're leaning toward the child-free choice, are you beginning to think that perhaps you are making a mistake, that you really won't be happy unless you have a child?

It's entirely natural to want the approval and understanding of those you love and respect, particularly your parents. After all, you spent approximately eighteen years in their home, listening to them, learning from them, internalizing their values and, unless you were particularly rebellious, trying to please them. It's a habit that's hard to break. But, at a certain point, you have to separate from your parents and carve out your own identity as an independent adult whose decisions reflect your needs, not theirs. Murray Bowen, Georgetown University psychiatrist and one of the pioneers of family therapy, calls this process individuation, and defines it as a way of coming to terms with one's parents, not by escaping, rebelling, or giving in to them, but by separating one's identity from theirs while maintaining a close relationship.

All of us want to relate to our parents as adults, but getting there can be difficult and threatening. It involves time, effort, and honest communication. It means that we have to accept responsibility for ourselves and give up the illusion that someone else will take care of us. And it means that our relationship with our parents will invariably change—and change, no matter how desirable, is always somewhat frightening. So, rather than risk such change, many people take the easy way out: handling parental pressure by giving in, running away or rebelling. In fact, the decision itself can be a form of rebellion, as the following stories indicate.

- Alan's parents are dying to become grandparents and his only sibling isn't married. But Alan is furious at his parents for a number of reasons, and even though he and his wife eventually plan to have children, he deliberately wants to postpone the pregnancy just to get back at them.

• Kathleen, a highly successful businesswoman who travels a lot, is angry because her parents keep telling her not to have a baby unless she quits her job. They're sure that she'll lose her husband, neglect her child, or both. Although she's leaning toward nonparenthood, she's now tempted to become pregnant, just to prove them wrong.

Poor Alan and Kathleen. Although they probably believe they're proclaiming independence by their acts of rebellion, they might just as easily have given in to their parents' wishes or avoided the subject completely. For when people rebel out of unresolved anger, give in out of a need to please, or run away, they are not making a real decision; they are just letting their parents' wishes dictate their actions. If frustrating or meeting your parents' needs is your major goal, satisfying your own needs becomes impossible. When you have to prove your parents right or wrong, you only end up wronging yourself.

To spring the parental pressure trap, you have to work toward genuine individuation by taking a trip back home, either literally or figuratively, and looking at your relationship with your parents as honestly as possible. Do you act like an adult when you're with them, or do you fall into old behavior patterns? When they raise doubts or criticize, do you immediately get angry and start to yell, as you did when you were an adolescent, or can you discuss the matter in a calm, reasonable way? Have you stopped to consider what *you* want? Are you aware of the differences—and similarities—between you and your parents?

If you're convinced that you'll never get through to them, or that they're hopelessly obnoxious, you're probably wrong. In fact, the intensity of your belief may be a sign that you're still playing the child's role at home, even if you're perfectly grown up with friends. But until you start acting like an adult, your parents are going to keep treating you like a child because that's the only way they've ever related to you. You have to institute the change, and you can begin by following these steps toward individuation:

1. Talk to your parents about their lives, their relationship with each other, and their parents. Try to focus on emotions, not just facts. If Dad quit high school when his father died, how did he feel about it? Share some of your own feelings. This can be a wonderful way to venture beyond chitchat to the deeper feelings that often go unexpressed between parent and child.

2. Spend time with each person separately ("Let's just the two of us go out for coffee"). Relate to each parent as a distinct individual, not just half of an indeterminate blob known as "my parents."

3. Try to recognize and refuse to participate in replays of old family scripts.

- One evening Tom and Christine told his parents they didn't know if they would ever have children. Tom's mother asked: "How could you be so selfish?" Tom pounded his fist on the dinner table and shouted: "You hypocrite! Don't you realize how selfish you are to insist on grandchildren?"

  Tom fell into a time-worn pattern of answering his mother's accusation with an even stormier accusation. The end result of such a pattern is that nobody listens and nobody learns.

It is better to calmly listen and calmly explain, trying to hold a conversation between the two adults you now are instead of between the parent and child you used to be.

If you're not ready to take these steps, or if your parents are dead, try the chair dialogue described in Chapter 3 (see page 28). Act out a conversation between you and your parents, playing yourself and each of your parents in turn. Even if they are still living, practicing these dialogues alone might give you enough insight and courage to risk an actual dialogue with Mom and Dad.

Before you start any serious discussions about the baby question, try to remember how you and your parents used to handle conflicts. What techniques did they use on you? What were your countertechniques? Use this information to avoid falling into destructive patterns that may have become habits over the years. Focus on the effective techniques, avoid the manipulative or ineffective ones, and watch for familiar manipulations on their part. Bear in mind, however, that you and your parents are different people now, and that more open and authentic ways of relating may be possible.

Although, in most cases, parents push for grandchildren, there are parents who take the opposite view. Some fear that their children will be unhappy as parents. Others don't want to be confronted with their own aging. And some women who take vicarious pleasure in their daughters' achievements fear that a baby will ruin career success.

Whatever kind of pressure you're facing, a trip back home is a must. Defying parental expectations, in whatever form they take, is not easy, but if you know what you're dealing with and what kind of changes you want to make, you can benefit from the experience. In fact, as the following story illustrates, it can promote personal growth by giving you the chance to improve your relationship with your parents and overcome your need for their approval.

David and Marilyn almost had a baby they didn't want. "We were afraid of disappointing our parents," David said recently. "We had always been model children. After getting straight A's in high school and college, we went to medical school just as our parents had hoped. Until the baby decision, it was easy to do what they wanted because we had always wanted the same things. Without questioning our motivations, we agreed that Marilyn would go off the pill when we finished our residencies and began our joint pediatric practice. But, thank goodness, she didn't get pregnant right away. Instead, she got headaches and I got nightmares. We asked ourselves why and concluded that we didn't really want children. We had just wanted to please our parents. We decided it was time to start asking what would please us. We want to work hard all day and play at night. After working with children all day, we don't want to come home to them at night, too."

"It was scary to tell our parents about our decision," Marilyn added. "We were tempted to pretend we had a fertility problem. But that was the coward's way out. So we told them. All four of them were shocked and angry. They tried to make us feel guilty. It would have been very easy to just stop talking to them.

"But the weird thing is, we have better relationships with both sets of parents than ever before. We took on my parents one week and David's the next. We listened while they told us why they felt we should have children. And they listened while we explained why we don't want them. We still don't see eye-to-eye, but at least we're beginning to accept one another. I feel like a real grownup for the first time in my life."

If you're willing to take the risks David and Marilyn took, you may be surprised to discover that your parents are capable of making some changes, too. And they'll be thrilled that you care enough about them to make the effort. Moreover, you may develop a new appreciation for your parents in the process. As you consider the responsibilities and sacrifices involved in parenting, you may come to realize just how tough the job is and how much credit they deserve for doing it at all!

THE FAMILY TREE

Family pressure doesn't necessarily have to be overt. Even if your parents are silent on the baby issue, you may still be influenced by family attitudes and values, often in ways you may not consciously recognize. According to Mel Roman, a noted family therapist and professor of psychiatry at Albert Einstein College of Medicine:

> We are all rooted to a vast underground network of family relationships, family patterns, family rules and roles . . . and we carry this network into any new family we form. We tend to overlook the power of the past in the choices we make and to underestimate the ease with which we fall into old patterns of behavior. . . . But it is not desirable to be bound to the past in destructive ways. In examining the family context that we have inherited from our families . . . we can attempt to separate the aspects of our past that can be put aside as old business from the useful aspects that can become new business in our current families.

Such an examination is especially important in the context of the baby decision. For when we think about becoming parents, we can't help associating ourselves with our own parents, and long-buried resentments and feelings about parents, children, and family relationships may get in the way of decision-making in the present. And if we don't stop to weed out the old business, we can't move forward with confidence.

An Unhappy Childhood

Some people are reluctant to become parents themselves because they have such negative feelings about their own parents and the way they were raised. "I only visit my parents out of duty," said one man considering fatherhood. "I can't stand the thought that my children would ever feel that way about me."

Are people who had unhappy childhoods less likely to want children? We don't know. Some professionals have linked the desire to remain child-free to a poor parental relationship. Others claim that those who choose nonparenthood are acting out their parents' unconscious desire not to have had them. But still others report that child-free individuals are no more likely than parents to have had an unhappy childhood.

If you're worried that you're choosing nonparenthood because your childhood soured you on family life, consider how and why you were unhappy and what you felt you missed. If your parents weren't affectionate, that doesn't necessarily mean you'll carry on the pattern with your own child. Perhaps your parents did indeed give you love in their fashion. Perhaps it simply wasn't enough for you, or perhaps you couldn't deal with the conditions, rejections, or put-downs that went along with it. Maybe someone else, an older sibling, a beloved teacher, a favorite aunt or neighbor, gave you the love you missed from one or both parents. Whatever the circumstances, it's important to recognize:

- The source of your ability to love. Who made it possible for you to be affectionate to your spouse or friends? Focus on that person or persons and build on those warm feelings.
- The fact that you can't make up to your child for the love you didn't get. If there wasn't a loving adult in your past, are you going to be able to give your child the physical contact and affection he or she needs? Experiment by "borrowing" a child, or spending time with friends' or relatives' children. Can you live with the closeness? Can you handle the demands? If not, perhaps you should not become a parent. You can still meet your need for intimacy by developing better relationships with friends, with your spouse, with your nieces and nephews.
- The fact that you will inevitably fail your children in some ways, although not necessarily as seriously, or in the same ways that your parents failed you. Remember, parenting is the one job no one can do perfectly.

Some people find it easier to express affection to children than to other adults. Were you taught that cuddling and physical contact was reserved only for children? Were the adults in your family cool and distant with one another? If so, can you give yourself permission to cuddle with your spouse? Experiment with this before having a child. If you can't loosen up with your spouse, a baby may make matters worse. Your spouse may resent the affection you shower on the baby and the three of you may get caught in an emotionally unhealthy triangle.

In some cases, an unhappy childhood is the sole motivation for choosing parenthood. You may unconsciously or even consciously want to give your child what you never had. If your father rejected you, you will love your child, by God! If your mother mocked you, you will respect and praise your child, by God! Unfortunately, this desire, well-intentioned as it may be, can create real problems for you and your child because it is based on the unrealistic hope that you can re-create your childhood and parent yourself in the way you'd always wanted to be parented. By fusing your identity with your child, you may hope to receive everything you felt you missed. However, raising a child won't satisfy your need to be a child, nor is your child the same person you are. When he or she doesn't respond as you would have, or show the appreciation you expect, you may be overcome by jealousy and resentment.

Obviously, a look back at your childhood is important, but you should not judge your ability to parent solely on the quality of your childhood or your relationship with your parents. Even if you hate your parents, that doesn't mean your children will hate you. You don't necessarily have to repeat their mistakes. If you enjoy parenting, respect your child, allow your child the independence he or she needs, and avoid your parents' errors, your children will probably feel very differently about you. The point is, unless you assess the impact of your past on your present life, you won't have enough information to make a thoughtful and rational decision.

My Parents/Myself

People considering the baby question often fear that they'll become their parents and lose themselves and their tenuous hold on independence. And in the grip of such a fear, they often respond by making a choice that seems to contradict whatever their parents stand for. If, for example, their parents were superparents, they may dedicate themselves to a career. If their parents placed career over family, they may respond by making children the center of their lives. However, because few stop to examine this fear in a more rational light, such people often don't realize that they are still imitating their parents—responding to subtle parental pressure—albeit in a different guise. The props and scenery may have changed, but the old script remains.

"My parents had nothing whatsoever to do with my baby decision," insists Marcia. "I decided not to be a mother because I knew I'd hate every minute of motherhood. My mother loved being a mother but I'd rather pursue my career as a dancer."

Marcia doesn't know it, but she's dancing in steps choreographed by—guess who—her mother. Marcia's mother was an accomplished artist who resented having to give up her career in order to have Marcia. She was depressed throughout her pregnancy. She responded by throwing all her thwarted ambitions into motherhood. She became a "perfect mother," but her buried resentment was conveyed to Marcia nonetheless. Her mother's overt message was "Motherhood is wonderful. You're the light of my life." Her covert message was "Don't fall into this trap; succeed, succeed, succeed."

Marcia's choice really is not a choice at all. Without realizing it, she's conformed to her mother's secret pressures. If she doesn't explore this issue, she's cheating herself out of adulthood. She's abandoned the parenthood wrapper but the package—a life of someone else's choosing—is the same as her mother's.

If Marcia finds the courage to go home again, she'll have a chance to untie the apron strings, explore both options, and make her own choice. If she decides to remain child-free, she'll be doing it for herself, not for her mother. If she has a child, it will be because she's listening to her own messages, not her mother's.

Lois's story illustrates a similar dynamic, although she was able, with help, to recognize and break out of the trap. A management consultant with a good marriage and three children, she confessed that she was very smug about being superwoman. "I thought I was showing up my so-called incompetent mother," she said. "When she had me, Mom gave up teaching to change diapers. Not me! I continued teaching at the university and hired a housekeeper to change my children's diapers. Mom never had any time to herself. Not me! I took one night a week as my special time all to myself. For months I thought I had all the answers, then suddenly I had to ask myself why I seemed to be on the verge of a nervous breakdown.

"In therapy I discovered that while the stage was different, the play was the same. My mother was a martyr at home; I divided my martyrdom between office and home. Mom put herself out to make the perfect dinner. I put myself out to make the perfect presentation. This was a wonderful realization because it made me look at both the strengths and the weaknesses that my mother and I share. It was only after acknowledging this that I was able to change my life. I cut down on my workload, stopped trying to entertain like Perle Mesta, and insisted that my husband and kids do housework."

Like Lois, many young women today don't realize that they're following in their mother's footsteps by embracing career achievement as blindly as their mothers embraced motherhood. In *Up Against the Clock,* a woman described her mother as "so bogged down with her kids that she had no life of her own." This sense of missing out propels many young women toward a choice that seems different, but is the child-free career woman or the woman juggling career and motherhood any less bogged down? As she races from appointment to appointment or office to day care center does she have any more freedom than her mother, who raced from supermarket to kitchen? The bogs may look different, but women are sucked in all the same. However, because it's easier to recognize old forms of enslavement than new ones, women tend to fall into this trap while boasting of their freedom. Perhaps because women are so conditioned to bypass their own needs in service to others, they still don't believe they're entitled to make choices that reflect the life they want for themselves.

The Comparison Game

Women who devote themselves to careers to differentiate themselves from their mothers often derive a false sense of strength and security by comparing their career achievements to their mother's lack of them. "I'm not just a wife and mother, dependent on others," they reassure themselves. "I have more control over my life." Consideration of motherhood challenges this assumption, threatening to expose their fears that they are really just as powerless, just as trapped by anatomy and societal expectations.

Moreover, if they do choose to become mothers, they believe they have to be as successful in the role as their own mothers were. "Who's the better mother (or who would be?)" is the question that dominates their thinking. Many fear that their mothers did a better job than they ever could or will because their mothers had more time to devote to the job and because they weren't as conflicted about it.

Since our mothers are our primary role models we tend to feel guilty if we don't live up to their image. Even if they smothered or overprotected us, even though we know the house doesn't have to be dusted every day, won't we feel guilty if we do anything less? However, if a woman is secure, she'll be able to cope with the idea that, in some ways, her mother might have been a better mother. And it's certainly true that most of our mothers know more about the practical aspects of parenting than we do simply by virtue of their experience. But this doesn't have to be threatening. Instead of competing and criticizing your mother for her lack of accomplishments, draw on her experience and acknowledge her wisdom in this area. Give her a sense of pride in this accomplishment and learn from her. This can be a wonderful way to foster a strong, positive bond with her. And even if you decide against parenthood, you'll know you're doing it for constructive reasons, not because you're afraid to compete or afraid that you'll end up as trapped and powerless as she was.

The flip side of this coin is the desire to become a parent simply to "show up" your parents and raise happier, more accomplished children. Such people aren't afraid of failing in the parenthood contest; they're sure, in fact, that they'll be winners. But this goal is as dangerous as having a child simply to make up for what you missed in your own childhood. Even if it were possible to evaluate objectively whether your kids turned out better than you and your siblings—which it isn't—your perfectionist expectations will ruin your relationship with them. Ironically, your obsession with success will make you a failure. You'll be so anxious and pushy that you will drive your kids crazy and they'll retaliate by rebelling against the very goals you've set for them.

My Mother/My Wife

Some people are less concerned about losing their own identity than losing their spouse. When they think about their husband or wife as a parent they become terrified because they associate their spouse with their own same-sex parent.

Lynn, a physicist so talented she was tenured at twenty-nine, terrified Fred when she announced her plans to take a leave of absence to stay home with the baby. When they'd originally agreed to have a child, Lynn had intended to continue business as usual. Now three months pregnant, she knits booties while chatting happily about the year she's going to take off. Fred is terrified. Is Lynn a new person? Is the familiar, safe wife gone for good?

Fred admitted he sometimes wished Lynn wasn't pregnant. He knew that his mother, a frustrated actress, had hated motherhood. She had poisoned his childhood with daily doses of "If it wasn't for you . . ." Now, he's confusing his wife with his mother. He's afraid, on some subconscious level, that Lynn will turn against him, blame him, as his mother did, for ruining her life.

The only way to overcome this kind of fear is by bringing it out into the open and discussing it. Lynn has to help Fred realize that her personality, her coping skills, and her career choice are very different from his mother's. Moreover, his fear can be put to good use, helping them both plan realistically so that motherhood is not a terrible burden for Lynn. Although such plans are only tentative at best, since they can't anticipate how they'll feel after the baby comes, open discussion can at least give them a handle on the situation.

Too many people working on the baby decision forget to go home, to explore their own past, often because they're afraid to discover that in ways they neither understand nor control, they're still not quite grown. But, as you've seen, the baby decision can be a unique opportunity to work on individuation and develop a genuinely adult and authentic relationship with your parents. By examining some of these subtle doubts and fears, you can come to terms with your past and put aside old business. And by acknowledging the similarities between you and your parents, you can begin to appreciate the real differences.

FRIENDS AND OTHER MEDDLERS

Twenty years ago, only the nonparenthood decision was sure to raise eyebrows and elicit unwanted and sometimes obnoxious comments and advice. Now, we've added a new prejudice to our repertoire. The fact is, no matter what you choose, you're bound to receive some flak. If you choose parenthood, the antichild-rearing contingent will look askance at your decision, wondering why you'd give up your freedom and independence for the thankless job of parenting. And if you make the child-free choice, the pronatalists, shocked by your shallowness and selfishness, will wonder what flaw in your character accounts for this "mad" decision.

Ironically, depending on what crowd you're with at the time, you may hear the very same accusation followed by a slightly different rationale. As the following choruses indicate, identical prejudices can be twisted to fit the values of either group.

PARENTS' CHORUS:	Child-free persons are immature. They don't want to grow up and accept the parenting role.
CHILD-FREE CHORUS:	Parents are immature. They just have children to please their parents as if they were still good little children.
PARENTS' CHORUS:	Child-free people are irresponsible. They want all the pleasure but none of the burdens of adult life.
CHILD-FREE CHORUS:	Parents are irresponsible. They just have kids because they feel like it. They don't stop to ask if they'll be good parents or if the world is too crowded for more.
PARENTS' CHORUS:	Child-free people are neurotic. Any mentally healthy adult would reproduce.
CHILD-FREE CHORUS:	Parents are neurotic. They force their kids to be extensions of themselves.
PARENTS' CHORUS:	Child-free people are selfish. They don't want to do anything for anybody else.
CHILD-FREE CHORUS:	Parents are selfish. They only think about themselves and their kids. They don't care about wider issues.
PARENTS' CHORUS:	Child-free people are afraid to take risks. They're scared to let go of the status quo.

CHILD-FREE CHORUS: Parents are afraid to take risks. They become parents only because they can't resist other people's pressures.

PARENTS' CHORUS: Child-free people will regret their decision later. Someday they'll wake up to realize they're all alone in the world.

CHILD-FREE CHORUS: Parents will regret their decision later. Someday they'll wake up to realize they sacrificed everything for kids who don't even visit them.

Sounds ridiculous, doesn't it, when we look at it this way? But, unless your family and friends are models of tact and understanding, you're bound to hear some of this. That's why it's important to learn assertive ways to deal with pressure before you've even made your decision. After all, how can you even think of jumping off the baby bandwagon if all your loved ones start jumping all over you? How can you consider having your IUD removed if your friends say you should have your head examined instead? Knowing how to respond assertively to meddling reminds you not only that you are the final judge, but also that you don't have to be devastated by disapproval. But before we delve into the specific techniques, let's take a look at what's behind the flak.

The "Babies Are Wonderful" Crowd

Why does the selfish nonparent stereotype persist despite research evidence and clinical experience to the contrary? Why do parents continue to pressure nonparents?

1. Ambivalence. There is no such thing as a parent who doesn't, on a bad day, regret having children, especially as he or she leaves a warm bed at 3:00 A.M. to comfort, change, or feed a screaming baby. Remember, many pregnancies that weren't unplanned *were* unquestioned. The parent who might be a nonparent, had that option been available several years

ago, is often the meddler today. Such a person often plays the "you'll be sorry later" record because he or she can't face the flip side: "I'm sorry now—I wish I had your freedom."

2. *Pure ignorance.* Many people aren't aware of the studies (see Chapter 7) that indicate that nonparents are at least as happy and as emotionally stable as parents. Such reports tend to be tucked away in professional journals that don't reach the general public. Also, people who don't know any nonparents personally have a hard time evaluating this "strange" option. And even if they do know one or two couples who have made that choice, they may consider them to be exceptions.

3. *An inability to recognize individuality.* Too often, we don't bother to notice that our closest friends don't share our needs and attitudes. We tend to assume they are just like us. If we have fun with our children, then everyone else would, too. We don't stop to think that Janet's passion for travel or Sid's desire for solitude may be squelched by parenthood.

Games Parents Play with Nonparents

In the grip of such feelings, people search for ways to vent them. But few are willing to be completely open and risk losing a friend, so they express their disapproval in less direct ways—by playing games.

A game is a social interaction which is in some ways dishonest and irresponsible. It is played for an ulterior motive. In many cases, neither the initiator nor the victim of the game is consciously aware of the payoff. Even though games serve a need, they are ultimately self-defeating. Honesty with oneself and others, though painful in the short run, leads down a longer path to fulfillment.

"You'll Be Sorry"

Lisa and Herb tell their friends that Herb has had a vasectomy. Jessie and Andy, parents of toddler twins, are shocked. "Won't you be sorry, later?" they ask. The *purpose* of the game is to "punish" the child-free person for the "sin" of freedom, for escaping 3:00 A.M. feedings and three million diaper changes. The *payoff* is seeing the child-free person squirm and counterattack. For the player, the counterattack proves that the child-free person *is* neurotic about the issue. And that "proof" serves to soothe his or her own doubts. The *price* is a phony, fruitless interchange in which neither person's feelings are revealed. The *countergame* should be an authentic dialogue in which the initiator admits his or her own regrets and jealousy of the nonparents' freedom, paving the way for the child-free person to discuss any doubts she/he might have. The players can understand and respect each other's choices and remain close friends despite their different attitudes.

"Ha! Ha! We Knew It All Along"

Joanna and Brad had decided to remain child-free when they were twenty-three, but changed their minds at thirty-three. When they announced Joanna's pregnancy at a party the response was so infuriating they wished they'd said nothing.

"Hah! The great child-free couple! You talked so much about your freedom and now you've found out how empty it really is. We always knew you'd change your minds!"

The purpose: to deprive nonparents of their right to change their minds. To express anger at someone who almost got away with "freedom," and to express relief that "you turned out to be like me, after all."

The price: the people who changed their minds feel angry and hurt. The bonds of friendship are weakened if not broken.

The countergame: an honest response to the change of heart. "Congratulations! What made you change your mind?" The newly pregnant couple could then explain why nonparenthood was right in the past and why parenthood seems right for the future.

Remember that people who change their minds are *not* ex-fools who have finally embraced an absolute truth. Their earlier choice was right at the time, but they are different people now, and the change reflects these differences.

Another variation of this game occurs when parents try to take some of the credit for their friends' new decision. "You listened to me at last. Because of my arguments, you have finally made the one true choice." In this situation, the players are wrestling for control.

"Do Me a Favor"

It's not easy to be the only child-free couple in a small town, as Kathy and Howie's story indicates.

They're called upon to do whatever everyone else is "too busy" to do: raise money for the local hospital, run the church bazaar and, of course, baby-sit for free, because they "have nothing better to do." While their friends may believe that nonparents are selfish, in fact, selfishness is a luxury Kathy and Howie can't afford. They're afraid to say no because that would prove that they *are* selfish.

The purpose: to convey the message, "Since you don't have children, you're obviously not doing anything important."

The payoff: ensuring that Kathy and Howie are as overburdened as they are so they won't have to feel jealous.

The price: Kathy and Howie feel so resentful that they don't do very well at the activities they're talked into. They're made to feel guilty about a perfectly good choice.

The countergame: Despite their fears of being accused of selfishness, Kathy and Howie have to start saying no to any favor they don't want to do. Accusations of selfishness can be countered with the assertiveness techniques described at the end of this chapter. They can insist that they're too busy with community activities of their own choosing to take on other duties.

Howie and Kathy also need the support of other child-free persons. If they can't find any on their home turf they can join the NAOP, which has a pen-pal club for members who would like to correspond with other nonparents. It also has a newsletter of great interest to child-free persons. (See Appendix C: Resources.)

People who choose to remain child-free have to develop armor, particularly women. Because motherhood has always been sacrosanct in our society, we've developed a whole set of myths and assumptions about childbearing:

- Pregnancy is a woman's most fulfilling experience.
- You're not a real woman until you've had a child.
- Motherhood is a woman's destiny.

Consequently, nonmothers get more black marks than nonfathers. The childless woman is shirking her role: she's cold, selfish, immature, neurotic. The childless man, on the other hand, probably has something more important to do; he's devoting his energies to his career. So it's not surprising that women are more upset by meddlers than their husbands are.

If you're hit by any of these accusations, recognize that sexism is an aspect of pronatalism and point it out to the meddlers. If you're a nonfather, listen empathetically to your wife's description of her frustrations. Offer her the support she needs to overcome them. Keep in mind that most people will judge her more harshly than they'll judge you.

The "Joys of Freedom" Crowd

Educating people about the child-free option is necessary and productive; pressuring couples to choose that option is not. Although nonparents still get the most criticism, there's an increasingly large group of people ready to point an accusing finger at you should you choose parenthood. And sometimes these are the very people who thought long and hard about both options! The problem is, they're not entirely comfortable with their choice.

- Eileen and Harvey finally decided to have a child. During Eileen's pregnancy, their best friends announced their decision to remain child-free. Eileen and Harvey jumped on them for making a big mistake. They lectured their friends on the "virtues" of parenthood and the "sins" of child-free living.

- After considering adoption, Joyce, a single woman, decided to remain child-free. When her best friend, Anita, also single, gleefully announced her pregnancy, Joanne tried to talk her into an abortion.

What on earth is going on? Why such violent reactions in normally easygoing people? The answer is simple: self-doubt.

Psychologists use the term "cognitive dissonance" to describe the act of selling someone else our own choice because we're jealous of *theirs*. Seeing others revel in the pleasure of the opposite choice makes us question the wisdom of our own. To reassure ourselves, we feverishly throw ourselves into telling the other person that our choice is not only right for us, but for him, too.

Ironically, it is often the less committed member of a couple who puts the most pressure on other couples because the partner who is more comfortable with the choice has less cognitive dissonance about it.

Games Child-Free People Play

Couples suffering from cognitive dissonance aren't always upfront with their attacks. Often, they play a game called "We Have More Fun Than You."

Although Keith and Sara have announced their plan to remain child-free, they are still uneasy about the choice. Their best friends have just had a baby and they drop by for a visit one night at eight. There's a charcoal smell in the air, but no steak in sight. Judy and Ralph open the door to give an explanation broken by the baby's screeches. While they debated what to do about Jennifer's colic, the casserole burned to a crisp. Dressed in their designer best, Keith and Sara observe that Judy's dress and Ralph's overalls are decorated in spit-up and squash. Ignoring both their friends' appearance and the baby, they begin to describe their plans for the evening—a French restaurant, a Broadway musical, and a cast party.

The purpose: to make their friends even more painfully aware of the gap between their past luxury and their present drudgery.

The payoff: to cover up their anxiety about their decision.

The countergame: 1. to continue working on the decision until it's more solid. 2. To empathize with their friends' frustration. 3. To realize that Judy and Ralph's decision to parent may well be right for them. To recognize that the difficulties of living with a newborn are temporary and that once life settles down for Judy and Ralph the gap between themselves and their friends will lessen.

"You're Just a Sheep"

In this game, nonparents claim superiority over parents by assuming that anyone who has carefully considered the baby decision would naturally decide against a baby. They believe, "We who don't have kids have total control of our lives. You parents have no control over yours."

The payoff: by feeling superior to parents, they mask their insecurity about nonparenthood.

The countergame: accept the wisdom of different strokes for different folks. When a nonparent feels insecure about his decision, that doesn't mean it's the wrong decision, just an unfinished one. After all, in a baby-peddling society, it's not surprising that those who refuse the purchase will sometimes feel uncertain.

The Conformity Syndrome

Sometimes nonparents accuse parents of giving in to society's expectations. In their opinion, child-free persons deserve a badge of courage for nonconformity. Although it's certainly true that in today's world nonparents make the less traditional choice and deserve a great deal of support and respect for their decision, we cannot stereotype parenthood decisions as conformist and child-free decisions as nonconformist. It's not that simple.

For example, sometimes what looks like conformity may really be a positive learning experience.

- In January, Bill and Marge consider parenthood. They're nervous and uncertain and they make lists of reasons for not having children. In June, their best friends give birth to a child. The following January, Marge is pregnant. Other child-free friends accuse them of conforming.

Are they guilty or not? Guilty, if Bill and Marge didn't want a baby but followed in their friends' footsteps anyway. Not guilty, if they really wanted a baby but were scared to jump off the fence. Perhaps it seemed less scary once they noticed that their friends not only survived but actually enjoyed parenthood. Maybe they had fun playing with their friends' baby. These experiences may simply have made it easier for them to do what they wanted to do in the first place.

Although they probably don't realize it, Bill and Marge benefited from two valuable psychological techniques: desensitization and role modeling. Desensitization is a process by which repeated small, safe doses of something scary reduces one's fear. Role modeling is the process of imitating the behavior of someone greatly admired.

The fact is, every decision contains some elements of conformity. Since there are going to be people criticizing both choices, the issue of conformity depends on the prevailing view of the social circle you're in. In a study of college students, Ohio State Professor Sharon Houseknecht found that those committed to nonparenthood had friends with similar commitments and/or friends who supported that choice. She concluded that the child-free choice could indeed be a conformist choice involving conformity to a small antiparenthood social group rather than to the larger proparenthood society.

If you have a baby shortly after one of your friends does, and the rest of your predominantly child-free crowd is shouting "conformist!," you could turn the tables on them and point out that you actually made the nonconformist choice in the view of most of the people you know. And if their doubts should get to you, check out the following considerations. You're guilty of conformity if:

- You haven't thought through the decision on your own.
- You have a baby just because you always assumed you would.
- You don't want your family or friends to think less of you.
- You want people to stop hassling you.

You're the only one who has the right to decide whether your decision is genuine. If you're comfortable with it, ignore the pointing fingers and remember that the meddlers are on the warpath simply to mask their own doubts or discomfort.

STILLING THE ANGRY VOICES

Before we begin to examine some of the techniques you can use to take the heat off yourself without alienating your loved ones, take a moment to study the Pressure Victim's Bill of Rights. Keep in mind that you have, at all times, the following rights:

- The right to choose whether or not to discuss the decision with a particular person.
- The right to be heard if you do wish to explain your decision to chosen people.
- The right to cut the conversation short or change its direction.
- The right to point out and object to the techniques a pushy person is using on you.

Dodging

This is a technique to use when you want to get a meddler off your back quickly. Simply agree with his or her viewpoint and don't add any fuel to the fire. You don't really have to agree; just acknowledge the possibility of some truth in what the person is saying. "You may be right about that. Perhaps it's true. Maybe I am selfish."

Social Awareness

This may be used by itself or as a follow-up to the "Why does it matter to you?" technique described below. Ask the person how he or she came to believe that one choice was better than the other.

A person who's pressuring you to become a parent may recall growing up in a pronatalist family, or being influenced by TV and other media. A person who's pressuring you to remain child-free may realize that his or her beliefs spring from "me" psychology, the feminist movement, or antinatalists who have swung the pendulum too far in the other direction.

Light Retorts and Humor

When somebody's meddling is making you sick, laughter may be the best medicine.

Eva's mother told her that nonparenthood was wrong because motherhood is natural.

"Oh, yeah?" replied Eva. "So are rattlesnakes, malaria, and poison ivy!"

Bounce Back the "Shrink" Ball

If someone tries to push you onto the analyst's couch, bounce back with a response such as: "What gives you the right to analyze me? I refuse to be your patient. I feel you are fighting dirty. How do you presume to know what's going on in my unconscious?"

Even people who have no trouble resisting amateur psychotherapists fall prey to real ones. And a friend or relative who happens to be a trained therapist can be very narrow-minded about the baby decision, especially *your* decision. You don't have to put up with slick pronouncements such as, "You don't want kids because your childhood was unhappy" or "You're only having kids because you want someone to control." Even a therapist whom you trust and whom you've asked for help should offer interpretations or advice tentatively. Put two therapists in a room to discuss a case and you'll have at least three interpretations of the client's behavior! You have the right to ask your therapist to explain his or her opinion as well as the right to challenge it.

"Why Does It Matter to You?"

Shift the focus from yourself to the pushy persons. Ask them where the push is coming from and why the issue is so important to them. It will help if all of you see that their statements are based on their values, not on some absolute truth:

JOAN: Is it true you're pregnant, Susie? (Sue smiles and nods.) I suppose I should say congratulations, but somehow I'm bothered. Have you really thought this thing through?

SUE: What is it about my being pregnant that bothers you?

JOAN: Well, it's your career! How can you possibly continue at the law firm if you have a baby?

SUE: I see, you're afraid that having a baby means having to let go of a career.

Notice the phrase "you're afraid." Sue has shifted the focus from herself to Joan. She can now say, "You may feel that a baby means the end of a career, but I don't see it that way."

DAVE: You can't mean you'll never have a child! I'm really upset to hear you say that.

GEORGE: What is it about my remaining child-free that bothers you?

DAVE: I'm afraid you'll regret it later when you're older.

GEORGE: I see. You believe that people without children end up being sorry.

DAVE: I sure do.

GEORGE: You enjoy fatherhood so much, I can see how you would have regretted not having children. But I believe I would regret *having* them.

Don't burn your fingers on a hot potato question or statement. Throw it back to the cook! Remember, people who are comfortable with their choice have no reason to be uncomfortable with yours. And don't worry about hurting their feelings when you throw their remarks back at them. They haven't worried about hurting you. Don't insult or psychoanalyze them, just tell them how the pressure makes you feel and find out what feelings prompted the push.

Explain

This technique is useful when you care about someone, want her to understand you, and believe that she'll really try to do so.

An explanation should be:

- Short and sweet
- Nondefensive and specific
- I-focused—emphasizing how *you* feel and what *you* feel and what *you* want; eliminating criticism of the other, especially saying, "You're conservative," "You're bigoted," etc.

Always keep in mind that *you're not obligated to explain yourself.* You're *choosing* to explain your reasons to this particular person and you can choose to stop midstream if the person launches an offensive. Here are some examples.

Richard talks to his parents about nonparenthood:

"Because you're my parents, it's important to me that you understand. Kate and I think we'd be bad parents because we'd resent the children. We both travel a lot for our political work and our jobs. We feel we'll contribute more to society by being enthusiastic workers than we ever could as reluctant parents."

Sandy talks to Gwen about parenthood:

"Gwen, I know you don't think I should have a baby, but because you're my best friend, I want to tell you why. At night when I meditate, I see myself holding and nursing a baby. I want a baby so much it hurts. Commercial artists are in demand, and I've looked into opportunities to freelance. Bob's going to gear down too. I feel I can meet my need to be a mother and a person too."

After the explanation, be prepared for the other person's response. If he or she continues to attack, use the "Why does it matter to you?" technique. Don't let yourself or the meddler forget the issue of individuality. No decision is right for everyone. The two of you are different people and you may make different choices. You might even invite the meddler to discuss why each of you has made a different choice. Is it possible that these personality differences attracted you and your friend to each other in the first place?

Sometimes, a meddler can point out issues you hadn't really thought about, and can actually help you make your decision.

Mary saw Ellen as so career-committed that she couldn't imagine her becoming a mother. Ellen listened carefully to Mary and decided she'd better do some more soul-searching and establish herself in her career before making a final decision one way or the other.

Corey felt uneasy about Dan's decision to have a vasectomy at age twenty-one, after just one year of marriage.

"Dan, do you really know what you're doing? I've seen the light in your eye when you wrestle with Eddie [Corey's toddler]. Shouldn't you give yourself a few years?"

Dan had to agree he was in too much of a hurry. He was terrified of abusing a child as his father had abused him. A vasectomy offered a guaranteed end to a cycle of misery. But he did enjoy children and he'd had an uncle who was very warm and loving toward him. Maybe another way to break the pattern would be to become a good father to his own child. He decided to postpone the procedure for a few more years, just in case.

It's important to separate real pressure from:

- Advice that is astute, open, and friendly, and offered in a way that you can take or leave.
- Advice or thoughts from a person merely sharing his own values, rather than pushing them on you.

Devil's Advocate

Twist someone's argument to fit your own choice. For example, if someone says you're selfish to plan not to have children, tell him, "Well, that's all the more reason to stay child-free, isn't it? Because selfish people make lousy parents." The same argument works as well for labels such as immature, neurotic, and unhappy. (Check the choruses on page 73.)

Refuse to Talk About It

This is a technique that pushes the listener away from you. Use it when:

1. You feel someone you don't want to be close to you is nosy and interfering.

2. You have tried to explain your leaning or decision to someone close to you and the person has not offered any support.

Simply say, "I don't care to discuss this. It's a personal matter," or, "You know, we've tried talking about this before, and we just never get anywhere. I'd rather not talk about it any more."

With an intimate, you might use a period of silence as a moratorium to unlock horns. Perhaps after a few weeks or months of avoiding the subject you and the meddler can have an honest, open dialogue.

However, if you do use this technique be prepared for accusations of neurosis.

"Look how uptight you are about the subject! Your touchiness just proves my point. Obviously, you're not really sure about this decision."

If this happens, respond with, "That's *your* interpretation of the subject. I think you're uptight about the subject or you wouldn't keep bringing it up!" Or, if you prefer, simply remain silent.

You Are Not Alone

Enlist someone else's help in coping with pressure. Ask your spouse or a friend to play a supporting role, but don't let them take the lead. This is your act and you won't respect yourself if you don't take responsibility for dealing with the situation.

You can also use a spouse, a friend, a counselor, or a workshop group to role-play ways to deal with pressure. This gives you a chance to hone your skills before you confront the meddler.

Begin by brainstorming a typical pressure situation. If nothing comes to mind, use one of these hypothetical scenarios:

- You tell your women's group that you're pregnant. Their response: "You've got to be kidding. You're only having a baby to avoid deciding what you want to do with your life."

- You tell your best friend, who's child-free, that you and your wife are considering parenthood. The next day you receive a special delivery package—a book about the miseries of parenthood.
- You and your husband are having his parents to dinner. Before your in-laws even take off their coats, they begin hinting about grandchildren.
- You are discussing your life plans with your boss and mentor. You tell him that you and your wife have decided to remain child-free. He responds, "But you can't really mean that. Of course you'll change your minds. Let's see, when does Anna turn thirty-five?"

Once you've chosen an appropriate scenario, act it out with your spouse or friend, using one of the techniques described above. Give each other feedback. Then, run through it again, using the feedback to strengthen your approach.

Have your spouse or friend play the pushy role while you play yourself coping with that person. Or, try a chair dialogue (see page 28) with the meddler. This will help you get inside the other person's skin and see why he or she is putting pressure on you.

"Which Technique Should I Use?"

To choose the best assertiveness technique for a given pressure, you should consider:

- Your own personality. What's comfortable for you?
- The other person's personality. Which technique is most likely to succeed with this particular person?
- Your desired goal. Do you want this person to open up or shut up?
- Your relationship with the other person. How close is it? Do you want to make it more distant by dodging or si-

lence, or closer by explaining in the hope of setting up a meaningful dialogue?
- How firm is your decision? Will pressure only get in the way or could it help test your commitment?
- Could this person help you with your decision? If so, maybe you should listen even if doing so is frightening and painful.

Although all of these techniques are useful, they are really just moves in a game, and the real key to coping with pressure is to recognize that:

- You are playing a game.
- You can choose whether or not to play.
- You can choose how to play it.

In fact, how you play the game is less important than the realization that you are playing one.

IS THERE AN END IN SIGHT?

As a final note of comfort, meddlers do give up and go home after a while. According to sociologist Jean Veevers, a pioneer in child-free research: "This social pressure seems to reach a peak for both husbands and wives during the third and fourth years of marriage—after sufficient time has passed for children to be 'expected' but before the couple has learned to deal skillfully with (or avoid) their social detractors."

So if you do decide to remain child-free, there will be less pressure as time goes on, and you'll be more skilled at handling it.

In light of this, you might wonder whether it's simply easier to play a waiting game. Rather than call attention to a shaky choice, why not wait until it's firm? And, in fact, there are couples who don't publicize until after they sterilize.

However, there are some drawbacks to presenting family

and friends with a fait accompli. For one thing, they just might have some helpful comments or insights. They might even surprise you and support your choice of nonparenthood. Or, their questions may help convince you that it's the *right* choice. In fact, telling a few people about your leanings and finding out how well you handle their reactions may give you the confidence you need to decide on nonparenthood. Finally, dealing with the meddlers can be a useful way of gauging the stability and progress of your decision. The more firmly the decision sits in your head, the more easily the pressures will roll off your back.

~§ 5 §~

Poison Vials

Most of us like to think of ourselves as rational individuals, able to separate fact from fancy and truth from exaggeration when we make a decision. And in most instances we can do just that. When a salesperson or real-estate agent extols the virtues of a particular car or home, we take their inflated claims with a grain of salt, nodding politely while we mentally total up the pluses as well as the minuses. After all, we're too sophisticated to believe everything we're told!

But, unfortunately, we're not as sophisticated when it comes to the baby decision. For we tend to believe everything we're told about the virtues and/or horrors of parenthood, forgetting that we're being subjected to just as much salesmanship in this regard, primarily because the salesperson is society at large. Twenty-five years ago we all accepted, without question, the notion that parenthood was the most fulfilling of experiences. Today, just as many of us believe that giving birth is tantamount to fighting a war, a war that will deprive us of peace, tranquility, sleep, and personal satisfaction. And, in the wake of these two extreme views, comes a whole flood of murky beliefs about both life choices, beliefs so popular it never occurs to us to question them. I call them poison vials because by polluting your mind they seriously hinder good decision-making. In this chapter, we're going to hold these beliefs up to the bright light of reality, to see how irrational they are.

POISON VIALS ABOUT PARENTHOOD

"Infancy lasts forever." People who are frightened by the endless demands of a dependent infant tend to forget that infancy doesn't last until age eighteen. In their view, once a baby always a baby. Actually when it comes to infants, what you see is *not* what you get, at least not for very long. Some time between ages two and four months you'll be washing less and sleeping more. If you want to be a parent and you're cowering in fear of an eighteen-year-old infant, you're running from an overgrown shadow of your imagination.

"I know I would resent giving up my freedom and that means I shouldn't become a parent." Every parent resents the loss of freedom at one time or another. Who wouldn't prefer a trip to Europe to a trip to the pediatrician? Who wouldn't rather listen to pure Mozart than Mozart adulterated by a toddler's wails? Happy parents aren't people who feel no resentment. They're the ones who live with the resentment because, on their parenthood scale, the pleasures outweigh the pains. And generally, they are also people who had already anticipated the resentment before becoming parents. They didn't make the choice while puffing on pipe dreams of perfect parenthood. They knew there would be times when they would fume with resentment. And they also knew that as their children grew, so would their freedom.

So the question to ask while working on the baby decision is not whether you would resent giving up your freedom. Of course you would. The question is: How much would you resent it? Enough to turn blue with depression and purple with rage, convinced that your life has been ruined? Or merely enough to turn green with envy occasionally when you think about child-free friends? The intensity of your resentment depends mostly on whether you feel a child is worth the sacrifices you *will* inevitably have to make. And if you do think a child is worth it, don't worry about resentment. When it comes, you'll be able to handle it.

"I should only become a parent if I'm 100% sure that's what I want." Children are never 100% wanted because their parents are humans who, by definition, never want anything 100%. We humans are ambivalent because we're aware of other possibilities, because we know we're giving up one thing to have another. Who doesn't have qualms about getting up in the middle of the night? Who wouldn't question the wisdom of an eighteen-year commitment, no returns, no refunds, no guarantees?

If you're reasonably sure you want children as you follow the steps in this book, go ahead and have them. *But don't expect total certainty.* In fact, if you don't have *any* doubts about parenthood, that would be cause for concern because it might mean you have unrealistic expectations about the joys of parenthood and your ability to be the perfect parent.

Two important factors in preparing for parenthood are forming realistic expectations and accepting ambivalence. By recognizing and accepting your own conflict and sharing it with your spouse, you will move toward an improved marriage and a better family life.

"We can't afford a child." Children *are* expensive. According to latest estimates, it costs about $100,000 to rear one child, not counting the cost of four years of college. Yet staggering as this figure may seem, chances are you could afford a child—if you wanted one. Although many couples decide not to have a second or third child for financial reasons, I believe the great majority decide against a first child for emotional, not financial, reasons. But it's much easier to blame economics than to admit you simply don't want children.

However, hiding behind the dollar sign cheats you out of

an opportunity for growth. If you want to develop your potential, you have to come out from your hiding place and openly confront a question: What is it in your life that makes you want to be child-free? What are the *emotional* treasures you'd have to give up if you had a child?

Most couples who choose to remain child-free have more than enough money to support a child. Many earn two professional salaries. They could actually afford to live better than most parents even if they have children, which is why they are often accused of selfishness. Yet these couples, who prefer to spend their money on activities other than parenthood, have more important reasons for remaining child-free.

"Everyone keeps telling us that kids are awful and that they'll ruin our lives." This assumption, which would have been an anathema in our parents' and grandparents' day, has become increasingly popular among certain groups of people, both parents and nonparents. What wonderful lives we would all be leading, they proclaim loudly, if these noisy, demanding, ungrateful kids weren't wreaking havoc on our lives and disrupting our sleep. The doomsayers view children as the dumping ground for all these frustrations. They tend to forget that child-free is not synonymous with problem-free. Time may be more available to the child-free, but it's still finite. We still have to make compromises, set priorities, and give up some pleasures for others. Such people also fail to understand the nature of children. Like Henry Higgins, who wanted to know "Why can't a woman be more like a man?," they want to know why a child can't be more like an adult. They view disobedience and misbehavior as a personal attack on their authority rather than the natural actions of someone who simply hasn't yet learned patience and control. One mother of two expressed it beautifully: "If there is just one thing I could tell your readers, it would be to think of children as smaller people, not as monsters or Martians." Although this woman's career as a mathematician has been hindered by her children, she has never forgotten that they are human beings, not in-

animate objects or malicious creatures out to block her path. It's a lesson we'd all do well to remember.

Raising children is difficult, and certainly not everyone should do it, but a decision to remain child-free should never be made on the basis of this inaccurate assumption because it cheats *all* decision-makers by stunting the growth they're entitled to. Although it's equally harmful to parents and nonparents, they suffer in different ways. When they fall prey to this assumption, nonparents stop too soon and parents go too far.

Nonparents don't bother to analyze the positive implications of their choice. It isn't enough to know why parenthood is awful, you also have to know why nonparenthood can be so fulfilling. What would a child prevent you from doing? Making laws? Flying planes? Writing books? Whatever your mission or your goals, are you arranging your life so you can really devote yourself to those goals? Are you taking the risks and making the commitments that will make these activities as satisfying as possible? If you choose nonparenthood simply because you're convinced that kids are horrible brats, you won't be able to make the most of your life without them.

Parents and parents-to-be, on the other hand, get carried away with unnecessary anxiety. They're the ones who expect every new stage and age to bring disaster, and they miss a lot of the fun of parenting. They're too worried and anxious to find any pleasure or fulfillment in their choice.

Many couples have told me that their worst postpartum problem was their own unrealistically negative expectations. In the old days, parents of newborns complained, "Nobody ever told us it would be so hard." Now that we're condemning parenthood and praising nonparenthood, we're hearing a new cry. "We never thought it would be so easy."

One young couple, ready to watch their marriage go down the tubes, was amazed to find themselves making love after putting the baby in his cradle. Expecting to hate the baby at 2:00 A.M., one father found rocking his daughter in the moonlight to be one of the high points of his day. Sure that only insanity led her to take a three-months' leave from her high-powered corporate job, one new mother ended up taking off the rest of the year because she was having so much fun. Obviously there are many people who would not find these experiences pleasurable, but painting an entirely negative picture of parenthood simply makes it needlessly frightening for those who really would have fun with their children.

When someone's in the midst of a tale of parental woe, listen with a critical ear. Ask yourself:

- Is this person giving me a realistic picture of parenthood or a caricature?
- Is this person sincerely interested in warning me about the problems of parenthood? Or does he or she have an ulterior motive?
- Does this person get a payoff for being unhappy? If I were in his or her shoes, would I cope better? If so, how?

If you're going to enjoy the life you choose, with or without children, surround yourself with happy people, not miserable ones. If you become a parent, find friends who not only vent their frustrations but also overcome them. If you remain child-free, look for role models too busy enjoying their freedom to bother attacking parenthood.

"I want to be a perfect parent and raise the perfect child. If I did any less, it would be terrible." Perhaps you think you're too worried, nervous, irritable, or moody to have a child. Maybe you're afraid you'll pass your neuroses on to your child. But chances are you're not any more neurotic than the rest of us, and what you're calling neuroses are only the normal conflicts and worries we're all subject to. There is no such thing as a perfect parent or perfect child. If you are a reasonably mature and satisfied adult who is eager to become a parent and willing to learn parenting skills, your child will, in all likelihood, turn out fine. Expecting yourself or your child to be perfect will only cripple your decision-making progress.

POISON VIALS ABOUT THE CHILD-FREE CHOICE

"I'm afraid I'll be sorry later, and that means I should have a child." You've made a careful, well-thought-out decision to remain child-free, but lately you've been plagued by fantasies of being sorry when you're fifty. Does this mean you should become a parent after all? Not necessarily.

Everyone will regret his or her decision. Regrets over what might have been are an inevitable part of life. Therefore, the question to ask is: "How strong will my regrets be?" It is also worthwhile to consider how often you may feel such regrets and how they will compare with your positive feelings toward your life choice. If you've thought about these issues, chances are your regrets will not outweigh your reasons for making your particular choice.

"I should remain child-free only if I have absolutely no desire for children." You can't expect an unequivocal choice. You just have to follow your overall leanings. You may have a strong desire for children, but an even stronger desire to pursue your own goals without the responsibility of caring for a child.

Elliot and Marla were fairly certain that the child-free choice was right for them, but occasionally pangs of desire for a baby held them back from a definite commitment. Upon closer examination they discovered that these pangs generally surfaced only on holidays when their young nieces and nephews were around. The rest of the time they rarely fantasized about babies; they were too engrossed in their careers and various hobbies. They realized they had been socialized to believe that "holiday time is kiddy time." This realization helped them make a definite commitment, and they redefined holidays as a time to enjoy the extended family they already had rather than creating a nuclear family they didn't want.

"Being a parent is the only way to meet my parenting needs." Most of us share a need to nurture, but remaining child-free

does *not* mean such needs will be thwarted. Moreover, it's possible that being a parent would be the *worst* possible way to meet these needs. So if you want to remain child-free, don't force yourself to become a parent just because you enjoy taking care of others. There are dozens of other ways you can nurture and create without becoming a parent.

"Everyone tells me I'd be a good parent, and that means I should be one." Mindy knows exactly what to do with other people's children. As head teacher of an innovative day care center, she's equally successful with the children she teaches, the staff she directs, and the parents she advises. But does enjoying other people's children mean that she would enjoy her own? Although her husband and friends are noisily pushing parenthood, Mindy hears a quieter inner voice whispering, "Peace, quiet, and solitude." She loves to meditate, read, sew, and listen to classical music. It would be hard to give up her quiet weekends for noisy babies.

The fact that Mindy has parenting skills doesn't mean she should become a parent any more than having mathematical ability means one should become an engineer. Only her inner desires can tell her whether or not to become a parent.

"Remaining child-free means you're selfish." As we saw in Chapter 4, this assumption is not only irrational, it's also completely arbitrary. It's a label that's tossed around casually and readily these days, but the definition of what constitutes selfishness can vary widely, depending on who's using the label. The fact is, there's simply no objective way to measure selfishness.

In my view, selfishness is an attempt to meet your own needs without regard for anyone else's. Self-love, on the other hand, means caring about yourself enough to do what's right for you, nourishing yourself in such a way that you can love others, too. And if you don't love yourself enough to make the decision that's right for you, it's unlikely that you'll be able to give your child the kind of love he or she needs.

Remember, too, that people who use this label are often guilty of an ulterior motive. Perhaps they are not happy with their decision, and in an attempt to justify it, they're trying to manipulate you.

"If we don't have a child, it's because we're chicken." The assumption that child-free couples are simply afraid to take a risk, that they are hanging onto a familiar life-style because they can't handle any change in their lives, is a popular one, especially among self-righteous parents. But in fact, cowardice or courage can be manifested in either life choice. The cowardly may have children because they're afraid of others' disapproval. The heroic may have children only by leaping over their fears, hoping for the best. Others certainly do remain child-free because change is threatening. But many choose the child-free option despite heavy social pressures and their own fears of regret, and show great courage in doing so.

"Remaining child-free means remaining the same." You're already child-free, right? So you know what to expect if you remain child-free, right? Wrong. Your life will change through the years whether you fear it or look forward to it eagerly. Child-free at twenty is not the same as child-free at thirty-seven or at fifty-six. You will certainly have many opportunities to grow and change with or without children.

"Children are wonderful. If I remain child-free, I'll be missing the ultimate life experience." Busybodies may ask you what the point of marriage or life is, if you don't have children. Parenthood is certainly a profound experience, but for some it would mean profound misery. Of course you'll miss something by not having a child, but if your talents, energies, and interests lie elsewhere, you would miss even more by having a child.

Poison Vials That Trouble Women

"I have to have a child before I turn thirty-five." Like thousands of other American women, you have decided to establish your career and devote time to marriage before even

considering motherhood. But now you're getting older and beginning to feel that time is running out. It is, but not as fast as you think. Although you may have been led to believe that age thirty-five is a time bomb, it's time to reconsider that assumption. Improved medical care and new knowledge make motherhood after thirty-five quite feasible. So take your hand off the panic button. You will have to make a decision, but not tomorrow, next month, or even next year. (See Chapter 9 for more information.)

"Having a child will ruin my career." Not so. First, it's important to distinguish between "destroy" and "delay." Ask any career woman who is also a mother if motherhood produced setbacks in her career. She'll be sure to tell you some lively stories, such as:

> Roslyn, a forty-year-old lawyer, went into labor while involved in a long-drawn-out, precedent-setting case. "Even though I'd already arranged for my partner to take over when I went to the hospital, I went to the labor room knowing I'd missed an opportunity in the courtroom."
>
> Marjory, a thirty-four-year-old corporate executive, was called out of a crisis in the boardroom to be told of a crisis in the playroom. Her five-year-old daughter had fallen off a climbing toy and had to be taken to the hospital.

But events like these generally cause slowdowns, not shutdowns, and for women who have consciously chosen motherhood the excitement of childbirth or the satisfaction of ministering to a hurt child offset the frustration of career detours.

I wasn't ready to become a mother until I realized that hundreds of successful career women were also mothers. They may or may not have worked when their children were young. They may or may not have been frustrated when they had to take time off. But for most of them, a child at home did not automatically lead to a fiasco at the office.

Of course, some careers are harder to combine with motherhood than others. A doctor can work part-time more easily than a concert pianist. And a slowdown or setback in one field can be more serious than in another. If you are too ambitious to tolerate *any* setbacks, or if your field is such that time off could end your career, you probably should not have children unless your husband is one of those exceptional pioneers willing to take most of the responsibility for the child. (For more information on combining career and motherhood, see Chapter 13.)

Poison Vials About Preparing for Parenthood

"Caring for a pet will help me evaluate my ability to parent." Some couples assume that their success or failure with pets is an indication of the kind of parents they'll be. If their dog or cat is the light of their life, they believe a child would be also. If they find the responsibility of caring for an animal burdensome, they think that the responsibility of caring for a child would be too exhausting even to contemplate. Are they right? Perhaps, but I wouldn't bet on it. People's feelings about children are different from their feelings about pets. Puppies have to be fed, walked, and trained, but they don't require round-the-clock attention, and they don't have to be fed or changed at 2:00 A.M. On the other hand, rearing a child involves more work, but it can also be more rewarding and more fun.

Although your feelings about your pet may tell you something about your inclination for parenthood, don't make the mistake of correlating the experiences. If you have a pet, ask yourself how you feel about taking care of it, what sacrifices you've made, and what the rewards are. Consider what these feelings might tell you about the baby question. Just remember that it's a big leap from pet care to parenting. Consider this clue to be just one of many. Your decision will be based on a combination of *all* your feelings about *all* the issues related to parenthood.

"Borrowing a child will tell us how we would feel about our own child." Child borrowing can provide useful information, or it can simply confuse the issue. It all depends on how you approach such an experiment and what you hope to get out of it. Let's look at two child-borrowing sessions to note some of the common pitfalls.

Heavenly Saturday. Frank and Evelyn borrowed a colleague's ten-year-old daughter Melissa for the day. In her frilly lace dress, with her curly blond hair, she could have posed for a children's clothing advertisement. She pranced around the zoo and giggled in the ice cream parlor. They all had a wonderful time, and Frank and Evelyn concluded they would enjoy being parents.

Unfortunately, what they don't know *will* hurt them. If Melissa hadn't gone out with them, she would have been at home driving her parents crazy. For Melissa wants to be the center of attention, not at the periphery of her parents' work activities. A dual-career couple, Melissa's parents form a clean-up committee of two every Saturday. So far Melissa has turned down all invitations to join the committee. In Melissa's neighborhood, there are few children and consequently there are many demands on Melissa's parents.

Even if Frank and Evelyn found they could cope with and perhaps end Melissa's complaints, they wouldn't necessarily be able to cope with parenthood. Enjoying the company of a pretty 10-year-old doesn't necessarily mean they'll love a screaming infant.

Hellish Sunday. Chris and Patty have borrowed a six-month-old named Joshua, and they're puzzled and frustrated. He's wailing at the top of his lungs and leaking from the bottom of his diaper. Neither bottle nor rocker nor pacifier will calm him, and his keepers are hardly calm themselves.

What happened to the cheerful cherub they fell in love with two months ago at his parents' house? Obviously Joshua's parents are competent to care for babies but they are not.

Obvious, but wrong. Two crucial events have taken place

between the two meetings. Joshua has changed: as a six-month-old he has just reached the age of stranger shyness. When they held him two months ago, he didn't realize as fully as he does now that Chris and Patty were *not* Mommy and Daddy. And his own parents had been there, providing a security base.

Also, Chris and Patty themselves have changed. Two months ago, the baby question was an open one, and they were relaxed about it. But now they've worked themselves into a panic: Patty's thirty-eighth birthday is approaching. So instead of playing happily with Joshua as they did before, they're looking at him anxiously as if his bald head were a crystal ball. Because they are tense, Joshua responds with tension of his own. And of course, his unhappiness upsets them all the more.

It's quite possible that Chris and Patty would love being parents if they just understood Joshua's stage of development and resolved some of their own conflicts about parenting. Like the pet experience, child borrowing can be a useful clue, but only if it's considered as just one of the many issues involved in the decision-making process.

Here are some guidelines to successful child-borrowing:

1. Borrow a child only after you have spent time with her while her parents are present. This will help ease stranger anxiety. Try to see the child more than once, under ideal circumstances (a Saturday barbecue when the parents and child are well rested), and again under worse circumstances (when the child is sick or when the parents have just arrived home from work exhausted and the child is hungry). Talk to the parents before you borrow the child to find out about her personality, how they handle various problems, what they do about crying and about discipline.

2. When you make arrangements for borrowing, make sure you have all the equipment you need to make the child comfortable: bottles, diapers, clothes, and favorite toys for a young child; perhaps a book or game for an older child. Ask

the parents whether they anticipate any problems and if ask for advice on how to handle that problem.

3. Borrow the same child over a period of weeks, and under different circumstances.

4. Borrow children of different ages to get an idea of how you feel about infants versus toddlers versus elementary schoolers.

5. Don't borrow a child if your spouse doesn't want to on that particular day. Or, if you do and your spouse doesn't, arrange to see the child alone.

6. Don't borrow a child when you're particularly upset about the baby issue.

7. Don't assume that child borrowing will completely resolve the parenthood dilemma.

8. Don't assume you'll feel the same way about the borrowed child as you will about your own. In reality, your feelings about your own child will be much more intense.

9. Discuss your feelings about the experience with your spouse. Listen carefully. Don't try to talk your spouse out of his or her positive or negative feelings because they differ from yours, and therefore threaten you.

10. Ask yourself these questions about child-borrowing:

Before you borrow a child:

- What do you expect to learn? Are your expectations realistic?
- Do you have a hidden agenda, such as the unexpressed hope that "If my spouse can just see how awful kids really are, he'll give up the idea of parenthood," or, "If she only sees how cute babies are, she'll melt and forget her desire to be child-free?"

After you borrow a child:

- What did you enjoy about the experience?
- What did you dislike?
- Did you take problems in stride or did you take them personally?

- How comfortable were you with physical closeness?
- Which age groups are most appealing? Why?
- Which age groups were least appealing? Why?
- Are you eager to borrow this child again? Why or why not?
- What does this experience tell you about your possible strengths and weaknesses as a parent? About your desire to be a parent?
- How did you as a couple relate to the child? Was there easy cooperation? Or was there competition over who could be the better parent? Was there any arm-twisting to involve a spouse who really wanted to be elsewhere? Were there times you wanted to talk to your spouse but the child got in the way? How did you handle that, and how did you feel about it?
- In what ways do you think you would respond differently to your own child than to this child?

"Changing my/our minds is a sign of weakness." Hogwash! I agree with Emerson that "a foolish consistency is the hobgoblin of little minds." Flexibility is a characteristic of happy people, and exercising it can lead to a more fulfilling existence.

Jackie and Ken were active members of the optional parenthood movement. At twenty-five, they had been certain they wanted to remain child-free. At thirty-five Jackie gave birth to a son.

"It was hard to tell everyone we changed our minds," Jackie said. "We had been on talk shows, published articles, spoken at rallies. Would we be the laughingstock of the child-free world?

"It didn't turn out that way. Our friends were surprised, but they respected our choice."

"We don't regret our involvement in the optional parenthood movement," Ken added. "In fact, we're still active members, supporting other people's right to remain child-free.

And we know our decision really was an option, not just something we fell into."

"We have to have two children if we have one." Grace is a victim of the all-or-nothing myth. "I think we could manage *one* child and two careers," she told me, "but I doubt we could manage two. We don't want a lonely, spoiled child. It wouldn't be fair. So I guess we won't have any."

New research is beginning to punch holes in old myths about only children. (For more information on this subject see Chapter 9.)

A FINAL WORD ABOUT POISONS

Because these beliefs reflect our society's values and standards, it's hard to escape their influence. They are communicated to us in dozens of subtle ways: in the voices of friends and relatives, in the books we read, and the movies we watch. But if you maintain some perspective, you can avoid their deadly influence. Recognize that they are simply arbitrary and often misleading attitudes, and try not to let them interfere with the decision-making process. If Columbus had believed, as most of his contemporaries did, that the world was flat, he would never have discovered America. Similarly, your mistaken assumptions can prevent you from making your own voyage of self-discovery.

⊰ 6 ⊱

But What
Would Gloria Say?

Alicia is well established in her career as a psychiatric nurse. She loves children and wants to be a mother as much as her husband wants to be a father. So what is holding her back? Her feminism is. Although she and her husband share all chores, and plan to share all responsibilities for child care, she wonders, "Can I really be a feminist and a mother, too? If I have a baby, will I be a traitor to the movement?"

Because I've heard similar sentiments expressed by a number of feminists considering the baby issue, it's important to ask: Does feminism preclude motherhood? The answer: *Absolutely not.* In the words of New York radio commentator Sherrye Henry:

> The very word "feminine" implicitly indicates the ability to reproduce. Must we deny ourselves the joy of our most natural function to become "feminists"? If so, take me off the lists. If my daughters decide not to have children—again one of the options they are fortunate to have—let them do so because their interest is simply in other directions, not because they think they must choose between motherhood and feminism.

Women who feel they have to make such a choice are missing the point of the women's movement. Feminism isn't simply about climbing the career ladder: It's about options and choices. In the old days before feminism and contraception, a woman could read only one kind of handwriting on the wall—the scrawls of children . . . and more children. And the woman who lived to be overwhelmed was lucky. Many of her less fortunate sisters didn't even survive childbirth. Now, thanks to feminism, women have many choices. But if we slam the door on the motherhood choice simply because we've been presented with the child-free choice, we're simply exchanging one prison for another, instead of opening the door to a whole array of possibilities.

In November 1979, in New York City, an important breakthrough took place—the first conference on feminism and the family. That same week, Betty Friedan published an article on that subject in the *New York Times.*

Friedan, who was the first to tell the world that women need work as well as love, was also among the first to remind us that women need love as well as work. Women, like men, have never been able to enjoy a balance between the two. In the past, women devoted themselves to love while men devoted themselves to work. Today, if we have not yet achieved a true balance, we have at least recognized our desire for it. As men take more time to enjoy their friends and wives and possibly their children, women are realizing that even though they want liberation, they do not want isolation. They want careers and independence but they want them within a framework of personal commitments that sometimes include children.

Although there are a few feminists who denigrate the choice of motherhood, especially as a full-time occupation, mainstream feminist groups have fought tenaciously for social change that would make motherhood more enjoyable. But it's not surprising that in the early days of its life, the women's movement focused more on career issues. They had to struggle to get women out of the kitchens and nurseries before they could send women back there, comfortable in the knowledge that it was a choice, not a societally imposed prison. But those ten to fifteen years of being told "thou shall not procreate" have deeply affected us. So even if the women's movement has shifted gears on the baby question, it may take time for our individual psyches to catch up. But catch up we must.

The point is, regardless of the nature or intensity of your involvement with the women's movement, feminism can coexist peacefully with either life choice. Even more important, it can enhance whatever decision you do make. As a feminist, chances are you'll find motherhood even more enjoyable and less stressful because you'll be aware of both the pitfalls and the ways to avoid them. And as a child-free feminist, you'll have a rallying point for your decision, which may be more satisfying as a result.

FEMINISM AND MOTHERHOOD

If it's common for women to have fantasies of being devoured by their babies, it's equally common for feminists to imagine that all the independence they've struggled so hard to achieve will be eaten away by a ravenous infant.

Perhaps you've spent years training for a career and you're finally beginning to achieve your goals. Maybe you've finally found a nonsexist male with whom you'd like to spend your life. Or perhaps you've spent years chiseling away at an unequal relationship and rebuilding it into something more balanced. So, frightening as the question may seem, you can't help wondering: "Now that I'm beginning to have it all, would a baby wreck it all?"

Certainly, nature is not an equal opportunity employer. You can negotiate behavior, but you can't negotiate biology. Even if your husband is genuinely nonsexist, he can't carry the baby for half the pregnancy or nurse for half of the feedings. And he won't need a few weeks' postpartum to get his strength back. Chore lists can be passed back and forth, but in terms of carrying and bearing a child, anatomy is still destiny.

Moreover, many women are dubious about pregnancy simply because it's such a graphic differentiation of the sex roles. The biological differences seem to symbolize the behavioral differences that may follow. And in our imperfect world, there's no guarantee that the burdens of child care won't fall primarily on a woman's shoulders. So in light of these very valid issues, any feminist, or indeed any woman, would be a fool not to cast an occasionally critical eye on motherhood. Yet the picture is not nearly as bleak as it was in the past. For it is not motherhood per se that is the problem; it is the institution of motherhood. And as a result of the pioneering efforts of the women's movement, the institution is beginning to change.

Let's take a look at some of the ways feminism is reshaping our definition and expectations about motherhood.

Fathers. According to Carol Nadelson, Vice-Chairman of the Psychiatry Department at Tufts University/Tufts New England Medical Center, the best thing that has happened to motherhood is fatherhood. "I think the problem has been that fathers have gotten left out of everything. If you really look at changing the model, you're also changing the role of the father."

Everyone in the family benefits when father is welcomed into the family circle rather than made to feel like a fifth wheel.

- Fathers enjoy being with their children and knowing they're important to their kids.
- Mothers can share both the work and the responsibility. Motherhood isn't as lonely as it used to be.
- Children are doubly blessed. When there are two bona fide parents, there are two benefits: First, two heads are better than one at coping with children's problems. Second, children feel more secure when mother isn't the only person in the world they can depend on.

Children. According to Nina Finkelstein, an editor of *Ms.* magazine, "Children integrated into feminist lives are lucky. I'm sorry that my own children didn't have that experience."

Children with independent mothers and intimate fathers grow up comfortable with independence and intimacy, regardless of their sex. Children in feminist homes also take pride in their contributions to the running of the household. When mother is no longer a slave, the child becomes more of a master.

Society. As Betty Friedan has pointed out, social conditions are a formidable barrier to many women who might choose motherhood: "How many women today 'choose' not to have children because they simply can't afford to stop working or because they can't count on adequate child care facilities?"

Why indeed should women have to choose between career and motherhood? Or choose both only to wind up too exhausted to enjoy either? The women's movement has been particularly vocal in pointing out, and working to eliminate, the evils of institutional motherhood. Feminists of both sexes have campaigned vigorously at the grass roots and federal levels to develop child care, family networks, parent support groups, and to institute changes in working hours to enable families to spend more time together. As these changes take hold women won't have to reject motherhood just because they reject martyrdom.

A feminist considering motherhood shouldn't simply ask whether or not she should choose motherhood. She should also ask, why does society make motherhood so difficult? Why isn't child care more readily available? Why are job-sharing, part-time jobs with benefits and flexi-time still so rare? For the feminist mother, a commitment to motherhood might be all the more fulfilling if it also embraced a commitment to broader social change. Far from being a traitor to the cause, she can use her knowledge and experience to become an important voice for the cause.

Childbirth. Feminist health care advocates, most notably the Boston Women's Health Book Collective, authors of *Our Bodies, Ourselves* and *Ourselves and Our Children,* have had an enormous impact on the nature and quality of childbirth. Women have taken back their bodies, becoming active consumers rather than passive compliers during pregnancy and childbirth. And fathers, instead of pacing nervously on the sidelines, now play a central role, acting as childbirth coaches. Our newborns are no longer rushed off to the nursery seconds after birth. They remain with Mom and Dad for an hour or two to allow family bonds to begin forming immediately.

Lifelines to new mothers. Through mothers' groups and individual counseling, in person and on the telephone, experienced mothers provide support and solutions to new mothers. Nothing compares with the relief of a new mother who has just discovered that other mothers share her feelings of fear, anger, loneliness, and frustration.

Role models. Because every woman is unique, no woman can simply repeat another's pattern and expect it to work for her. Nevertheless, as we grope in the dark, hoping to find new ways to mother, we can't help looking around for some shining examples. Observing and talking to women who have chosen not to be mothers, who combine career and motherhood or who manage to be full-time mothers and yet wholetime selves, make us feel less alone and guilty. Moreover, working mothers can serve as mentors for other working mothers, offering useful advice about child-care and ways to cope with the dual pressures of job and family.

Advice for Feminist Mothers

Let yourself enjoy motherhood. Some feminists try to reconcile the dichotomy between feminism and motherhood by downgrading the role and not letting themselves express any motherly feelings. Seemingly desperate to reassure themselves that their brains haven't turned to mush, they return to work before they're physically and emotionally ready. Nervous about falling into the stereotype of the gushing, proud parent, they are quick to change the subject if asked about their kids. And when they do discuss motherhood, they often emphasize the difficulties rather than the joys. One feminist mother, Alice Abarbanel, described this problem: "Now I see that a lot of my words to other people, especially women's liberation women, were partially to impress. I feel I bragged about my negative fantasies of killing Amanda and didn't talk about or let myself feel many positive or 'typical' ones."

Part of the problem, once again, is overidentification with our own mothers. If their dictum was "Speak of love but keep silent about anger," we take the opposite view because we fear that in following in our mothers' footsteps we'll also experience all their frustrations and resentments. But we are not our mothers and the world is not the same. If we deny ourselves this gift, we are accepting the sorrows of motherhood while rejecting the joys. And we are denying our children the attention and love they need and deserve.

Feminist literature: a new kind of mothers' manual. Postpartum, with both of my children, I fed myself on feminist literature while feeding milk to my daughters. Doris Lessing, Adrienne Rich, and *Ms.* magazine spent as much time in the rocker as my girls did—baby in one arm, book in the other. It was my way of reassuring myself that I was still a feminist and an intellectual even if I was now a mother.

Angela Barron McBride and Alice Abarbanel report experiences similar to mine but they both felt uneasy. The combination of mothering babies and reading feminist literature seemed schizophrenic to them. However, self-condemnation for this perceived inconsistency is unfair. If you become a mother, recognize that your feminist beliefs will make motherhood more manageable. And women's books and magazines can play a special role in keeping you linked to feminism.

How Feminism Helps Nonmothers

A vehicle to fulfillment. Thanks to feminism, women can find fulfillment in nonmothering ways: through careers, artistic endeavors, political and social activism. All of the above can fill one's need for what Erik Erikson calls generativity— that is, a need to feel creative and to somehow contribute to the quality of life for future generations.

High self-esteem. In the past, women who chose not to mother were labeled selfish, immature, cold, and neurotic. Now, women choosing to remain child-free can see their decision as a strength rather than a weakness. Both the women's movement and the optional parenthood movement have reminded us that our value as individuals is not limited to our reproductive value. And the child-free woman is a living demonstration to other young women of the viability of nonmotherhood.

Here are some special contributions you could make as a child-free feminist:

- Work wholeheartedly for political and social change rather than splitting afterwork hours between kids and campaigns.
- Help organize and improve day care.
- Serve as a mentor to younger women in your field.
- Be a special friend to someone else's child.
- Educate girls and young women about feminism.

As a teacher, a counselor, a Scoutmaster, or just as a pal to your friends' children, you can:

- Help girls to grow up strong, active, and self-confident and to recognize all the educational and career opportunities open to them.
- Teach boys to value their own feelings and nurturing abilities and to commit themselves to equal rights.

PEACEFUL COEXISTENCE

There is room in feminism for both choices, and it's important for women who make opposite choices to support each other. Sexism and pronatalism are related. Contempt for child-rearing is contempt for both women *and* children. When child-free women scorn motherhood, they scorn not only women with children, but all women. In the words of Adrienne Rich: "Any woman who believes that the institution of motherhood has nothing to do with *her* is closing her eyes to crucial aspects of her situation."

Motherhood gives women a feeling of community, a link with other women past, present, and future throughout the world. Even if we choose not to have our own babies, we can choose to be proud of other women's babies as one of the many possible fruits a woman can bear. We can recognize and value our own nurturing qualities, even as we develop assertiveness and competence. It is possible to reject motherhood for oneself without rejecting women who are mothers.

Similarly, feminist mothers need to support child-free women. They must recognize that a nonmother does not escape sexism merely by remaining child-free. She may avoid the burdens of motherhood, but she'll still have to face the stigma of nonmotherhood—and it's a stigma that persists, even today.

Even among feminist mothers themselves, there are often two groups: the playroom group and the boardroom group. Part of the problem is cognitive dissonance (see page 79). Many women are so afraid they've made the wrong choice that they'd rather not spend any time with those who have made a different choice—a choice that might seem more reasonable if they look too closely.

Bertha, a child-free feminist, laughs while watching her friend Debra's toddler daughter reading *Of Woman Born*—upside down. She wonders, "Will I be sorry later?" Debra, meanwhile, envies Bertha's freedom to pursue her journalism career and campaign for the ERA. Debra, who has organized a popular and successful play group and a mothers' group, also sometimes envies another friend, Randi, a mother of two who holds down a full-time teaching job. "Am I lazy? Am I afraid of success?" she asks herself. Rat-race Randi, in turn, envies Debra the luxury of leisurely play. She feels guilty about leaving her children with a day care mother, and at night she's often too tired to give them much attention. And on it goes . . .

The truth is, we need each other. If we want our children to come of age in a world that respects diversity, we must respect each other's choices. If we're too insecure to band together, we're going to be divided and conquered by the sexist opposition.

Child-free women can keep mothers posted on events they may have to miss. Mothers can give nonmothers accurate battlefield reports rather than armchair observations about parenting. Their testimonies are important data for planning social change.

Women who have made opposite choices can also meet some of each other's personal needs. For example, Elaine sometimes takes Cathy's daughters to a park on Saturday afternoons. Elaine gets a chance to enjoy two little girls without having to take on the hassles of motherhood. And Cathy gets a chance to soak in a bubble bath or work in her studio. Whenever Elaine, who lives alone, wants a feeling of "family" she can get it at Cathy's house, as she often does on Sundays and holidays.

FEMINISM AND THE FUTURE

According to the members of the Boston Women's Health Book Collective, "the 'personal' and the 'political' are inseparably intertwined. . . . For many of us, motherhood has been our most radicalizing experience." It's one thing to hear other mothers describe their frustration; it's quite another to live with it. Mothers are potential social activists because of their frustration. Traditional women who might otherwise turn their backs on the movement, join when they realize that sisterhood is an alternative to suffering; that mothers' groups are an antidote to loneliness; that politics and group activism may be the only route to social change.

Psychoanalyst Jean Baker Miller and writer Erica Jong have both given considerable thought to the problems all mothers face.

Dr. Miller says, "Motherhood shouldn't have to be incompatible with developing other parts of oneself. All of our institutions, schools, workplaces, and graduate training, are very much *not* what they should be, which is geared so that women can have children and participate without being penalized. And there's no reason that could not be done."

No reason, that is, except social prejudice. No reason other than our archaic belief that children are their mother's concern, not their father's or society's.

As Erica Jong points out:

We live in a country where there are no public facilities for changing a diaper, putting down a screaming child, nursing in public places. Our libraries, theaters, schools, supermarkets, airports have no child care facilities whatsoever. . . . If we truly want to integrate feminism and motherhood, we must demand that society become more hospitable to the needs of women and children. The cards are deliberately stacked against us and since most of our legislatures are filled with men who have nice wives at home to raise their kids relatively uncomplainingly, our grievances will never be understood.

But things *are* getting better. Feminism has already made a difference in the lives of thousands of women *and* men. More and more, congressmen's wives are not going to stay home and make life easy for their husbands. They're going to be in their own offices working hard at their own careers. And more of our legislators are going to be women, many of whom will also be mothers. But most important of all, as women and men begin to enjoy the rewards of a less constricted existence, they will demand action from our nation's leaders.

What is motherhood? Is it the loveliest of daydreams or the ugliest of nightmares? It can be either, said feminist leader Charlotte Perkins Gilman; it depends on the society in which a mother lives. Gilman portrayed motherhood as bliss in *Herland,* a Utopian fantasy novel. She portrayed it as blight in "The Yellow Wallpaper," a surrealistic story of postpartum depression. The difference in the two experiences lies in the social backdrop. In "The Yellow Wallpaper," the woman who goes mad is a victim of a patriarchal society. Her husband and her doctor forbid her to work. In *Herland,* however, where motherhood was the be-all and end-all of existence, women were active and assertive.

Pessimists may rush to point out that men did not exist in Herland; therefore motherhood can't be pleasant if men are present. But I'm not convinced. I've been impressed by the feminist families that I've met and observed. They haven't solved all the problems, but they're working on it, and finding a great deal of satisfaction in doing so.

≈§ξ≈

Step Three

———————

Considering
Happiness

❧ 7 ❧

Which Way Happiness?

There are as many ways of defining happiness as there are
ways of being happy. For some couples, children are a
necessary ingredient; for others, they would simply spoil
the broth. The very fact that you're conflicted about the baby
issue indicates that you could probably find satisfaction in
either choice. But it's equally true that one choice will, finally,
seem more appealing. "Aha," you say, "but how can I figure
that out?" By understanding what happiness means to you; by
recognizing the impact that your attitude toward happiness
will have on the decision-making process; and by considering
what each choice can offer in terms of your own definition.

In this chapter, we're going to look at some of the building blocks of happiness and examine how they relate to the
decision-making process in general and to each life choice in
particular. Once you have a handle on some of these issues,
you'll be in a better position to make the choice that will lead
to the sometimes elusive goal of happiness.

But suppose you don't even have a handle on happiness itself. Should you base your decision on who you are now, or
who you would like to be in the future? I believe you have to
base it on both. A good baby decision should fit comfortably
now, yet allow ample room for future growth. We are all subject to doubts and depression. If on your good days you don't
want children and on your bad days you do, you probably

should remain child-free. Your fantasies of children as res-
cuers are only fantasies; you'll be sadly disillusioned if you
expect children to bring you happiness. Suppose, however,
you sing lullabies on your good days, and think about vasec-
tomies on the bad ones? Then you should probably delay your
decision until you feel more positive about parenthood even
during the bad times.

Remember, there is no such thing as the perfect decision.
Some ambivalence is par for the course. In fact, a characteristic of a happy person is the ability to make the best of a
decision, regardless of the outcome. If you are unhappy now,
is it because you expect too much? Do you really have to
change your life itself, or do you simply have to readjust your
definition of happiness? Keep this idea in mind as you consider the issue of happiness.

BUILDING BLOCKS OF HAPPINESS

Adventure

If you're not adventurous, you won't be able to make a good
decision. You have to leave the safety of the status quo and
sail through the storm of new possibilities if you want to get
anywhere. And you also have to face the danger of making the
wrong choice.

If you remain child-free, you have an obvious edge over
parents in the amount of time and energy you have available
for both physical and intellectual adventures. But many nonparents don't take advantage of their unbounded opportunities
for adventure. Those who, year in and year out, work at the
same job, eat at the same restaurants and take the same vacations, don't have much sparkle in their lives. In contrast, parents who backpack or climb mountains with their children,
take them to a new museum or park every weekend, and who

make up stories and games with them are reaping a maximum of stimulation out of a minimum of opportunity.

Obviously, there is a potential for adventure in either choice —if you are willing to seek it. The question to ask yourself is, "What kind of adventures would I enjoy more?" Would parenting be an adventure or just a nightmare? Are you willing to give up big chunks of time, energy, and money that could be channeled into other forms of adventure that you enjoy? Are you willing to plan ahead, arrange child care, and pinch pennies in order to seek adventure with your family? Similarly, will you use the time and freedom you have as a nonparent to add variety and spice to your life?

Risk

It takes courage to bring a child into this world when there are so many unknowns. And it also takes remarkable courage to remain child-free in spite of outside pressures. Either choice can represent a step forward toward growth or a step backward toward safety, and you are the only one who can distinguish between the two motivations. As with the adventure question, you have to ask yourself, "Which risks do I want to take? Which ones will help me become more like the person I want to be?"

Spontaneity

Spontaneity, doing what you feel like doing, when you feel like doing it, is an important element in everyone's life, but it should not enter into the decision-making process itself. You can't just throw out the pills or walk into the vasectomy clinic because it feels right at the moment. Remember, you'll have to live with that split-second choice for a lifetime.

Being a parent fosters spontaneity in some ways and

squelches it in others. Children's silliness and their ability to live in the present allow their parents the freedom to revel in their own childlike qualities and to focus on the present. But in other areas of their lives parents lose a great deal of spontaneity. Their sex life (is there privacy available?), their social life (is there a baby-sitter available?), and their mobility (are schools and playmates and child care available?), require much more planning when children are involved.

Obviously, then, nonparenthood offers a greater potential for spontaneity. If you're child-free and you have a craving for Chinese food, you can head for the Peking Restaurant without having to call up a baby-sitter. You can make love on the living room rug without having to worry about being found there by a child. But, ironically, many child-free couples take this kind of freedom for granted, and associate true spontaneity with the uninhibited behavior of children. If you're basically interested in nonparenthood, don't be swayed by this belief. There are other ways to get rid of your inhibitions than by asking your offspring to function as your therapist. You *can* learn how to enjoy the child in you without having any of your own.

Flexibility

People who can roll with the punches are usually freer to make a decision because they can either live with the consequences or rethink the decision. Of course, the baby decision is different because once you have a baby or a vasectomy you can't rethink the decision quite so easily. But, despite these limitations, it is still possible for a flexible person to make healthy adjustments to a less-than-perfect decision.

Suppose you have a child and discover, too late, that you've made the wrong choice. If the decision was made responsibly, you will have some loving feelings toward children or you wouldn't have made that choice in the first place. You don't owe your child the perfect childhood; it wouldn't prepare him or her for our imperfect world anyway. You just owe the child love, respect, attention, and discipline. Parenting groups and professional counselors could help you feel more at ease about parenting. You might also enjoy your child more if you made some changes in your life. If you were home full-time, perhaps returning to work would help ease your boredom and resentment. If you were working full-time, switching to a part-time schedule might make you feel less overburdened.

Similarly, if you were sterilized because you were convinced you'd never want a child, you can still change your mind and adopt. And, of course, there are dozens of ways to enjoy children without having your own.

Flexibility is particularly important in the decision-making process itself. According to Gail Sheehy, in our twenties we tend to do what we think we *should* do; in the thirties we do what we *want* to do, and in the forties, we question *whatever* we've done. The point is, as your life changes, your attitudes and feelings about children will change, so it's vital to be as flexible and open as possible about the baby decision. Don't take any drastic steps that could preclude a later change of heart. If you're in your twenties and believe that you'll never change in any way, you're either wrong or stagnating.

Mortality

Birth and death are inextricably linked. It has been noted that a pregnancy often follows an unexpected death in the family. On some unconscious level, it seems to be our way of replacing our lost beloved and assuring the continuity of the family. And on a more conscious level, children seem to be our passport to immortality—the means through which we can live on after we die.

However, there are other ways to defend ourselves against death. According to Yale University psychiatrist Robert Jay

Lifton, there are four other paths to immortality besides parenthood:

1. Theological immortality—a belief in an afterlife and the spiritual conquest of death.

2. Creative immortality—a legacy of creative work or social change.

3. Natural immortality—a feeling of "being survived by nature itself, the sense one will live on in natural elements, limitless in space and time."

4. Psychic immortality—the achievement, through meditation or other mystical experiences, of a feeling of oneness with the universe, a feeling that transcends death.

Now consider all four sources above, as well as Lifton's fifth mode—biological immortality through parenthood. What combination of modes seems right for you? Do you consider children necessary passports to immortality? If you have a child, will his or her existence help or hinder you from achieving other forms of immortality?

Although some couples choose parenthood as a way of coping with fear of death, for others this very same fear is a major impetus for delaying the decision. Having children, or even thinking about having them, reminds us that there will soon be creatures in this world who will outlive us. In fact, I believe that some of the anxiety about the age thirty-five cutoff is really displaced anxiety about the age seventy-five cutoff. The certain ticking of the death clock is much more frightening than the uncertain ticking of the birth clock, and it's easier to think about the cutoff we'll survive than the one we won't. By avoiding the issue altogether, we can pretend that we're not getting older.

However, we can only live fully if we accept the fact that we are going to die. As Lifton and others point out, when we repress the reality of our death we also repress our humanity. Thus, by coming to terms with the baby question, your life will be richer whatever you decide because you will have had the courage to accept aging and death.

Mission

Martin Buber wrote: "Every person born into this world represents something new, something that never existed before, something original and unique. . . . Every man's foremost task is the actualization of his unique, unprecedented, and never recurring potentialities. . . . ."

What is your goal, or goals? Do you want to become president of your company, a political leader, a successful artist, a social activist? Or do you want to focus your energies on human relationships, spiritual development, personal growth, or simply enjoying being àlive? As you think about your mission and how the question of children relates to it, keep the following issues in mind:

1. Your mission is your means to happiness. If you find a meaningful purpose and devote yourself to it, happiness will result. But remember that yesterday's mission may not be today's. Your goals will change as your life changes.

2. Although a sense of mission is essential to your happiness, rigid adherence to an old mission is not. It's possible to be totally committed to political change, career goals, or art for the next ten years and then to commit yourself totally to parenthood for the following ten years. You have to ask yourself whether you would feel any sense of mission in parenthood. If the answer is no, but you think you would enjoy parenthood, consider whether parenthood would prevent you from meeting your other goals.

3. It's possible to have more than one mission. A child-free person might be equally committed to career goals and to social activism. A parent might be equally committed to a canvas in the studio and a child in the home. However, if you have too many goals, you won't be able to fulfill any of them. Although two or even three goals are possible for some people, for others only one passion at a time is feasible.

4. For some women, the decision to combine career and motherhood is a genuine decision to fulfill two missions. For

others, the same choice is simply a way of creating so much "busy work" that they won't have to face up to other goals that are somehow threatening. Abraham Maslow coined the term "Jonah complex" to describe this "fear of one's greatness." He also defined it as the "evasion of one's destiny," or "running away from one's own best talents."

Why should we fear our greatness? Maslow offers three reasons: (i) fear that others will envy us; (ii) fear that we'll be overpowered by ecstasy; and (iii) fear that we will be "punished" for daring to be great.

You may also be reluctant to work toward your goals because you are:

- Afraid of failing
- Unwilling to make the sacrifices involved
- Afraid of making a big change in your life. (Will your family and friends still love you? Will you ever have leisure again?)

As part of the decision-making process, you must consider whether your decision is influenced by a desire to escape your destiny. Do you want to be a mother because you'll shine at motherhood or because you are afraid of shining at work? Are you considering a pregnancy simply to protect yourself from the perils you perceive in success?

For Cassie, becoming a mother was an attempt to run away from her talents; she had been told she would soon become a partner at the law firm if she just kept up the good work. Three months later, she got pregnant, began to work part-time, and seemed to lose all interest in the job. Cassie knows that success in her field is the goal she really wants to strive for, but she's afraid she'll lose her husband if she dedicates herself to this mission. Her mentor is a divorcée; her other female colleagues are single. Her husband, an untenured humanities professor, is jealous of her accolades. She wants to keep him and she's afraid she won't be able to if she continues to achieve. She's also tired of working like a slave and of being envied by her friends. For Cassie, the decision to get pregnant was a decision "just to be a normal person and have a kid." But Cassie is playing with fire. She's going to resent giving up her commitment to career success eventually, and by then it may be more difficult for her to return to her field.

When they made their baby decision, Kay and Jason carefully considered her dedication to sculpture and his to political work. It sounded good on paper but a look at another piece of paper, their weekly calendar, showed very little time was actually devoted to her art or his politics. Jogging, Yoga lessons, Chinese cooking, and Japanese meditation all got in the way of their real work. They accuse themselves of laziness, but their real problem is fear. Anyone who can run so many miles and make it to so many classes on time isn't lazy. Kay and Jason are just plain scared.

- What if their friends envy or turn against them once they're successful?
- What if they fail; people will laugh at them. If they don't try, then they can't fail.
- How would success change their lives, their relationship, the way they spend their leisure time?

How does parenthood or nonparenthood relate to your potential for greatness? Is parenthood actually your vehicle to greatness? Would it seriously threaten your chances of achieving greatness? Or can it exist in tandem with your other goals?

Solitude

Solitude is an opportunity for contemplation, meditation, and self-discovery. It's not the misery of being lonely but the bliss of being alone. But many of us throw ourselves into an array of activities in a desperate attempt to avoid such self-exploration because we're afraid of the feelings—anger, jealousy, fear, helplessness, unworthiness—that we may find lurking in our psyches. However, we can't discover all of our positive strengths while we're bottling up all the negative emotions. We have to be comfortable enough with ourselves to let all kinds of feelings come bubbling up during the quiet times.

Of all the components of happiness, the craving for solitude is the one that clashes most brutally with parenthood. It's hard to hear the whispering of your inner voice over the wailing of a toddler. But ironically, parents sometimes make better use of their limited opportunities for solitude than nonparents do with their unlimited ones. Parents tend to appreciate solitude in the rare moments they can find it. And they often exploit what I call "nighttime solitary confinement." Believe it or not, children do sleep sometimes, especially at night. During those hours, some parents find they actually have more time for themselves than they did when they were child-free. Why? Because when they were child-free, they were never home. Now that children force them to be home and to be "on" most of the time, they appreciate and attend to the silence when they get it.

If you crave solitude, are you getting enough even without children? Would you be happier in a career where you freelanced or worked by yourself most of the time? Do you need to say no to more social engagements and yes to more "self" engagements?

If you're leaning toward parenthood, how would you and your spouse arrange for quiet time? Remember, too, that the issue of solitude is not solely a function of whether children are present or baby-sitters are available. The nature of your work is also important. If you are a mother of one quiet twelve-year-old and/or work full-time in quiet surroundings, you may enjoy more solitude than a child-free pediatrician or sales executive. Although it is possible to find private time as a parent, it's not easy, and if you require a great deal of solitude, consider that very carefully before having a child.

Freedom

Most of us tend to think about freedom as if it were money —accepting without question that more is better. But, like money, how it's used is often more important than how much there is. In fact, social psychologist Eric Fromm claims that many people would prefer the oppression of totalitarianism to the anxiety that comes with freedom: anxiety about making choices and taking responsibility for them. That's why so many couples who are anxious about the baby decision try to escape from their freedom of choice through an "accidental pregnancy" or what I call the "child-free drift." And there are other escape hatches as well. If you have a child because "everybody should become parents," or remain child-free because "nobody (except saints) should become parents," you're *not* exercising freedom of choice; instead, you're allowing societal values to dictate your decision.

Of course, there are many people who err in the other direction, seeking freedom at all costs. But if freedom is the ability to make a commitment based on your needs rather than on some external standard, total freedom abdicates any commitment whatsoever. Fear, not of responsibility but of commitment, propels such people to avoid ties of any kind. And, as a result, there's also no meaning or intimacy.

Freedom and commitment are interrelated, and both are necessary to a fulfilling life. As part of the decision-making process, you should consider not only whether you want to commit yourself to a child, but to whom or what *else* you want to commit yourself.

Becoming a parent doesn't necessarily mean giving up freedom; it often simply means exchanging one kind for another. Some parents claim that the activities they had to give up were empty in comparison to the fullness of life with children. In contrast, nonparenthood will give you more freedom in the abstract sense, but it will be an empty sort of freedom unless you make that choice because your life is full of something else. Nonparents can exercise their freedom by choosing life goals more suited to them than parenting.

Intimacy

You were not born in a vacuum and you can't grow in one, either. Although popular psychology would have you believe that you have to choose between personal growth and caring relationships, in reality growth occurs only in the context of such relationships. A healthy loved one encourages and supports your growth. Moreover, if you are too scared to get close to others, you will also be too scared to grow. People grow in relation to others, or they don't grow at all.

If you choose to remain child-free, you are *not* relinquishing your potential for growth and intimacy. You will have two precious commodities—time and energy—to nurture already flourishing relationships and build new ones. You will not have to readjust your comfortable old marital relationship for a new baby. Nevertheless, don't assume that your marriage or other relationships will stay exactly the same. They may deepen, change direction, or even end. Such change is inevitable, and the important questions to consider are: How do I want these relationships to grow and change? How do I want to grow and change within them?

Parenthood, on the other hand, will both fulfill and frustrate your needs for intimacy. The early child-rearing years double your opportunities for commitment and caring, but *more* doesn't necessarily mean better. Are you and your spouse secure enough to share the spotlight with a baby? Will you resent the baby because he's getting some of the attention that used to come to you? If you can't make love at noon, will you still want to make love at midnight? If you and your spouse are not as close as you'd like to be, are you hoping a baby will fill the gap? In all likelihood, a baby won't fill the gap; he or she will only widen it.

A Sense of Family and Community

• It's Thanksgiving Day at the Nelson household. Eric is carving the turkey while his wife Rhonda ties a giant bib around eight-month-old Tommy, who's been weaned to table food in the nick of time for a taste of turkey. Other guests include Tommy's older sister, age two, five of his cousins, two sets of aunts and uncles, and four grandparents.

• The Price home is just as crowded, but with a different sort of family. Dick and Rita, like most of their guests, are child-free by choice. Dick's law partner and best friend, Tony, and his wife, Amanda, have grown children on the other side of the continent. Lilly, who collaborates with Rita on art projects and who is divorced, brought along her twelve-year-old son, Mike. Mike is playing Ping Pong with Chuck, Tony and Amanda's grandson who's visiting from New York. This is the seventh year in a row that the same group of people has gotten together for Thanksgiving, a remarkable record considering that five of them live out-of-state.

Everyone needs a family. In fact, part of our need for intimacy is a need for the warmth and closeness that the old-fashioned extended family seemed to offer. "Two against the world" is a great theme for love songs and soap operas, but it's not enough for most of us. No matter how "perfect" your spouse may be, he or she can't possibly meet *all* your needs. And even if he or she could, how would you ever cope with widowhood or divorce?

We all need to feel connected to others, to know that there is more than one phone number to dial when we're depressed, more than one kitchen that's always open for tea and sympathy. This is one of the reasons why so many people mourn the loss of the old-fashioned extended family, all those aunts, uncles, and cousins living close by. Today, our high divorce rate and our penchant for mobility make it unlikely that many of us will have that kind of extended family—at least one that's related to us by blood.

But we can form our own families, as Dick and Rita did. Many couples feel that these "chosen" families meet their need for a sense of community better than their own blood relatives ever could. In fact, in our nostalgic longings, we often forget the petty bickering, the feuds, the jealousies we had to put up with in our "blood" families. We look back through the proverbial rose-colored glasses. The point is, you can have an extended family whether you're a parent or not.

Jane Howard is a single woman who belongs to a number of chosen families. In her ground-breaking book, *Families,* she describes several "found" families. According to Howard, ties are very strong in families that come together because they care about each other rather than because they are forced together by accidents of birth.

What are the requirements of a strong family bond regardless of the nature of the tie?

- Involvement. A feeling of commitment; a feeling that "these are my people through thick and thin."
- Continuity. An expectation that you will see these same people on a regular basis, over time.
- A crossing of generational boundaries. Having your own child or seeing your own parents may be about as appealing as a fingernail scratching across a blackboard. But to feel comfortable about your past as a child and your future as an older person, you have to have contact with persons under twenty and over fifty.
- Maintenance. A willingness to build relationships through entertaining, writing letters, making phone calls, and sending gifts. You have to give as well as take to keep a family going.
- Flexibility. An ability to coddle when someone needs

compassion, and to stand back when someone needs independence.
- Coordination. Every family needs a person who, in Ms. Howard's words, is a "switchboard operator," someone to keep track of family members' activities and whereabouts.

A "found" family network is not for child-free couples only. Even if you choose to have a child, you'll want an extended family with whom you can share both the joys and the burdens of the children.

Think about your current extended family. Is it a blood family, "found" family, or a combination of the two? How would your relationship to it be affected by parenthood? By a definite commitment to the child-free choice? Would a child mean more or less contact and harmony with this family?

If you do decide to have a child, don't underestimate your need for continuing contact with your family. Don't make the mistake of assuming, as our society has for years, that the nuclear family can be all things to all members. If you are cut off from your "blood" family and your "found" family is child-free, will the members support your decision to become a parent? If not, will you be able to maintain these old ties, or will you have to form new ones?

If, on the other hand, you are still close to your own family, are you prepared for changes in all family relationships after you have a child? Your parents may view your decision as a sign to let out the reins: now that you're a parent, you're no longer their baby and can do what you want. Or, they may decide to pull in the reins: now that you're a parent you need to be told how to take care of your child, a service they, as experts, can provide. Child-free couples, on the other hand, tend to worry that without children to form a nuclear family of their own, their connections to others will fray over time. The question that haunts them is: "When I'm old, will I be all alone?"

But there is no justification for having a child as protection against the loneliness of old age. Although many people do receive help and comfort from their adult children, many others don't. If you are worried about old age, but not interested in parenthood, use your energies to prepare for the future. Invest the money you would have spent on your children to build a nest egg for your retirement. Find a large circle of friends and meaningful activities, and you'll be well prepared for old age.

Happiness and Marriage

Is there any truth to the increasingly popular claim that lullabies are death knells to a perfectly good marriage? I do not think so. I view this as a pendulum swing. We've gone from the old myth that children save bad marriages to the new myth that they ruin good ones. Years of marital and family counseling have shown me how easy it is to scapegoat children; to claim that life was heaven before children came and hell after. That's much easier than taking responsibility for the situation. *If* your marriage is good; *if* you both want a child; *if* the child is planned; *if* you and your spouse discuss the potential problems and stress both before *and* after the birth; *if* you make time for each other, then your relationship will not suffer. Of course, that's a lot of "if's." But there are plenty of "if's" in any marriage, whether children are present or not.

If you both want a child very badly, you may feel closer than ever after the baby's birth. Moreover, discovering how well you cooperate on late-night feedings, spelling each other during crying jags, supporting each other through blue periods, and coordinating child care can make you both realize how strong your relationship really is.

There is no doubt that the early years of parenthood are very stressful. Nor is there any doubt that people who are unwilling to endure those stresses would be happier and more productive if they remained child-free. But if you both want children you needn't fear for your marriage.

However, if the strength of your marriage is based on the creation of your own little private world of two, a child may indeed weaken the relationship. In many relationships, one spouse is dependent on the other, and he or she may feel very threatened by the prospect of a child. If either you or your mate is fairly dependent:

1. Don't have a child. It would be a mistake for you as individuals and as a couple. If you *both* don't want a child, don't have one.

2. Try to work on the dependency issue. Consider the following possibilities: (a) Individual counseling for the dependent spouse to help him or her recognize and overcome whatever is blocking growth. (b) Marital counseling to work on the changes necessary in the relationship if the dependent spouse is to grow. The nondependent, nurturing spouse may have a "need to be needed." If so, he or she may need help adjusting to the spouse's increasing independence.

You are the only one who can judge what effect a baby may have on your marriage. But remember, a baby can't improve or ruin a marriage—only you and your spouse can do that.

Some people argue that the skills called for in a good marriage are totally different from those in parent-child relationships. I disagree. Here are the skills that are essential to both:

- The ability to be physically affectionate.
- The ability to communicate, including intimate sharing, listening, and problem-solving.
- The ability to make a commitment despite the risks involved.
- The ability to accept the other's uniqueness rather than treating that person as an object or extension of yourself.
- The ability to be flexible and to make compromises.
- The ability to give and to find pleasure in giving.

Marriage and parenthood differ not so much in skills required but in the choice of beneficiary.

What the Experts Say About Happiness

Research studies can't tell you whether or not you will be happier as a parent or a nonparent, but they can tell you a thing or two about the happiness of other parents and nonparents:

- Nonparents are at least as mentally healthy as parents.
- Child-free marriages are at least as happy as marriages that produce children.
- People are most dissatisfied with their marriages during the years they're raising children. Marriages are most successful prior to the birth of the first child and after the youngest leaves home. And they are most troubled when there are very young children in the home.
- Even though married people with young children are less happy and more stressed than married child-free persons, the differences are not considered statistically significant. Married people with young children are much happier than single people and much more similar in their happiness to child-free couples than they are to single persons.
- Despite the stress children put on marriage, one nationwide study reported that many more parents felt that their children had brought them closer together rather than pulling them apart.
- Marriages are happier when a couple has successfully controlled fertility; that is, a couple who either has no children or no more than the number they wanted. Couples who conceive accidentally are not nearly as happy.

Although there are many different ways to interpret these studies one clear statement can be made: No couple should have a child unless both really want one. There is no justification for claims that children are essential for happy lives or happy marriages. A person deciding to remain child-free is *not* condemning himself or herself to a lower quality of life, a bad marriage, or poor mental health.

However, research is not a crystal ball. It *is* useful for:

- Shaking up old assumptions like "marriages with children are happier."
- Justifying a new lifestyle: "See, child-free people are mentally healthy after all."
- Suggesting new angles you may not have considered. "Maybe social pressures have influenced us more than we realized."

But research should *never* be taken as gospel simply because no scientist is infallible, least of all the social scientist. All data are influenced by the questions scientists choose to ask and by the way they ask them. Moreover, both researchers and their respondents are influenced by current social myths. So when you read a study, consider these guidelines:

1. Who did the study? How might the researcher's professional affiliations or personal beliefs affect both the questions and the answers?

2. How did the author come to his or her conclusions?

3. Do the parents and the child-free couples fall into the same socioeconomic group so that meaningful comparisons can be made?

4. How do the researchers define "child-free"? Many studies are difficult to interpret because they lump together child-free persons who are merely delaying parenthood, would-be parents who are infertile, and couples who definitely plan to remain child-free.

5. How does this study apply to me and my spouse? How is each one of us similar to the people studied? How are we different?

6. Get more information. You may be able to contact the researcher through his or her university to get a reprint of an

article or references to books or journal articles. Even if you don't have a strong social science background, you may be able to get more out of the original journal article than you could in a summary found in a newspaper article or pamphlet.

If you and your spouse have a good relationship and you're both very positive about having children, don't let the research discourage you. Because you value children, you'll be able to deal with the stress. And if you don't want children take heart in the fact that most studies indicate you'll be at least as happy as parents are, if not happier.

~§~

Step Four

_____

Making
the Decision

ᨠ 8 ᨡ

Tug-of-War, or
What to Do
When Couples Conflict

In the healthy confrontation neither person loses sight of the
fact that each is seeking to express the truth and find a meaningful way to live. In a true confrontation, the persons always remain persons. And because there is awareness and knowledge
and sensitivity, the argument, the face-to-face struggle, follows
its natural course and opens new pathways of relatedness.
    —CLARK MOUSTAKAS

Probably the hardest decisions of all are the ones made by
couples in which one person wants a child and the other
does not. Although many marital conflicts can be resolved
through compromise, there is no such thing as half a baby.

Even couples who are in the habit of listening to each other
may turn a deaf ear during baby conversations. It's hard to
accept someone else's needs if they clash so brutally with your
own.

Existentialist theologian Martin Buber describes two kinds
of relationships, the I-thou relationship and the I-it relationship. In the former a person talks with respect and listens with
understanding. In the latter, a person relates to the other as
he would to an inanimate object—ignoring the other person's
needs while pushing to get his own way. While a good marriage is, by definition, an I-thou relationship, a marriage full
of I-it interaction tends to result in unhappiness, if not di-

vorce. But even happily married couples can slide unknowingly into an I-it relationship when considering the baby dilemma. There are two reasons. First, most couples aren't accustomed to such major conflict since people generally marry someone whose needs coincide or at least do not conflict with theirs. But the baby decision can divide otherwise compatible couples. When they said "I do" to marriage, they may have also said "I do" or "I don't" to children, only to change their minds a few years later. Second, the stakes are high either way, and accepting your partner's choice may seem like Russian roulette. People feel much too strongly about the decision to be able to compromise. Even in an excellent relationship, your spouse may suddenly seem like an ominous barrier between you and your goal.

What generally happens when a couple disagree? There are four possible outcomes:

1. They postpone the decision until agreement is reached at a later date.

2. The ambivalent spouse agrees to the choice of the spouse who feels more strongly.

3. One spouse twists the other's arm.

4. The spouse who feels more strongly about the issue resorts to devious tactics to push for his or her choice. This is similar to arm-twisting, but the methods used may be more subtle.

Obviously, the first possibility has the least potential for harming the relationship, as long as the postponement period is mutually agreed upon, and as long as the couple set a definite date for reevaluation. Postponement gives both spouses a chance to think over the issue privately and in a less tense atmosphere. Often, they are more willing to negotiate and compromise the second time around. Remembering their earlier battle can motivate both to find a better way this time.

The second solution can be a good one if the ambivalent spouse is genuinely ambivalent and can swing either way. In such a case, he or she generally would be able to find either choice satisfying. However, ambivalence sometimes may mean that one spouse simply hasn't had the time or the chance to make his or her own decision. Sensing this, the other spouse may play on this perceived weakness by pushing for his own choice and making it difficult for the other to come to a personal decision.

Frances definitely doesn't want a child. Mark, her husband, makes faint murmurs from time to time about wanting one, but says, "There's no point in asking myself what I want, since it's obvious I'm not going to get it."

For whenever the baby issue is brought up, Frances's usual habit of good listening flies right out the window. She says she wants Mark to deal with the decision, but whenever he starts to talk about it, she finds a way to stop him. No sooner does he open his mouth to say that he might like a child than Frances cuts him off with five reasons why he doesn't *really* want one.

Why does such a loving, empathic person suddenly become so insensitive and inconsiderate? Because she feels guilty about depriving her husband of children. And to deal with her guilt, she tries to convince herself that she knows what he wants better than he does. She is probably right in her assertion that he would have to give up a lot of things he likes if he had a child. And if he did an emotional tally of all the pros and cons, perhaps he *would* come out with a glowing *C* for child-free. But if she's wrong—if he comes out with a *P*—then she has to deal with her guilt.

The moral of the story: if you want to *resolve* the issue, *involve* your spouse. Consciously lock your mouth shut while he or she is talking. Give feedback to show that you understand. Remember that expressing feelings about the situation, empathizing with your spouse's feelings and deciding what to do about the feelings are three separate processes.

Why is it so important for Mark to make his *own* decision even though he knows they won't wind up having a child? Because coming to terms with the decision gives him a basis for a more committed and meaningful life. If he decides he wants a child, he can set about finding other ways to meet this desire. As the Turkish proverb says, "He that conceals his grief can find no remedy for it." And if he decides that he doesn't want a child after all, he can think about what major life commitments would give him the greatest satisfaction. He will be ready to make these commitments once he has come to terms with the decision not to parent. And he won't be able to accuse Frances of twisting his arm, thereby playing on her guilt.

Games Couples Play

Arm-twisting, in any form, is dangerous. Whether you issue a direct ultimatum or resort to more devious manipulations, you are treating your spouse as an object by refusing to listen to or respect his or her wishes. Although, in some cases, the pressured spouse accepts the outcome cheerfully, trying to make the best of it, this is rare. Resentment about the arm-twisting is bound to bubble up, and the pressured spouse may assume a martyr role, blaming the other if the decision doesn't work out well and playing on the other's guilt. Sometimes, in fact, the pressured spouse may allow the situation to occur because he or she unconsciously seeks the martyr role as a way of later manipulating the other.

Although the direct approach is the best, many couples can't or won't relate that way. Instead, they resort to games based on arm-twisting or subtle manipulation—often with disastrous consequences. Let's take a look at some of these games and how they can be avoided.

"Baby, You Can Twist My Arm"

In this game, the spouse who feels more strongly about the issue (often the more dominant spouse) speaks out loud and clear for his or her choice, and the other spouse gives in without stopping to consider if it's the right choice for both.

The payoff: avoiding a fight.

The price: lack of mutuality and autonomy in the relationship. The victimized spouse usually plays a game of his or her own: "Look what you've done, it's all your fault." If the decision was proparenthood, when things go wrong he or she can cry, "Don't blame me; it was your choice." If the decision was nonparenthood and the couple is later unhappy for *any* reason, the victimized spouse can always say, "I bet we would have been better off with kids. You never gave me a chance to have them. Look where it's gotten us."

The countergame: The victimized spouse should respond to the attempted arm-twisting by saying, "I understand you have very strong feelings about this. I have some feelings too, although I haven't thought them through yet. Let's plan a time to discuss this. We're talking about *my* child, too, and I need to find out how I feel so I can participate in the choice."

The Avoidance Game

In this game, one spouse, usually the one who wants a baby, tries to get the other to talk about the issue. The other usually says, "Later." He or she is always too tired or too busy for the baby decision.

The payoff: avoiding a difficult issue.

The price: retaliation by the eager spouse. The uncomfortable sensation of living with an unsolved problem, one that may linger in the air indefinitely.

The countergame: Make a date with your spouse to discuss the issue. If your mate is pressuring you for a baby that you don't want, be honest about your feelings.

Actually, some spouses who press their mates in this fashion are disappointed and frightened when they get a direct response. They may even unconsciously bring up the subject precisely when their spouse is engrossed in another activity. Why? Because they enjoy the role of the "good guy" who wants to resolve the issue, while also enjoying the security of the rebuff that's sure to come. They may even complain to others about their spouse's reaction while failing to recognize their own avoidance behavior.

A variation of this game can occur when a spouse leaning toward nonparenthood wants to get sterilized or otherwise resolve the issue once and for all. Again, the avoiding spouse would be better off expressing his or her doubts directly rather than merely avoiding the issue.

"Shrink"

In this game, one spouse uses psychiatry in an attempt to shame the other into a desired decision. While the most common form is amateur psychiatry, the game may be even more deadly when the partner playing this role is a professional therapist. Here is how one husband played amateur psychiatrist.

Sally wanted to remain child-free; Bert wanted a child. He went to the library and spent all day copying quotes from psychoanalysts who claimed that women who wanted to remain child-free are running away from their destiny and trying to be men. He presented his findings to Sally with the zealousness of a D.A. who's gotten the goods on a thief.

The payoff: Bert expressed his hostility and frustration to Sally.

The price: Sally was angry and hurt, and more determined than ever to remain child-free.

The countergame: Bert should express his desire for children and his disappointment that Sally doesn't share this desire directly. He and Sally have to recognize that both have a right to their own opinion.

Bert can make progress by changing "you" messages to "I" messages.

Not: "You're unfeminine because you don't want children," or, "You're neurotic."

But: "I feel disappointed. I want to be a father, and I can't help hoping you'll continue to consider the possibility of becoming a mother."

As a result of the "I" message, Sally may be able to reconsider and even change her mind. At the very least, marital communication has been improved, and Sally will feel that Bert respects her even though he disagrees with her.

"Sneak"

This game is played when one spouse, usually the wife, sabotages birth control in order to conceive against the other's wishes. It's hard for men to play this game because their wives generally take more responsibility for contraception than they do.

The payoff: getting a desired baby without having to negotiate with one's spouse.

The price: resentment on the part of the deceived spouse. A weakened marital bond.

The countergame: The spouse who wants a child should directly communicate his or her wish and try to negotiate. During the negotiation, he or she might try to meet the need for a child in other ways, such as baby borrowing.

A variation of this game can occur when one spouse secretly practices birth control even though the couple has ostensibly agreed to have a child. But the subterfuge is bound to come out sooner or later, when the deceived spouse's suspicions are aroused and he or she suggests fertility treatment. And the negative consequences of such dishonesty will begin to eat away at the relationship even before the treachery is discovered.

"The Courting Divorce Game"

In this game, the spouse who wants a child manages to twist the other's arm. What the acquiescing spouse doesn't

w is that the other has an unspoken agenda—"I want this
d more than the marriage, and I'm going to have the child
.. matter what. If the marriage fails, I'll still have the child."

The payoff: the player gets a child—come hell or high
water.

The price: dishonesty will undermine the relationship in
some way.

The countergame: admit your feelings to your spouse. If
you and your spouse want to agree on this risk together, that's
one thing. But an agenda like this isn't just unspoken; it's
unfair.

Games should be avoided at all costs. No matter how
tempting it may be to push, especially if a gentle, or even not-
so-gentle, nudge seems likely to get you what you want, the
consequences won't be pleasant. The antidote to pressure tactics is direct, honest communication, which brings us to the
key to resolving the tug-of-war:: *The desired product—a mutual decision—will only be as good as the process—mutual
communication.* In other words, by listening carefully to one
another, without trying to manipulate and without getting
angry or defensive, you will demonstrate your mutual love and
respect, and you will be less likely to spiral down into an I-it
relationship.

This kind of dialogue indicates that you accept your spouse
as a human being in his or her own right who exists for more
than your pleasure. It shows that you accept your spouse's
right to seek his or her own identity and fulfillment. And even
though one of you will not get what you want, you have both
been validated as human beings and as spouses.

Decision-Makers' Bill of Responsibilities to Spouse

You are obligated to:

- Listen to your partner's needs, desires, arguments, concerns, preferences.

- Give verbal feedback to show that you understand his or her point of view.
- Explain your needs, desires, arguments, concerns, preferences, rather than assuming that your spouse can read your mind.
- Recognize that your preference is simply that—a preference, and that neither your choice nor your spouse's is right or wrong in any absolute sense.

FIRST AID FOR BATTLING COUPLES

By now, I hope you and your spouse are ready to discuss the issue openly and honestly. But before you do, it might be a good idea for both of you to ask yourselves the following questions. You may come up with some insights that will lead to a faster solution and, at the very least, you'll both have a clearer sense of *all* the issues involved.

1. How unhappy would you be if you agreed to your spouse's choice? Could you be happy with either decision? Are you caught up in an unnecessary power struggle?

2. Are you totally opposed to your spouse's choice or just ambivalent? After doing the exercises in this book and discussing issues with your spouse, can you think of any advantages of doing what he or she wants?

3. Do you object to your spouse's decision itself or rather to the feeling of being pushed? If it's the latter, then ask your spouse for a pressure-free moratorium period to give you a chance to make your own decision.

4. Is the disagreement unconditional or are you simply battling about specific conditions, such as (a) when to have a baby; (b) how much money can be saved first; (c) whether you can afford a child on one salary or even two; (d) whether career issues have to be resolved or career training has to be completed; (e) incompatible childbearing approaches; (f) natural pregnancy versus adoption; (g) the division of labor

that would occur after parenthood; (h) the need for more time before deciding; (i) a fear of risk-taking; (j) unresolved ambivalence.

5. Are you presently or potentially in agreement with your spouse but exaggerating your disagreement in order to get bargaining power for resolving other problems? If so, why are you doing this? Do you fear that you can't get what you want from your spouse if you go about it in a more straightforward manner? Discuss this and try to arrive at more direct ways of working out difficulties.

6. Were you originally drawn to your spouse because of the very same nurturing qualities that now attract him to parenthood? Or were you attracted by your spouse's desire for independence and solitude, qualities that now propel her toward the childfree choice? If so, what would you, your spouse, and your marriage lose in terms of those qualities if *your* choice were selected?

Working It Out

Here is how one couple negotiated a compromise. Bettina definitely wanted a baby. Hal was not only uncertain about fathering but also unwilling to talk about it. One day the couple managed to knock down the barrier.

BETTINA: Why do you always change the subject whenever I ask you about having a baby?

HAL: Because I just don't see how it would work out.

BETTINA: Why shouldn't it work out? Don't you want to have children as much as I do?

HAL: Well, I don't know. I guess I want a baby, but I don't think it makes any sense to have one. Look, you complain as it is about my working so hard and not being around much nights and weekends. You want me to take more responsibility than I do. If we had a baby, wouldn't you be even more resentful? You'd have even more work, and I just wouldn't be able to be much help.

BETTINA: Wouldn't be able to or wouldn't be willing to? Lots of men are taking half the load of housework and child care and still managing to get ahead at work.

HAL: But those men are sacrificing their career success. They're just not going to go as far because of their family. That's fine for some men, but it's not fine for me. I'm not willing to slip behind just to have a family. I do think I could offer a child a lot of love and caring. But I can't see myself taking the time to do all the day-to-day diapering and doctor's appointments.

BETTINA: Well, I want to have a baby, but I sure don't want to have to do all the work. I know what you're getting at. You want to have your cake and eat it, too. You're saying to yourself, oh, good old Bettina, I know what I'll do. I'll say I don't want a baby even though I do. Poor thing is so desperate to get pregnant she'll agree to anything. I'll get her to say she'll take responsibility for the baby. You get the pleasure of fatherhood while *I* get all the miseries.

HAL: Bettina, maybe I *am* doing that. I don't know. I'm certainly not doing it on purpose. I do want a child but not if it's going to mean sacrificing my career. I don't *feel* like I'm playing a game. I'm really in a quandary. I do want a child, probably as much as you do. I just don't know how we can work it out.

BETTINA: I'm willing to do more than you. I always have, even though I've never liked the situation. But I refuse to be Cinderella. What are we going to do about it?

HAL: For one thing, let's not force ourselves to decide right this minute. If I hit you with an ultimatum like "the baby's all yours or else we're not having it," I know you'll just fume. If I agree to have a baby and promise to do more than I really will, I'll be unfair to both of us.

BETTINA: So how can we work this out? Let's see, what if you agree to think about, say, spending Saturdays being responsible for the child? Maybe one day off would be enough for me.

HAL: That is something to think about. Maybe if we didn't have a baby for another two or three years, I might even *want* to gear down a little. I've seen Bill and Harry do that at work. They used to burn the midnight oil a lot more than they do now. They seem to spend more time with their families than they used to. And maybe if I get another promotion or two, we'd be able to afford a housekeeper. That would take a lot of the burden off you, and it would take pressure off me.

BETTINA: That sounds okay—I guess. I can't help resenting the sexism in getting yourself out of the housework by paying somebody else to do it. But it does sound like a possible way of having a kid without ruining either of our lives.

HAL: Yeah, it really seems more workable now. Do you feel better about all this?

BETTINA: I'm still upset, and it's far from resolved, but I do feel more optimistic. I feel better now that you're finally willing to listen and to think about compromises.

HAL: And I feel better, knowing that you're not out to take my career away from me. Why has it taken so long to have this talk?

If you've discussed these issues and you still don't seem to be making any headway, think about these alternatives:

- Consider counseling (see "Help," Chapter 10, page 196).
- Consider postponing the decision, perhaps even indefi-

nitely. As I said earlier, postponement can be constructive or destructive. It's generally constructive if you set specific goals for a specific period of time. It's generally destructive if it leads to the nondecision to be a nonparent (child-free drift) or the nondecision to be a parent (an accident). Nondecisions cheat you out of growth opportunities, and make it easy for you to feel sorry for yourself and to blame your spouse or fate for the outcome. However, if the decision is driving you apart, an agreement to do absolutely nothing may be the only way to defuse serious conflict. Put the issue on a back burner, even for a year or two if necessary, and then try to confront it again. But if you decide to do this, avoid a permanent nondecision by agreeing to bring up the subject at a later date.

Take a reading on the intensity of both your own and your spouse's feelings about the issue. If your spouse is ambivalent and you feel strongly about a particular choice, see if time and perhaps some compromise can win your spouse to your point of view. But remember, compromise does *not* mean manipulation. However, if one of you really wants a child and the other is just as vehement about remaining child-free, you are almost certainly better off choosing nonparenthood. It's easier for an unwilling nonparent to meet parenting needs outside the home than it is for an unwilling parent to tolerate a child in the home. This is the one parenthood situation that could easily lead to divorce.

Don't Become a "Single" Married Parent

Perhaps you've thought about solving your dilemma by becoming a "single" parent in a married household—telling your unwilling spouse that you'll take all the responsibility for the child. *Don't do it.* It's impossible and disastrous to live in a house where there is a child present—your child—and avoid any involvement. If two people have their arms around each other and one plunges into a pool, the other is going to get just as wet. There is no such thing as a one-parent family in a two-spouse home.

Jay and Audrey considered such a solution because Audrey desperately wanted a child and Jay was just as adamant about remaining child-free. They were so impossibly deadlocked that Audrey considered telling Jay, "Okay, you don't have to be a father. Just get me pregnant and I'll do the rest. I'll change all the diapers, arrange all the child care, and even pay all the child's expenses out of my salary. You won't even have to hold it if you don't want to."

Luckily, Audrey decided not to follow through because in such an arrangement both spouses would lose. Jay would lose his coveted child-free status. Audrey would have to accept the sometimes delayed gratification of "single parenthood" while Jay enjoyed the immediate pleasures of remaining "child-free." Or trying to. Because his alternatives are guilt at staying uninvolved or resentment at getting involved against his will. Audrey cannot drastically change her life—by becoming a parent—without drastically changing her husband's life. Jay is a stickler for neatness, but would have to put up with mess. Jay loves silence, but would have to put up with noise. Jay loves Audrey's undivided attention, but he would have to share her with the baby.

What would happen if Audrey ran a 103-degree fever and the baby needed to be fed in the wee hours? What if they had tickets for a special concert and the baby-sitter canceled at the last minute? Hearing the baby-sitter blues would be a poor substitute for his favorite music. In such situations, Jay would have to pay the price of being a father even though it was Audrey who ran up the bill. And Audrey would have to pay the price of Jay's resentment and endure the consequent deficit in their marriage.

Furthermore, consider how a child would be affected by

living with a parent who's uninvolved or only reluctantly involved. As a psychotherapist, I have worked with hundreds of such parents and children, and observed the emotional anguish of all involved.

When a couple seriously entertains such an idea, the spouse who wants children either:

- Mistakenly assumes that once the baby is born the reluctant spouse is going to turn into a parent—if not a model parent, at least a functioning parent. But the result is more likely to be a malfunctioning marriage and family.
- Consciously or unconsciously decides that having a child is more important than staying married. This can, in fact, be a roundabout, "safe" way of drifting toward a desired divorce without ever having to take responsibility for it.

If you don't want a child and your spouse does, can you think of some way to help him or her meet those intense needs to parent? For example, if your husband wants to borrow his nieces and nephews on Saturday afternoons, maybe you could take over the bill-paying he usually does then in order to give him time for his "children." In this way, you can show respect for your husband and for his desire to have something you don't want. You can make him feel loved and understood despite your disparate attitudes about parenting. And it also indicates your willingness to make some compromises, despite your unwillingness to have a baby.

BEFORE YOU HEAD TO THE DIVORCE COURT . . .

If you are considering divorce over this decision, proceed with caution. Although very little research has been done so far, based on studies I've read and the cases I've come into contact with, I don't believe couples get divorced over the baby issue alone. Generally, there are other factors involved that are at least as important, if not more important. But it's very easy to blame the baby issue for the breakup of a marriage because it's tangible as well as being a convenient scapegoat; you don't have to blame yourself or your spouse, or hang out other dirty family linen on the public clothesline.

Phyllis, a systems analyst, and Ben, the owner of a successful chain of local pizza restaurants, had been married for two years. One night, Phyllis came home from an awards banquet to find divorce papers and a note on the kitchen table. The note said that since she didn't want children and he did, the marriage was over. Phyllis was shocked. Ben hadn't even given her an ultimatum—"Have a baby or else!" He had just assumed he knew the outcome of such an ultimatum, and had acted accordingly.

At least that was the way it looked at first. After they had been separated for a month, Phyllis found out that Ben had a girlfriend who was pregnant. "Ben wanted a different kind of wife," Phyllis said. "Not just one who was willing to be a mother, but also one who would stay home and keep a beautiful house, entertain his business associates, and greet him at the door with a martini, a newspaper, and a smile. He got Sheila pregnant as a convenient out. Baby or no baby, our relationship would have ended soon. He didn't reject me for refusing to be a mother so much as for insisting on being an independent, achieving woman."

In situations like this, it's not the baby question but rather role expectations that sever a marriage. The knot is untied because the husband wants a "traditional wife" package, of which children are only a part. And the woman leaves not only to avoid becoming a traditional mother, but also because she doesn't want to become a traditional wife. Ironically, such men often would actually prefer not to have children—*if* their wives gave them what they consider the "proper attention"!

If you are considering divorce because you want a baby:

1. Is more than the baby issue involved? What else do you

fight about? How else do you feel your spouse fails to meet your needs?

2. How will you handle the decision if you remarry? Can you be sure a solution will be any easier the second time around?

- If your new spouse is your age or older, he or she may already have children from a previous marriage and be uninterested in others. If so, would your new stepchildren satisfy your parenting needs? It's also possible that your new mate would be just as committed to the child-free choice as your present spouse.
- If your new spouse is younger than you, he or she may be unprepared to make a baby decision for a number of years or may already have decided to remain child-free.
- Your new spouse may already be sterilized. If so, he or she is unlikely to favor adoption or artificial insemination even if these alternatives were acceptable to you.
- Even if you're lucky enough to find a new love who would make an ideal parent, you may not be lucky enough to find one who would also make an ideal spouse.

3. Have you considered the pros and cons of single parenthood? (See Chapter 9).

4. Do you have realistic expectations about parenthood? Do you think parenthood is so wonderful that it might be worth risking the end of a good marriage? If so, your expectations are unrealistic. The frustrations of parenthood, especially in the earliest years, often outweigh the rewards. You're bound to wind up disappointed and blame the child for depriving you of your spouse. You may well make the child feel guilty or take it out on him or her in some other way.

Is Counseling the Answer?

You should seek counseling for this conflict if:

- You find it impossible to talk about it or to get your spouse to talk about it.
- You've followed the advice in this chapter and still feel hopelessly embattled.

You will probably need private sessions—just you, your spouse, and a counselor—rather than an ongoing group or a special workshop. The group format is useful for exploring issues, overcoming fears and misinformation about life-styles, and making life plans. But ordinarily group sessions will not allow enough time for a full exploration of the conflict between you and your mate.

The Second Time Around

Simon and Judy's marriage seemed to be made in heaven— the first year, that is. At their first anniversary dinner, Judy made a toast: "May we have a little one to celebrate by our second anniversary."

Simon choked on his shrimp cocktail. When he stopped coughing he looked at Judy as if Dr. Jekyll had suddenly turned into Ms. Hyde. "But, Judy! Why spoil all this? Do you have any idea what a kid would do to our marriage?"

For the moment, joyous thoughts of their marriage were overshadowed by gloomy visions of divorce. This was not a new subject for the couple, only the idea of *their* divorce. For their two-year affair had resulted in marriage only after Simon's twelve-year marriage had finally ended in divorce. And when Simon moved out he didn't just leave a wife. He left a family, a girl of eight and a boy of twelve.

Although Simon loves his children, he never chose to have

them. Simon may have walked down the aisle, but his first wife, Marge, waddled. She was five months pregnant with child number one. And child number two was conceived under the same circumstances: Marge claimed to be taking the pill, but, in reality, she wasn't.

But surely, you ask, surely Simon and Judy must have talked about the baby decision before they decided to marry. The whole truth is that they half-talked about it. Because their feet weren't touching the ground, they neglected to cover the baby decision territory. They knew they wanted to be in bed for a 2:00 A.M. cuddle, but they hadn't discussed whether they would get out of bed for a 2:00 A.M. feeding. They knew they wanted to be free to be seen in public, but they hadn't discussed whether they'd be seen in a sportscar or a station wagon. Both had been aware of Judy's interest in children, and both had mentally filed this under *L* for "later." The question was just too scary. After all the emotional trauma they had gone through to be together, surely they wouldn't let a teeny tiny baby issue keep them apart?

"We'll cross that bridge when we come to it," they had agreed, and promptly pushed the issue aside. And on their first anniversary, they found themselves wobbling on that rickety old bridge, which alas, they would have to cross.

If you want to be a parent and you marry someone who already has children from a previous marriage, you can expect the tug-of-war to be more intense for the following reasons:

1. *Differential willingness to sacrifice.* The ABP (Already Been a Parent) has experienced both the joys and stresses of parenthood, and the idea of starting all over again can be quite repugnant. For the NBP (Never Been a Parent), on the other hand, the pleasure of having a baby in the house outweighs the sacrifices involved during the early years. The trade-off seems worth it. But the ABP has already experienced those pleasures firsthand, and in his or her eyes the sacrifices definitely outweigh the joys.

2. *Economic considerations.* Many ABP's have to make

child support payments, and the idea of new bills may be quite frightening. If the budget is stretching to care for two existing children, perhaps it will burst with a third.

3. *The power struggle issue.* Sometimes the NBP isn't really sure she wants a child but is testing the ABP spouse to see if he loves her more than his ex-wife. Will he give her everything he gave his first wife?

Having a child can be a way of competing with the ex-wife. In this situation, the second wife not only wants to replace the ex-wife in her husband's affections, but she also hopes to replace the ex-wife's children with her own children.

Exercises for the Second Time Around

SEPARATE FACES (For the ABP)

Are you blurring your ex-wife and your present wife into one image of Wife-as-Mother? Try to imagine your ex-wife's face. Now imagine your wife's face. Picture a solid white line between them, separating them in your mind. Now try to figure out how much of the unpleasantness of your first parenthood experience stemmed from the unpleasantness of your first marriage. How would parenthood be different with your present wife? Are you making an unfair assumption that all women mother in the same way your ex-wife did? You chose your second wife because you thought you would be happier with her. Is it possible that you would enjoy her children more than your first wife's? What characteristics does she have that might make her a better mother? Are they the same characteristics that make her a better wife, for example, affection, patience, an ability to communicate?

Share this exercise with your wife. Ask her if she thinks you're confusing her with your ex-wife. Let her tell you why and how she thinks she would be different from your first wife as a parent.

The goal of this exercise is to make sure that your desire to remain child-free is based on a clear conviction of what's best for the two of you, not on a mistaken blending of one wife with the other. This does not mean that you should have a child; it merely indicates the importance of uncovering the real issues.

It's quite possible that confusing your former wife and your present one clouds other couple issues as well, and so doing this exercise may improve your marriage as a whole.

INNER JOURNEY (For the NBP)

Have you considered the possibility that you are competing with your husband's ex-wife? Are you sure you want children for their own sake? Do you enjoy time spent with your step-children? Is it possible that your relationship with them can grant you any parenting satisfaction? (Scratch that possibility if the "children" are grown up or nearly so!)

Remember that the stepparenting relationship is shaky. The kids may be cold or indifferent to you now, but might warm up to you later. Try to project what your relationship with them might be like in a few years, once you've gotten to know each other better and they've come to accept your presence in their lives (and you've come to accept their presence in yours). If you have already experienced moments of pure liking for them despite some strained interactions, then it's a good bet the "stepping" experience will be positive for you.

Consider some substitute parenting experiences. Do you think some of these might be satisfactory? Would your husband help make it possible for you to participate in these activities?

A FINAL WORD ABOUT CONFLICT

Although conflict is never pleasant, take comfort in the fact that it often leads to growth—both personal and as a couple. Weathering this storm successfully can draw you closer together—if you are both willing to be honest and direct, and make compromises when necessary.

Before Aileen's engagement ring ever touched her finger, she and Roger had agreed that they would never have children. Roger thrived on cleanliness, order, and quiet; children meant dirt, disorder, and noise. The good life he envisioned meant coming home from his law practice to a peaceful dinner with his wife. Aileen readily agreed. As a doctoral candidate in physics, she wasn't sure she could combine her career with motherhood.

Eight years later, Aileen discovered that she had a strong desire to become a mother. Although she repressed it because she knew Roger would be miserable as a father, she became increasingly depressed. Whenever Roger mentioned a vasectomy, she changed the subject. Roger was not unaware of her conflict. He had noticed the mixture of pain and pleasure on her face when she played with her nieces and nephews. He didn't want her to be unhappy, so before committing themselves to the child-free choice, they went to see a counselor.

Questioning their decision did not make them change their minds. They agreed that remaining child-free was the only way to remain married, and having Roger was more important to Aileen than having children.

But putting their cards on the table made them both feel better. As they discussed their conflicting desires, Aileen realized that her depression was a vague mourning for the children she would never have. Because she had never openly admitted her feelings, she had never openly mourned. But if she failed to do so, she might remain depressed indefinitely. With the therapist's encouragement, she allowed herself to grieve. It was a stormy month. Aileen, crying for her "lost" children, lashed out at Roger for depriving her of them. They were both frightened by her anger. They discovered that they didn't know how to be emotional with each other. Both had come from homes where emotional expression was unwelcome. Both had chosen "safe" careers—science and law—that placed no demands on them to be human. Through counseling, they learned to face their emotions and talk about them together. They became closer and more affectionate as a result.

Because Aileen had acknowledged her need for mothering, she could do something about it. She started "borrowing" her three-month-old niece on Sunday afternoons. She enjoyed this substitute mothering. Although it would never make up for her childlessness, it was a meaningful alternative.

During therapy, Roger discovered that his perfectionistic expectations for himself and others contributed to his desire to remain child-free. He thought he had to be the perfect father for the perfect child. Although he still wasn't ready to be a father, he realized that he could work on this problem. He began keeping a diary of these unreasonable expectations, and made a check mark on a record pad every time he stopped himself from making an unfair demand on himself or his co-workers. Over the next few months, the demands decreased and he even began joking about them.

A year has gone by. Aileen and Roger still don't plan to have children. But now they have made a real decision, not a phony one. They're comfortable with themselves and with the decision.

Their story illustrates some of the ways couples grow during the decision-making process:

- Learning how you as a couple handle conflict and make decisions
- Recognizing and expressing emotions
- Recognizing weaknesses and correcting them
- Noticing needs and fulfilling them

Learn from Roger and Aileen. Use your conflict not only to resolve the baby issue, but to find new and better ways of relating to each other.

❧ 9 ❧

A Parenthood Sampler

To make the best possible decision, you should have as much information as possible at your fingertips. And in this chapter we'll be examining some of the options you might want to consider before you make your final decision.

BREAKING THE AGE BARRIER—DELAYED PARENTHOOD

Who is that woman sitting on the park bench, bouncing a husky six-month-old on her knee? Her hair is streaked with gray and laugh lines stretch out from her eyes. You can see that she's between thirty-six and forty-five, but you aren't sure about her relationship to the baby—is she mother or grandmother? These days it's impossible to tell. More and more women are opting for motherhood after thirty-five.

Advantages of Delayed Parenthood

- Because you're older and wiser, if you decide to become a parent, you're probably making a better decision than you might have when you were younger.
- Older couples are more willing to settle down. If you've already been in almost every country or vacation resort

you can think of, you're less likely to chomp at the bit if you have to stay home. And despite the persistence of this stereotype, most older couples have no trouble adjusting to being tied down even though they are used to so much freedom. You may not compare with Mr. and Mrs. Walton, but you probably have more patience and tolerance to bring to parenthood now than you would have had when you were younger.

- You are likely to be in better financial shape, and therefore more likely to be able to hold on to your standard of living and to hire household help and baby-sitters.
- If either of you wants to cut back to part-time or take a year off, it's easier if you're both established professionally. And of course, your increased nest egg facilitates such cutbacks.
- Because you're older, you may be better at combining career and motherhood. In *Passages,* Gail Sheehy claimed that few women could integrate career and motherhood before their thirties.

Disadvantages of Delayed Parenthood

- The medical risks for both mother and baby are higher. And the possibility that the baby will have a birth defect such as Down's syndrome (mongolism) is also greater.
- Some older parents find that they don't have enough physical energy to keep up with their kids. It may be harder to play ball with them, or take them on camping or hiking trips.
- Your child has a greater chance of losing you to death or illness before he's grown up.
- You may never get to see your grandchildren, even if your child decides to become a parent.
- You may have to face the problems of retirement and empty nest at the same time. Even if this sounds like

double-barreled freedom, it could also turn out to be double-barreled depression.

- If you take several years off from work, you may have trouble going back. Even if you "dress for success," your wrinkles and gray hair may deprive you of jobs for which you're qualified. Of course, you are less likely to run into this problem if you achieve career success before becoming a mother.

- If you're thirty-eight when you give birth, then you'll be fifty-six by the time the child is grown. You may wind up envying your friends who had their children at twenty and emptied their nest at forty.

- If you have fertility problems, they may get worse as you get older.

The Medical Story

Although the chances of fertility problems, miscarriage, and birth defects increase with age, your chances of having a healthy baby are excellent! Statistics across the board are less relevant than the characteristics of the woman stretched across the examination table. If you're healthy, eat well, exercise, and have good prenatal care, your chances of having a healthy baby are *better* than those of a younger woman whose health is below par.

Furthermore, it is now possible to test for Down's syndrome before the baby is born, thanks to the medical procedure known as amniocentesis. This procedure, done in early pregnancy, draws a small amount of amniotic fluid from the uterus. Laboratory analysis of the fluid can test for Down's syndrome as well as a wide variety of other genetic abnormalities. If the child is abnormal, a couple can then consider abortion rather than carrying the baby to term.

However, it's important to realize that amniocentesis isn't magic. It has its price:

- There's a 1% chance the fetus will be harmed by the procedure.
- You won't get a money-back guarantee. Complications resulting from pregnancy, labor, or delivery could still harm the child in some way. And there are no tests for abnormalities due to genetic mutations or for certain birth defects.
- Abortion is a serious matter. An abnormal fetus is still a fetus. A decision to abort would be painful, even if you decided that it would be less painful than bringing such a child into the world. And by the time you got the results of the amniocentesis, you would be about twenty weeks into your pregnancy. You'd already be showing and the baby would be kicking. Moreover, it would be too late for a simple D & C abortion at a clinic. You would have to go to a hospital for a more complicated and riskier procedure.

Although most women who undergo amniocentesis come through with no ill effects, to be told that their baby is just fine, it's important to realize it's not a miraculous, trouble-free procedure.

Fertility Problems

It's no coincidence that books about delayed parenthood and about infertility are coming out in droves. According to many doctors, there is a connection between late motherhood and infertility, and it's not due to age alone.

- Women who have been on the pill for many years may not start to ovulate even after they've stopped taking the hormones.
- IUD wearers may contract IUD-related infections that make it hard to conceive after the device is removed.
- Earlier abortions or venereal disease can affect fertility.

Obviously, if you've been sexually active for ten to twenty years, your chances of having one or more of the above problems is greater than if you were younger.

Can you get a fertility checkup in advance? The answer is yes and no. You can get some raw data about your present fertility, but nobody can guarantee your future fertility. Dr. Albert Decker, medical director of the New York Fertility Research Foundation, recommends that couples who want to delay parenthood visit both a urologist and a gynecologist to look for any signs of trouble brewing. A man can be tested for general health and sperm count; a woman can be examined for problems such as endometriosis and pelvic inflammatory disease, and can talk to her doctor about her menstrual history. Of course, the only proof of fertility is a pregnancy, and today's fertile couple may be infertile tomorrow. But this kind of information, limited though it is, can help you make a more informed decision about delaying pregnancy.

According to Dr. Sherwin Kaufman, a gynecologist associated with Planned Parenthood of New York City, a woman who is fertile at thirty probably will still be so at thirty-five, but one who was borderline at thirty may be infertile by thirty-five.

If you suspect that you have a fertility problem—defined as a failure to conceive within six months to a year—see a fertility specialist. Based on his advice, you'll then have to choose the more preferable course: trying to get pregnant now even though it may not be the ideal time, or banking on the chance that you will be able to conceive later on.

Most experts now recommend that any couple over thirty who haven't conceived within six months see a fertility specialist. Even if you have some trouble getting pregnant, the latest medical techniques may be able to help you. (Also, see Appendix C: Resources, for information about Resolve, a national group offering support and counseling to infertile couples.)

Infertility isn't only a medical problem; it's a psychological problem as well. Infertile couples often view it as a personal failure, believing that they are somehow less masculine or feminine because they are unable to bear children. In addition, they have to deal with extreme disappointment and feelings of shame and embarrassment. Therefore, it is sometimes a wise idea to seek professional help. Like any other problem, it has to be faced before it can be solved. When couples try to pretend it doesn't exist, as Jane and Charlie did when they played the "We Don't Want Children Anyway" game, they simply set themselves up for more suffering.

Charlie and Jane feel frustrated and ashamed because they have been unable to conceive. They can't bear others' pity, curiosity, or worse, advice. So they tell people who are unaware of their problem, "We don't know whether we want children or not. They're a lot of trouble. We're thinking about remaining child-free."

The purpose of the game: avoiding some of the pain of infertility.

The payoff: preserving self-esteem and avoiding a sense of shame.

The price: first, many people see right through this game; second, the pain of infertility remains.

The countergame: Charlie and Jane should admit to each other and to themselves the intense pain and stigma they feel. They need to acknowledge their hopes and mourn their loss. They need not and should not tell everyone they know about their problem, but they can stop being dishonest. They might say, "We think we would like a child some day," rather than, "We're thinking of remaining child-free."

If you do have a fertility problem:

- Admit to yourself and to your spouse that the problem exists and that it hurts.
- Get medical help.
- Consider psychological counseling if you're having trouble coping with it.
- Explore the possibilities of a good life without children.

This differs from the game because you are admitting that you're making the best of an unfortunate situation.

Motherhood over 35 Is Not for Everybody

Couples choosing to have their children later in life are overwhelmingly positive about their decision. And with new medical developments and longer life spans, this choice will become even more feasible in the future.

However, as positive as delayed parenthood can be, we should be careful to avoid another pendulum swing: from "all mothers should be under thirty" to "all mothers should be over thirty." We don't need new molds, we need genuine and realistic choices.

For many women, motherhood before thirty is equally positive. Those women who want to have it all, but not at the same time, may want to put their energies into parenting first and focus on work in their later years. This can be a good choice for a woman already in her mid-twenties who hasn't made a career commitment yet. By the time she decides what she wants to do, and establishes herself in that career, she may have trouble getting pregnant. If she's eager for a baby she might not want to take that chance.

The point is, let's keep this option an option, let's not turn it into rubber stamp.

ADOPTION

Adoption, regardless of its other advantages and disadvantages, certainly tests your motivation for parenthood! Because you have to put up with a lot: agencies, home visits, interviews, waiting, waiting, and more waiting.

So why adopt?

- One or both of you are infertile.
- You have one or two biological children and want another child, but you don't want to contribute to the world population problem. You also want the satisfaction of providing a good home to a child who really needs one.
- You have one or more biological children, and have tried again, but with no luck.
- You are a single woman who wants to become a mother. For various reasons, you prefer this option to pregnancy or artificial insemination.
- You're a single man who wants to become a father.

Advantages of Adoption

1. Careful decision-making. The process that most adoption agencies follow—careful evaluation, probing interviews—forces you to take stock of your potential for parenthood, and encourages you to make a really thoughtful decision. If you're less than certain or markedly ambivalent about parenthood, you're not likely to get a child.

2. The satisfaction of offering a child a loving home. The experience of consciously choosing a specific child rather than having the child selected by biology can be very rewarding.

3. The chance to skip infancy. If you don't think you would enjoy a baby or a toddler, you can skip these earlier stages entirely by adopting an older child. Bear in mind, however, that older children sometimes have severe emotional problems, and coping with their needs and demands can be even more demanding and frustrating than caring for an infant.

Disadvantages of Adoption

1. Scrutiny. Going under an adoption agency's magnifying glass can be painful, embarrassing, infuriating, and frustrating. So can the long wait that's often involved.

2. Sacrifice. Adoptable children may be physically or mentally handicapped. They may have been physically or psychologically abused by their natural parents, by foster parents, or by child care workers in institutions. They may have been traumatized by war or other disasters. Therefore, it can be quite difficult for you, your spouse, and the child to adjust to each other.

Even if the adjustment is successful, it is definitely not going to happen overnight. It can take months, even a year or more, to win the child's trust, and to learn how to handle crying jags, disobedience, tantrums, or complete withdrawal on the part of the child. And just when you think all these hurdles are behind you, something can happen to upset the child and cause a relapse. When that happens, you'll probably feel that you're back at the very beginning of the obstacle course, although that's not the case. The problems will be easier to solve by virtue of your greater experience and the relationship you've been able to build, but a great deal of patience and sensitivity will be required.

This period of adjustment, or should I say ordeal, can wreak havoc in a marriage. Sometimes an adoption is followed by a divorce. I believe this usually happens only if the marriage was poor to begin with or if one spouse twisted the other's arm. If you have a strong marriage and you both want the child, the adoption will probably work out and your marriage will survive.

Adoptive parents do have the opportunity to get to know the child before making a final decision, but in the first flush of excitement, potential problems are often overlooked. Although, technically, a child can be returned to the agency, this decision is psychologically devastating for child and parents alike. Children who are waiting to be adopted often have terrible doubts about their self-worth and lovability. The experience of being "tried out" by a family and then returned to an agency can only exacerbate such doubts. So if you do decide to adopt, be sure you can follow through.

Guidelines for Persons Considering Adoption

1. Do some reality-testing. Have you been too caught up in romantic notions to ask and answer realistic questions? Are you fully prepared for the sacrifices as well as the gains?

2. Talk to successful adoptive parents. Discuss the problems they have faced, and find out how they have coped. To get the broadest picture possible, talk to parents who have adopted newborns, older children, handicapped children, disturbed or abused children, foreign children or children of different races. Investigate as broad a spectrum as possible. Is your level of patience and tolerance equal to theirs? Could you cope with the problems they have had? Although it's unlikely that your problems would be the same (or necessarily as severe), the more you know, the better prepared you'll be. And you'll make a better decision, too.

3. Face disappointment about infertility. If you're adopting because of fertility problems, make sure you don't leave any unfinished business behind. You have to mourn the biological child you will (probably) never have before you can welcome an adopted child into your life. Otherwise, you may consider the child a second-rate substitute at best, and you won't be able to give him the first-rate love he deserves.

4. Consider the rest of the family. If you have biological offspring, have you considered their needs as well as your own? If they are old enough, discuss the possibility of adoption with them.

Nora and Calvin are thinking of adopting a Vietnamese child who lives in a foster home. Their four-year-old, Missy, has been included in the picnics and outings that the adoption worker has arranged. Nora and Cal tell Missy they are thinking of having Ricky come to live with them. They read children's books on adoption and ask her what she thinks of Ricky's coming to live with her. At first she is all excitement. Then she starts asking whether Ricky will sleep in her room and eat her food. Nora and Calvin firmly tell Missy that her room and her food and her parents' love are all hers to keep; that there will be different food, a different room and different love for Ricky.

5. Be realistic about potential problems. If you adopt a mentally, emotionally, or physically handicapped child, are you still planning to work? Will your agency let you work after the child comes to live with you? You may find it even harder to juggle career and child than if you had your own baby.

If you're considering adopting a child of another race or culture, have you considered all the angles? *You* may be open-minded, but what about your family, friends, and colleagues? Are they tolerant enough to accept this child? If not, think about the effect on the child as well as on your relationships with them.

It would be a pity to give in to shameful prejudice when you're ready to accept a child with open arms. But you really should stop and consider whether you're prepared for the up-hill battle that will be required. And no matter how much you love and want the child, she *will* suffer if many or most of the people in your life—friends and neighbors—make her feel unwelcome.

Moreover, many racial and ethnic groups oppose interracial adoption on the grounds that it deprives the child of his or her cultural and community ties. If you do adopt such a child, will you be able to teach her about her heritage and establish a sense of ethnic pride? If some of your friends, neighbors, or colleagues share the child's background that can be extremely helpful. But if this is not the case, it still is possible to give the child that sense of pride by taking her to cultural events and by making new friends who do share her heritage.

Although adoption of a child who is different in some way turns out to be very satisfying for many families, it's important to assess in advance how satisfying it would be for you and for the child involved. Each situation is unique, depending on the people involved, so you can't *base* your decision on someone else's success or failure, although you certainly can and should take that person's experience into account.

Adoption is a loving and often very rewarding act. But the adoption decision, like the baby decision, must be based on scrupulous self-questioning and not on careless romanticism.

To find out more about adoption, read the books suggested at the back of this book. To apply for adoption, contact your county department of social services or look up Adoption Agencies or Social Services in your Yellow Pages.

SINGLE PARENTHOOD

Thank goodness for options. Today if you're not the marrying kind, you can still be the parenting kind. In this section, we won't be talking about people who became single parents through divorce or death. We'll be talking about women and men who consciously choose to become parents on their own, without a spouse.

Why Be a Single Parent?

There are a number of reasons for choosing single parenthood. Some people simply don't want a spouse even though they do want a child. Others would prefer to be married, but haven't found the right person yet. Single parenthood, for many, is a better alternative than marrying the wrong person in hopes of getting the right child. This is especially true for women nearing the end of their childbearing years. Most don't have the time to wait for the right man to come along. For this reason, more women than men choose this option, although single men are successfully adopting these days. And as nurturance becomes a more valued male quality, I think we'll see more adoptive single fathers.

The typical single mother who's a parent by choice is a college-educated career woman in her late twenties to mid-thirties who's either divorced or has never married. Having a child is more important to her than having a husband. She knows that she may find a husband at forty or forty-seven, but she can't wait that long for a child. She may have wanted a child for a long time, but "delayed her gratification" until her schooling was finished and her career was underway. But when the "right" time came, Mr. Right hadn't yet shown up. Or, in the case of a divorcée, Mr. Right turned out to be Mr. Wrong.

Joys of Single Parenthood

- An intimate relationship with a child. Discovering the pleasure of sharing, caring, and commitment with another human being. Some singles feel their lives are lonely and meaningless, devoid of human connections. A child can provide meaning and stability in one's life. However, this should be a benefit, *not* a motivation for choosing single parenthood. If you have a child because you're lonely or unhappy, both of you will suffer.
- The satisfaction of doing things your way. Spouses often disagree about child-rearing tactics, and power struggles are common. As a single parent, you can call the shots and make all the decisions.
- In the case of adoption, the joy of providing a good home to a needy child.
- A new self-respect for having the courage to make a choice that's right for you even though others may disapprove.
- A sense of pride in being able to manage parenthood without a partner.
- A sense of interdependence. You may never have realized how loving and caring your family and/or friends were until you needed their help—caring for your sick child, relieving you for an afternoon, and so on.

Difficulties of Single Parenthood

- You may feel very isolated at times as a one-parent family in a two-parent world. And you may feel overburdened both psychologically and financially.
- Your social life and your life as a parent may clash. Your child may resent your lovers, your lovers may resent your child, and you may resent everybody. Dating becomes more difficult since time is less available and child care arrangements have to be made. However, some single mothers report an improvement in their relationships with men because they can enjoy men more once they no longer have to consider them as potential passports to parenthood.
- You're soloing in a job that's tough even for two. Can you handle the frustration, the isolation?
- You may encounter prejudice from unexpected quarters, such as family and friends whom you thought would be supportive. Such disapproval can be hard to handle, especially if you weren't prepared for it. And even if you're expecting it, living with it may be more difficult than you thought it would. You may even resent the child, consciously or unconsciously, for straining your relationships with family and friends.

It's Your Choice

Despite these difficulties, there is one important compensation: you've chosen to be a single parent voluntarily and consciously. In contrast, those who become single parents through divorce or death are thrust into the situation involuntarily. The divorced single parent has to cope with the additional burden of feelings of failure and disappointment. As a "single single" parent, you're in control of your destiny; the problems are easier to face because you chose them in the first place and you're prepared for them. The divorced parent, on the other hand, expected to share the responsibility and may be ill prepared to go it alone. Moreover, all too many mothers who are married might as well be single for all the help they get from their husbands.

Considerations for Potential Single Parents

1. What is your financial situation? Can you reasonably support a child? If you want to work part-time after the child's birth, or after you adopt, will you be able to afford to? Are you considering living on welfare? If you want to continue working full-time, what sort of child care can you get, and how comfortable will you feel with it? Can you afford a child? Are you willing to cut down on travel, movies, dinners out? Can you live on a tighter budget? Remember, the money you've been spending on yourself will have to be spread to cover two.

2. What is your social situation? If you are in a relationship, do you want your lover to be the biological and/or psychological father? If so, how will this affect your relationship? Are you harboring unrealistic hopes that he'll decide to marry you? And if another man serves as biological father or as the major father figure, how would your lover react?

How will a child affect your relationships with your friends —male and female?

3. What is your family situation? Will your parents, siblings, and other relatives be supportive or critical? How will a child affect your relations with them, both negatively and positively? If these people are conservative, will they accept the child once they get to know him? It's important to distinguish between hostile criticism and sincere concern for your welfare. Are they expressing narrow-minded or rigid attitudes or are they asking important questions that you may not have considered carefully enough? And if they are just narrow-minded, can you live with the hostility, or perhaps even out-

right rejection of you and the child? Can your child live with it as well?

4. What is your support system? If you have your own baby, who would coach you through childbirth? Who would help you when you got home from the hospital? Who would you visit on Sunday afternoons? Where would you and the child spend Christmas? Would you be able to call someone up and say, "This kid is driving me crazy. Do you have time to talk?" Or, "Could you come over and stay with Susie while I go out for a while?" With whom will you share the bad moments (terrible twos, high fevers) and the good (first tooth, a blue ribbon at the science fair)? You may not need a husband's support, but you will need somebody's. That somebody can include lovers, friends of both sexes, family members, and paid help. No happy, single parent truly parents alone. If she lacks a co-star, she'll need a whole cast of supporting actors instead.

5. Can you establish a comfortable balance of independence and interdependence? Are you independent enough to raise a child on your own? Can you also allow yourself some healthy dependence, asking others for help when you need it?

6. Are you choosing single parenthood for any of the following *wrong* reasons:

- Do you hope that parenthood will frighten off potential lovers who threaten your security? If you have a child, do you believe you'll be less of a catch? If so, you'd be better off dealing with this problem in therapy than using your child as a shield. And there's no guarantee the shield will work!

- Do you believe that a child will overcome your feelings of loneliness? He or she may, for a few years, but older children generally spend more time with their peers than with their parents. And then they leave home. A solid love relationship, on the hand, might last forever.

- Do you want to prove that men are unnecessary, that you can do anything and everything all by yourself?

- Do you like being in control, and believe you can control a child better than an adult? Would it be easier for you to be intimate with a child than with an adult? Again, these are problems to be worked out in therapy, *not* through your child. If you become a parent for either of these reasons, you're likely to become tyrannical or over-protective, and your child may rebel against you.

7. What resources are available in your community? Are there single parent support groups that can offer emotional support as well as practical assistance with housing, jobs, and so on? It's really great to share joys and frustrations with others in your situation. Are there any single mothers around with whom you might want to live? Any communes that include parents and children, both married and single?

If you know other single parents, ask them about their experiences, both pro and con. If you can, spend some time with them to see what their life is like. Compare the similarities and differences between their situation and reactions and yours.

8. How will you go about getting or having a child? You have three basic options:

- A biological pregnancy
- Artificial insemination
- Adoption.

Let's consider some of the advantages and disadvantages of each.

Pregnancy Through Intercourse

Women who decide to conceive through intercourse, rather than via artificial insemination, have two alternatives: to choose a man with whom they have a committed relationship, or a man they know casually. In either case, a woman has to decide whether to be honest about her objectives. A number of women are taking men to their beds without laying their cards on the table. They reason that if their lover knew they were trying to get pregnant he might refuse to cooperate, end the relationship, or try to get custody at some later point. Therefore, by not telling, things will be less complicated. However, when a single woman is trying to get pregnant the relationship *is* complicated and there's no getting around that fact.

First, consider what might happen if the man involved is a longtime lover whom you don't want to lose. What will you do when you get pregnant? Pretend it was an accident? Admit that when you got under the blanket you pulled the wool over his eyes? Either way it's not likely to improve the relationship.

Suppose the potential father is a new lover. You might argue that sex is taking place between two consenting adults. But just because a man has consented to intercourse doesn't mean he has consented to fatherhood. You are taking the liberty of making a parenthood decision for the two of you. Some women counter by saying, "Well, men have always used us for sex, leaving us with unwanted babies in the process. Why can't we use them for babies that we *do* want?"

The reason is that men as well as women are entitled to make decisions about the fate of their bodies. They should be able to decide whether or not to become fathers. Even if you are willing to take complete financial and psychological responsibility for the child, a man shouldn't be put in the position of being unwittingly irresponsible. There are many conscientious men who wouldn't like the idea that a child they fathered is being raised by somebody else.

Perhaps you think that what he doesn't know won't hurt him, and you may be right. But it *will* hurt you and your baby. A good parent-child relationship must be based on honesty. What kind of relationship will you have with your child if it's tainted by deception from the very beginning? When you use a lover as if he were a non-anonymous sperm bank, you are falling into the kind of I-it relationship we discussed earlier. (See page 145.) And if you treat your baby's father in this fashion, can you be sure you won't treat your child the same way as well? If you disregard someone else's feelings and rights to get your own way in one area, you're likely to do so in other areas of your life, too. And you're not only cheating the man, you're also cheating your child out of his birthright —two parents who cooperated, knowingly, in his conception.

Another problem is that at some point your child will ask you about his or her father. You will either have to pretend you don't know or admit that the father has never been told. Obviously either of these responses could cause anguish for both you and the child, not to mention the father, should you or the child contact him several years after the fact.

Unfortunately, legal morasses may prevent you from being open with your lover even if you are so inclined. According to attorneys specializing in family law, if a man knows he's your baby's father, he can sue you for visitation rights and/or for custody, even if you're not married and he previously signed an agreement waiving paternal rights and you previously signed an agreement not to demand child support.

Even if you don't tell him the baby is his, if he suspects it is, he can file a paternity suit. If the appropriate blood tests, etc., establish him to be the father, he can sue for visitation rights and/or custody.

At any rate, if you are considering single motherhood, you would do well to consult an attorney specializing in family law. Then you can make an informed decision.

Artificial Insemination

This procedure has an advantage in that the anonymity of the father is guaranteed. For this reason, women who want to ensure that the father will never try to see the child, become involved in his or her life, or sue for custody, often choose this method. Other women are drawn to artificial insemination because it does not involve possible persuasion or exploitation of the men in their life. However, arranging for it can sometimes be a problem. If you are interested in artificial insemination, contact a women's health clinic, a hospital obstetrics and gynecology clinic, or a private doctor.

Adoption

It's easier for single persons to adopt today than it was in the past. The policy began to change when agencies realized that a single parent was better than no parent at all for hard-to-place handicapped or older children. Then they began to see how successful single adoptions can be. In fact, under some circumstances, they are even more successful than conventional two-parent adoptions. Children whose parents quarreled constantly sometimes do better with just one parent, for instance. And a child who was abused by his father may adjust better to living with a single mother than he would to a mother-father combination. One loving happy parent is certainly better than two unhappy ones. And a single parent's attention is not constantly divided between a spouse and a child, so the child gets a lot of needed attention. For more information on adoption, see the preceding section.

ONLY CHILDREN—A SINGULAR SOLUTION

True or false:

- Only children are spoiled.
- Only children are selfish.
- Only children have more emotional problems than other children.
- Only children are lonely.

False, false, false, and false. Exciting new research by social scientists Sharryl Hawke and David Knox indicates that only children are more creative and well adjusted and get along better with their peers than other children. Their research involved 750 subjects over a period of four years. But even in the 1950s, well before these researchers began their study, there was evidence pointing in the same direction.

Why, then, does the myth of the unhappy, lonely, only persist? I think there are three reasons:

1. Onlies who *are* unhappy are often victims of self-fufilling prophecies. Because professionals told parents that their only children would be unhappy and maladjusted, they expected them to be. On top of that, many parents felt guilty about not giving their child a sibling. So they overprotected and spoiled them to compensate for their guilt. Overprotect and spoil, and presto—you have an unhappy child!

2. In the past, parents of only children generally didn't choose the option. For one reason or other, they couldn't have another child, and they themselves were disappointed and unhappy. The child naturally picked up their feelings and began to feel that he wasn't enough to make his parents happy. And in such an atmosphere, how can a child grow up happy?

3. Cognitive dissonance rears its ugly head once again! Parents overwhelmed by a harvest of children disparage the less burdened parents' "puny" crop. A relatively peaceful one-child home can be a painful reminder of the confusion of one's own life. Many a parent's unconscious takes care of the pain by focusing on the supposed miseries of onlies and their families.

According to Margaret Mead, the one-child family is the family of the future. She thought women would marry and have one child relatively late in life in order to be mature enough to integrate motherhood and career.

If you are a two-career couple, having an only child may be the perfect way to have your cake and eat it, too. You can reap all the rewards of parenthood without being overwhelmed by too many burdens.

Advantages of an Only Child

- You spend fewer years raising young children, so you're less tied down. And you don't have to spend as many years worrying about child care or as many dollars paying for it.
- You can involve the child in your work and your social life. It's not so hard to take one school-aged child to a friend's house, to a meeting, or even to work, but just try taking two!
- You have more time and attention to give one child. It's hard enough to juggle one child and a career, but when you have two children, what little "quality time" you do have has to be juggled between both.
- Even if you're a full-time mother a one-child family may turn out to be the most satisfying. You have the time to paint, dance, do volunteer work, or pursue the activities you like. Or you might want to revel in motherhood, making natural baby food, starting a play group, and picnicking in the backyard. There are mothers who love these activities with one child, but who would not enjoy them as much with two.
- Two children are noisier than one. If you must have a house that rivals a monastery, then you shouldn't have a child. But if you want a relative balance of child and quiet, you'll be more satisfied with just one child.
- Two children are more distracting than one. If you have two young children, you have to put up with a lot of crying as they noisily compete for your attention. And heaven help you if it escalates! And as siblings get older, you have to referee a lot of fights.

Are there any disadvantages to an only child? Some only children demand a lot of attention because they lack companionship. You can solve this problem by helping your child make arrangements to be with his friends, but this doesn't always work. Winter snowstorms and summer vacations may deprive your child of companionship, while other children have siblings as built-in companions. However, don't let this problem hold you back from having an only child. Most parents of onlies prefer the hassle of social arrangements for one child to the hassle of total responsibility for two.

Other onlies don't demand attention, but they get it anyway! As one described it: "I think about my folks as Mama and Papa bird—each perched on one of my shoulders."

As the parent of an only child, you do have to be careful not to smother or overprotect the child, or make him the repository of all *your* dreams and hopes. All children need independence, need to make their own decisions and dream their own dreams. If you give your only child these gifts, rest assured he'll be neither lonely, unhappy, spoiled, nor selfish.

DECIDING TO HAVE A SECOND CHILD

Couples who make the first baby decision carefully often become careless about a second (or third). They assume that since one child has been fun, two children will be twice the fun. Although you can't be sure that your pleasure will be doubled, you can be sure that the workload will be tripled, at the very least. According to most parents, one plus one equals 200% more stress. One mother of three says, "Two is three times the work of one and three is ten times the work of two." So think twice before you decide on two, and read the preceding section to make sure you're not falling prey to only-child myths.

The only *good* reason for a second child is a strong desire for one. And even then, you have to ask yourself:

- Can we afford another child financially and psychologically?

- Can the world's population accept another contribution from this family?
- Are we willing to be *much* more tied down than we already are?
- What do we want from the next child that our first child can't give us? Are our expectations likely to be met by a second child?

As you work on your second baby decision, make sure you're not considering another child for any of the following reasons:

- Your first child is becoming too grown up and independent, and you want someone you can cuddle and control.
- You need a change in your life; a new meaning.
- You're tired of being pressured to have another child, and it seems easier to give in.
- You believe the myths about only children. You think you have to give Billy a little sister.
- You want a child of the opposite sex.

If this last reason hits home, consider why it is so important to you. If you're the mother of a boy, do you want a girl so she can become the kind of woman you always wanted to be? If you're the father of a girl, do you feel a son will somehow validate your masculinity? There are many hidden agendas involved in a desire for a child of the opposite sex and none are healthy for parent or child. If you would simply enjoy a child of the opposite sex, is there an already existing boy or girl with whom you could develop a special relationship instead? For instance, if you love little girls' dresses, could you shop for your niece? Could you toss a football to your best friend's son instead of to your own? And what will you do if the child turns out to be the "wrong" sex? Try again? And again?

Finally, if you're thinking of having a second child as a companion to the first, consider the possibility that it might be a lot less draining to arrange a social life for one child than to rearrange your whole life for two. Also there are no guarantees that siblings would actually enjoy each other's companionship.

The "Don't Confuse Me with the Facts" Game

Let's take a look at what can happen if you make the second baby decision carelessly, or if you base it on a fantasy rather than an assessment of the practicalities involved.

Adrienne and Jake have always cherished dreams of a family of four in a big white house in the country. Their reality: not four children but one, a toddler named Chris. Not a large house in the country, but a small apartment in the city. There isn't enough money for more children or more space. Jake is a paraprofessional counselor with high job satisfaction but low pay. Adrienne is home with Chris full-time. The couple vaguely considers finances, but dismisses the question with platitudes such as, "Where there's a will, there's a way." They are forgetting about their budget and their contraceptives.

The purpose of the game: to avoid looking at the realities that would lead to a decision to forgo or at least delay child number two.

The payoff: getting child number two.

The price: Jake and Adrienne are going to be pinched tighter than ever before. And they'll feel like kicking themselves for their impracticality. They may be in such dire straits that Adrienne will have to work, abandoning her commitment to raising young children full-time. She'll have to leave two children in day care instead of being home with one.

The countergame: Adrienne and Jake should sit down and go over their budget. They should ask themselves how and when another child might fit in. They should:

- Seriously question why it's so important to have another child, and ask themselves how they might otherwise fill the need. For instance, if they want companions for Chris, he and Adrienne might join a play group. Or Adrienne could become a day care mother.

- Consider ways to boost their income. Jake could look for a higher paying job. Adrienne might consider supplementing their income with freelance or part-time work.

The moral of this story: be honest and realistic about your ability to cope with a second child both financially and emotionally. If you can, that's great. But if you can't, think twice before you get in over your head.

STEPPARENTING

It's the easiest way and the hardest way to become a parent. It's also the fastest and the slowest. There is no labor, but there's lots of work. There is no pregnancy, but there's a long period of adjustment.

The problem with stepchildren is that they have been brought into the world by someone else—someone who, in all probability, is not one of your favorite people. It's not easy to accept a living reminder of your mate's first marriage. Nor is it easy for a child to accept your intrusion into the place that "rightfully" belongs to his *real* parent. And in the child's eyes, you're not only a rival to his mother, but to him as well. Once you move in, can he be sure his father will still give him as much attention?

And if the children are not simply occasional visitors, but will live with you instead of the other parent, all these problems are intensified. Such is the stuff that stepparenting is made of. That's why many family counselors advise premarital counseling for marriages that involve stepchildren.

Although difficult, stepparenting can be a satisfying experience for both parents and children. How satisfying you might find it will depend on some of these factors:

- What relationship, if any, do you already have with your potential stepchildren? Have you had at least some positive experiences? If not, is it reasonable to hope things will get better?

- Children who act beautifully toward Mom's boyfriend or Dad's girlfriend can turn ugly as soon as they hear the first strains of a wedding march. Could you cope with this turnabout?
- How specific are your plans? Have you and your intended discussed whether the child(ren) would live with you? If they won't, have you agreed, at least in a preliminary way, on the number and duration of their visits? Of course, you can't be categorical about this, but you can establish loose guidelines. Will you have to add on to your existing home or move to another one?
- Go through your datebook to look at last month's activities. How many of these would you have to give up or arrange differently once the kids are part of your life?

Survival Tips

- Expect things to get worse. Realize that even a friendly stepchild may become unfriendly after the wedding. And in response, your own feelings of goodwill may dry up. All the best intentions in the world may make no difference when every overture on your part draws cold silence or icy indifference. Try to get through this time by talking about your bad feelings with your stepchild and your spouse. Try to show the child that you still like and respect her even though you're both angry and uncertain just now.
- Expect things to get better. If you reject the unacceptable behavior while letting the child know you accept him or her, things will eventually improve.
- Tell the child that you know you can never compete with or replace the other parent. Acknowledge the other parent's specialness to the child. Tell him that you know

your relationship will be different, and hope it will be good.

- If you're becoming the stepparent of a teenager, don't expect anything except survival. Parenting teenagers is rough enough for biological parents and rougher still for stepparents. You should not try to be an authority figure —your spouse will have to play that role without you. Your relationship has to be more that of a teacher or older friend.
- If you decide to have a child of your own, your stepchild will probably be jealous, angry, and hurt. It is important for all of you to discuss your feelings about the baby.

Don't wait until the situation has become impossible before seeing a counselor. If you do, you may already be locked into some hard-to-escape patterns.

_____

Help!

The big moment has arrived. You've done all the exercises, you've thought about all the issues, you've talked to your spouse, your family, your friends. Both you and your spouse are pretty sure you know what you want, but you're still scared. Why? Because when you make a change, any change, some last-minute panic is perfectly normal. So don't assume that your sudden paralysis means that you've made the wrong decision. You probably haven't. But before you throw away your contraceptives or rush out to buy a twenty-year supply, read over the guidelines that follow. If, after you've finished, you are still convinced that your choice is right, accept those lingering doubts as par for the course and act on the decision. However, if your doubts intensify, that could be a sign that you haven't done enough work on the decision. If so, give yourself some more time and consider seeking some professional help.

1. Think child, *not* children. Baby decisions should be made one at a time. Nature may give you twins, but you ought to at least decide on one pregnancy at a time! Don't fall into the trap of believing that if you have one child you have to have another. There's no reason in the world why you shouldn't have just one if that's what you want. So if you want one child, go ahead and have it, and put away thoughts of another until

the time is right. When you are ready to make the next baby decision, your experience as a parent will make that decision much easier.

2. If you are both certain that you want to have a baby, but you're just afraid—of a change in the staus quo, of the responsibility—try to overcome your paralysis.

(a) Try a chair dialogue (see page 28) by yourself or with your spouse, and talk out some of your fears. Role-play some of the scenarios that seem frightening. Are you afraid your husband won't find you attractive during pregnancy? Are you worried your wife will become too wrapped up in the baby? Are you nervous about handling a newborn, about dealing with illness? By acting out your fears, you may be able to conquer them, especially with your spouse's support. It can also be useful to role-play in reverse, acting out each other's fears to get some insight into one another. If you step into your partner's shoes, and vice versa, you'll both be in a better position to support and help each other when real problems come up.

(b) Realize that some of your fears cannot be overcome beforehand. If the baby decision is right for you, you'll adjust. Parents who claim that their children ruined their lives are, for the most part, people who should never have had children.

(c) Waiting may only make things worse. If you know you want children, but haven't been able to say "Tonight's the night" for six months, it may become only more difficult as each month goes by. Remember the first time you stood on a diving board, frozen with fear. The longer you stood and stared at the water, the harder it became to take the plunge. Sometimes you just have to dive in right away.

(d) Consider switching to a riskier contraceptive. By using foam or condoms, you will move toward pregnancy less abruptly than if you went straight from the pill or IUD to nothing. Or, use contraceptives occasionally, but not every time you make love. This is a good way to test the strength of your choice. If you've absolutely panicked about having sex without protection, go back to safer contraceptives and do some more work. Your baby decision was premature.

(e) Realize that you may not get pregnant immediately. Unfortunately, many couples anxious about the decision expect to conceive immediately, perhaps hoping that pregnancy will magically dissolve their ambivalence. And when they don't conceive right away, they panic. The best thing to do is to accept the tug-of-war within you and learn to live with it.

3. If you still have serious doubts, remain child-free. If you're child-free and you change your mind, you do have three options: a pregnancy, if it's not too late; adoption; or substitute gratifications such as special friendships, volunteer and professional work with children. But if you have a child despite your doubts, the options are limited. Of course, you could put the baby up for adoption, but that can create so much emotional trauma and guilt that it's worth considering only under the most extraordinary or desperate circumstances. So if your doubts are more intense than the normal last-minute panic, listen to the important message they're giving you.

SEEKING PROFESSIONAL HELP

Finding this decision painful doesn't mean you need therapy. When you examine your past it's not unusual to find some painful memories. When you consider your possible future as a parent or nonparent, it's not unusual to feel sad about the road not taken. A child-free man contemplating a vasectomy may mourn the son he'll never teach to ski. A woman who's trying to get pregnant may mourn the freedom she feels she's giving up. Don't be afraid of your pain. It simply indicates that you're really working on the decision. Only if it becomes intolerable is it a reason for seeking professional help.

If any of the following situations apply to you, seeing a counselor may be a good idea.

1. You're frustrated because you've spent six months or more on the decision, and you haven't made a bit of progress.

2. You and your spouse are poles apart. One of you says "Now!" and the other says "Never!" Before calling a counselor, reread "Tug-of-war," Chapter 8. If you're still at loggerheads, then you probably need professional help.

3. You're too "stuck" to do the exercises. If you draw a blank when you close your eyes, your unconscious mind is clamped shut. Seeing a counselor can help loosen you up.

4. You've done the exercises and you are disturbed by what you're discovering. You may be threatened by the choice you're leaning toward, or perhaps you're coming to the un-nerving realization that you have a lot of emotional problems to resolve. Talk to your spouse and friends first. If this doesn't help, maybe a professional will.

5. You and your spouse can't even converse on the subject long enough to find out whether or not you disagree. Perhaps you or your spouse absolutely refuse to discuss the issue. Or maybe one or both of you are getting hung up in long silences or making accusations rather than speaking openly.

6. You're leaning toward parenthood, but one of you was abused as a child. Perhaps you're worried that if you become a parent, you will fall into the same abusive pattern with your child. Or perhaps you have an emotional problem that makes you doubt your ability to be a good parent. Spending some time working with a professional can help you figure out whether you could parent happily and successfully.

CHOOSING THE RIGHT KIND OF HELP

The Baby Decision Workshop

A special workshop focusing solely on the baby decision may be conducted by a psychotherapist, counselor, or teacher.

It may be a one-shot deal for a day or a weekend, or it may meet one evening a week for several weeks. What purpose does a workshop serve?

- It gives you an overview of what's involved in making a baby decision.
- It offers you tools in the form of exercises and activities that help you get a handle on the problem.
- It allows you to share your confusion and your solutions with others, getting and giving feedback and support.
- It shows you how others are dealing with the baby decision. Listening to other people's struggles can help you sort out your own, especially if their values, needs, and interests are similar to yours.
- If they are leaning in a particular direction, you may be more inclined to consider how their choice applies to you.
- It offers you and your spouse an opportunity to talk in a nonthreatening atmosphere.

You can usually attend without your spouse if he or she won't come. Some groups are for women only, but most encourage couple participation. They also welcome singles considering parenthood. If a workshop is full and there isn't another one scheduled for some time, ask the workshop leader (if he or she is a therapist) whether you and your spouse could set up a few counseling sessions.

A good workshop will have the following characteristics:

- A workshop leader who accepts the validity of both choices.
- A balanced format consisting of presentations, informal discussions, and values clarification exercises such as the ones in this book.
- A group large enough to bring in a number of viewpoints but not so large that you'll feel too shy to talk.

If you are unsure about whether a workshop is right for you, or if you would just like to find out more in advance, don't hesitate to call the leader and ask some questions such as:

- What is your professional training?
- Are you open to both choices?
- What decision did you make? (If the leader is defensive, angry, or uncomfortable about answering this, you don't want to be in the workshop.)

The leader's decision needn't reflect the choice you think you're leaning toward. And if he or she is any good, that won't even be an issue. All you need is someone who will support and accept the choice you do make because it's the right one for you.

You can also ask the instructor to send you a course outline and provide the names of former participants. Call some of these people and ask them how helpful they found the workshop and whether they thought it was slanted toward either choice.

Individual Therapy

If a baby decision workshop can be said to give you an overview, individual therapy will provide an underview—the counseling will be more intensive and you'll cover more personal territory.

You can set up a specified number of individual sessions, four to six, for example, to work solely on the baby decision. Or you can keep them open-ended to explore not only the baby decision, but related personal growth issues. This is up to you and your therapist, and depends on what you feel you want and what your therapist thinks you need. But you don't have to sign your life or your wallet away. You can just see a therapist for a few goal-oriented sessions.

Individual therapy is appropriate if:

- You've attended a workshop and want to explore your decision or your conflicts about it more fully than you could in a group.
- You're already familiar with the issues and busy exploring them, but want some expert help in sorting them out.
- You're disturbed by what you're learning about yourself or concerned about your ability to be a good parent.
- You want to remain child-free, but you're overwhelmed by guilt about disappointing your parents, or having difficulty withstanding the slightest pressure from the meddlers in your life.

Couple Counseling

If you and your spouse are in serious conflict over the baby decision, marital counseling may be appropriate. But resolving mutual conflict isn't the only reason to seek such help. You may just want an objective third party to help you explore the issue together. Since it takes two to decide (or should), joint counseling sessions can be very useful.

Here are some special tips about couple counseling.

- To save time and money, prepare in advance. Do the exercises in this book before your first session. That way you will already have pinpointed your trouble spots and can get right to work on them.
- Tell the therapist you want help making a decision, not a personality change. You may want to plan for a specific number of weekly sessions, say five or ten.
- Feel free to visit and talk to more than one therapist before committing yourself. Some therapists don't charge for a first visit. Even if you do have to pay regular fees, it may be more economical in the long run to see more than one before deciding which one will give you your money's worth.

What to Look for in a Therapist

Choose a therapist whom you like and can talk to easily. He or she needn't specialize in the baby decision, although it is helpful if the therapist has worked with children and families and has some experience with both the joys and sorrows of family life. However, your own feelings are the most important barometer. If you like and trust the therapist, that's more important than degrees earned, licenses held, or years of experience.

If you can't decide between a workshop and counseling, remember that a workshop goes wider and therapy goes deeper. A workshop covers a lot of issues but not as intensively. In counseling you'll delve into the specific issues that are most germane to *your* baby decision. And with a growth-oriented therapist, you'll discuss the implications your choice has for personal and marital growth.

How to Find Help

- Contact the NAOP (see Appendix C: Resources) for a list of fertility decision counselors and workshop leaders in your community.
- Check your telephone directory for the nearest Planned Parenthood or Family Service Agency. You'll find them by name in the white pages or under Social Services in the Yellow Pages. Also check the Yellow Pages under Birth Control Information and Marriage and Family Counselors.
- A women's counseling center may offer help or refer you to an appropriate counselor.
- University departments of family studies, education, psychology, or social work are possibilities for both service and referrals.

- Try word-of-mouth. If you have friends who have been to a workshop or tried baby decision counseling, ask them what it was like and whether they were satisfied. Therapists your friends have found helpful in nonbaby-related personal or marital counseling might be able to see you or refer you to someone else.
- If you live in a small town that doesn't have any family service agencies or family planning centers, your local community mental health center or county department of social services may be able to help.

The baby decision is a life choice, not a sickness. Having trouble with it doesn't necessarily mean that you need outside help, and seeking such help definitely doesn't indicate weakness, neurosis, or failure. It means that you're taking new strides toward growth.

❧❧

Step Five

_____

Acting on Your Decision

⋞ 11 ⋟

Yes,
We Have No Children

You've finally made the big decision and you're going to commit yourself to a child-free life-style. But now that you've got it, what are you going to do with it? In this chapter, you'll learn how to maximize the pleasures of non-parenthood.

LIVING WITH THE CHILD-FREE CHOICE

1. Get off the hot seat. You don't have to justify your decision to *anyone* (except yourself and your spouse), unless you *choose* to do so.

2. Peel off the selfishness label and tear it to shreds. Your choice makes you no more selfish than a parent. And if being happy and productive in your own way is selfish, then revel in your selfishness!

3. Spring the perfection trap. Nonparents sometimes feel so guilty about their choice that they try to compensate by becoming superachievers in other areas of their life. They feel that if they're not going to have kids, they have to do something spectacular instead. But liberation from unwanted parenthood should not translate into enslavement to unreasonable self-demands. And ironically, by striving to be unusually productive in your work to make up for the "sin" of not being productive as a parent, you are actually defeating your pur-

pose. To be truly creative, you have to be both willing to risk failure and relaxed enough to play around with ideas and possibilities.

4. You have as much right to be "ordinary" as anybody else. You have not committed a sin by not having children; you have nothing to atone for. Your talents will emerge more easily if you don't impose excessively high expectations on them.

5. Allow yourself solitude. Ironically, some people who decide to remain child-free because they crave solitude never take advantage of it. They get caught up in a whirlwind of activities that precludes any quiet time. Why? They fear solitude because when there are no distractions unwanted thoughts and fears can't be ignored or repressed as easily. Few of us like to face our problems head-on, or admit that our marriage, our work, or other parts of our life are not as satisfying as we would like them to be. But solitude is a golden opportunity for growth. And compared to parents you're blessed with a wealth of it. Don't pass up your special opportunity for quiet time to meditate, daydream, fantasize, pray, or plan.

Don't overload yourself with activities that prohibit solitude and relaxation. Ironically, even pursuits that seem to encourage growth, such as yoga classes, journal or dream workshops, or encounter groups, can actually hinder it, if you take on too many at one time. You will end up spending too much of your spare time rushing from one to another, instead of working on and experiencing each activity, and as a result, you won't benefit much from any of them.

6. Find a path to immortality (see page 127). Can you live with the fact that you will die some day? Have you figured out what you'll be leaving behind? Your answers to these questions indicate whether or not you'll regret your decision in the future. If you feel creative and productive, if you believe your life has had meaning and value, then it's unlikely that you'll regret your decision in later years, although you may have occasional doubts. But they're normal, and they'll pass quickly.

7. Make the most of your marriage. You're lucky. Because

you don't have children, you have time and energy to lavish on each other. And you'll both benefit—research indicates that child-free couples are quite happy, possibly happier than those with children.

8. Share. Because you don't have a shared interest in a child, pick a special project that you can work on together. For many child-free couples, such projects evolve naturally. If this isn't the case for you, choose one consciously.

Set aside time for each other. Even though some couples choose nonparenthood in order to protect their relationship, they may become so involved in various activities that they spend little time with their spouse.

9. Develop a family system (see page 135). Who would you turn to if your spouse died? With whom do you spend holidays? Do you have any ties with people under sixteen or over sixty? Family ties are important, and if you're not close to "blood" family—either physically or emotionally—create a "chosen" family with friends, colleagues, neighbors, and so on.

10. Don't feel guilty. Child-free couples sometimes feel guilty, as if they're getting away with something. It's a little like being the only person sipping lemonade in a hammock while everyone else is working in the hot fields. But you needn't feel bad. You're being excused from the burdens of parenthood, but not from the burdens of life.

11. Get together with other nonparents. Join the NAOP (see Appendix C: Resources). If there is a local chapter in your community, attend meetings. If not, see if you can start one.

Making It Final—Sterilization

If you and your spouse are certain you won't ever want children, you will probably consider sterilization at some point, either a vasectomy for the husband or a tubal ligation for the wife.

The decision to be sterilized actually involves two *separate* decisions: first, the decision not to have a child; and second, the decision to close that option off forever.

Sterilization offers the following advantages:

1. An end to worry about contraceptive failure. Many couples report that their sex life improves after sterilization. Women in particular say they never realized how much fear of pregnancy affected their sex lives.

2. An end to anxiety about possible long-term effects of the pill or IUD. An end to the inconvenience of the diaphragm and other methods.

3. A rite of passage. Sterilization can be a turning point resulting in a burst of creativity in another area of your life. By closing the door to parenthood permanently, you may be more open to new possibilities and interests, and you'll have more time and energy to pour into them.

4. A sense of closure: an end to a long, involved decision-making process. (Of course, no decision is completely final. Even if one spouse is sterilized, a couple could still adopt. And if a husband has had a vasectomy, his wife could consider artificial insemination at a later date.)

The major disadvantage of sterilization is its irreversibility. Like a decision to have a baby, a decision to be sterilized is irrevocable. For this reason I suggest the following:

1. Be cautious about getting sterilized in your twenties. Some people are so certain they would never want children that they undergo sterilization procedures while in their early or mid-twenties. If you and your spouse are quite sure you will never want children; if you would find an accidental pregnancy or abortion totally unacceptable; if you are worried about contraceptive side effects, sterilization may be the contraceptive of choice. And more and more people in their twenties are making that choice. However, it is possible that you will change your mind about children when you're older. For that reason it may be a good idea to wait awhile before making this decision.

Child-free television commentator Betty Rollin describes her doubts about sterilization in the under-thirty crowd. "You can't assume your present feelings are going to be with you forever. People often change their attitudes as they get older. I think that choice is one of the great gifts of life and, in a sense, early sterilization deprives one of having that choice." And Carol Nadelson, a Boston psychoanalyst and vice-chairman of psychiatry at Tufts New England Medical Center says: "I see a lot of people who decide to become parents in their late thirties or early forties."

One of the reasons why people change their minds in their thirties or even early forties is linked to Erikson's concept of generativity—a concern with nurturing and guiding future generations. This need generally doesn't surface until the late thirties or early forties. And although you can meet it in other ways—through creative work, by associating with other people's children—as most child-free people do, you may wish to reconsider parenthood at that time.

For women, a change of heart is possible when they reach their mid-thirties especially those who embarked on a career at age twenty-two and have had fifteen years of professional success by age thirty-seven. By that time, many are:

- Ready for a change. They want to try something new and different.
- Ready to shift from a work ethic to a family ethic. Whether they take a few years off, continue working full-time, or switch to part-time, they are ready to shift their focus.
- So well established in their work that it's easier to combine career and motherhood. And the frustrations of coping with a double life may seem less taxing when they're older and wiser.

Their husbands may also shift their psychic energies from career achievement to personal relationships. If both partners are now willing to spend time parenting, having a baby becomes more feasible than it was when the couple were in their twenties and too busy establishing their careers to consider parenthood.

But suppose you're in your twenties, have given this matter quite a bit of thought, and want to be sterilized. Is there an acid test for sterilization readiness?

According to Maxine Ravech, sterilization counselor at Preterm in Brookline, Massachusetts, taking responsibility for oneself is the dividing line between the twenty-three-year-old who's mature enough to be sterilized and the one who isn't. "If I hear someone saying to me, 'I know I could be wrong, but I do understand that sterilization is irreversible, and I believe this decision is right for me,' I think that person is mature enough to understand the meaning of sterilization." If you can agree with this statement, if you think you could live with regret should it ever materialize, you are making a mature choice.

2. Don't get sterilized until you've been married or in a committed relationship for at least a year. Feelings about children are sometimes linked to our feelings about our mates or lovers. One woman who didn't want any children with her first husband couldn't wait to get pregnant with her second. In fact, happy parents who thoroughly planned their parenthood report that conceiving and giving birth was a way of celebrating their union and their love for each other.

Although your image of a child in the abstract may seem like a devil, your image of the potential child of someone you love may seem like nothing less than an angel. Therefore, give yourself some time to ensure that your feelings about your spouse and your relationship won't affect your feelings about a child.

3. Give yourself time to let the decision jell. If you are considering sterilization now, wait six months to a year before taking any action.

Does your interest in the idea fluctuate depending on your moods, or is it steady? This should not be a spur-of-the-moment decision. If you have given it the test of time, the sterilization decision will probably not be a mistake.

4. Don't get sterilized if your spouse still wants a child. I've already stated my belief that you should never have a child unless you *both* want one. By the same token, you should not make such a final sterilization decision until your spouse has come to terms with the child-free decision itself. Your spouse must be allowed to express anger and disappointment, mourn, and find substitute ways to nurture. If you simply make a unilateral decision and top it off with an unalterable sterilization procedure, your partner is going to feel steamrolled.

5. The spouse who is more committed to nonparenthood should be the one to undergo sterilization.

Even when both partners agree to remain child-free, typically, one will be more certain than the other. "I had a tubal ligation," Angela reported, "because I was more committed to nonparenthood than Doug. He was willing not to have children. He enjoys the peace and freedom of our life as it is now. And he gets 'fatherly' satisfaction from his activities with his Boy Scout troop. But if something happened to me, or if we split up, it's quite possible that he would want a child by a different wife. I've been positive ever since I was a child that I didn't want children, so it made more sense for me to be sterilized."

6. If you do get sterilized:

(a) Don't panic if you have some qualms just before or after the procedure. It's natural to have a few regrets, but if you've made a careful decision, you'll probably live quite happily with it.

(b) Seize the opportunity to make new life plans. Now that you don't have to use your nest egg for a nestling, you may want to use it to test your own wings. Perhaps it's time to realize your dream of owning your own business, or to take a less profitable, but more exciting job. Or perhaps you can take the trip you've always longed for, up the Himalayas, or down the Amazon.

(c) Be choosy and careful in announcing your action.

Should you tell, and if so, how and to whom? The advantage of an announcement is that it will put an end, once and for all, to all those tiresome questions and pressures. It also allows you to share your excitement, relief, and your sense of freedom, and it keeps your intimate friendships honest and aboveboard.

On the other hand, if you don't share the news, you won't have to deal with possible rejection, anger, and hostility, often in the form of endless lectures. And if you have any lingering doubts about the wisdom of your decision, these lectures can be intolerable.

If you're like most people, you'll probably tell those people who will support your action and avoid telling many who would disapprove. But there are some people, your parents, for example, who may have to be told even though the telling won't be pleasant. And even if you decide against sterilization, you will have to tell your parents that you've decided to remain child-free. Either announcement may evoke shock, hurt, disappointment, and anger. So when you make the announcement, keep the following points in mind:

1. Keep an adult perspective. Now that you're grown up, view your parents with an adult's eyes rather than a child's. Try to avoid slipping into old parent-child patterns. Focus on understanding and sharing and try to prevent the discussion from degenerating into a destructive pattern of lecturing and being lectured to.

2. If you don't share the news, are you protecting them or yourself? Some people don't tell their parents because, ostensibly, they don't want to hurt their parents' feelings. But, more often than not, they're really trying to avoid being hurt themselves. But you'll all suffer if you persist in saying "Maybe some day" when you had a vasectomy ten years ago! Eventually, the truth will out and everyone will be hurt.

3. Empathize with their feelings of disappointment, hurt, and anger. Let them mourn. You've taken away what they

believe is their right to grandchildren. Don't take away their right to inevitable human reactions. You don't have to agree with their attitude or feel guilty about it, but you can say, "I can understand why you feel that way."

4. Listen. Pay close attention to your parents' reactions. If you don't respect their feelings, you can hardly expect them to respect yours. You and your parents may never agree, but you can offer each other compassion and understanding.

5. Realize that their expectations of grandparenthood were realistic. The child-free choice was unheard-of when you were born. And during all the years your parents raised you, there was no reason for them to doubt that they would have the pleasure of knowing your children. It's hardly surprising they're disappointed. Try teaching them about the child-free choice. Give them this book and some NAOP pamphlets. Share with them what you've learned from your own experience, from other child-free couples, and from your reading.

6. Give them time. They may come to accept your decision once they get used to the idea, especially if they see that you and your spouse are happy and productive.

7. Help them find other satisfactions. If they already have other grandchildren, or if you have siblings who might eventually have children, remind them of this. Try to help them find other ways to get involved with children. Gently and tactfully suggest that they consider:

- Becoming foster grandparents to a family whose "real" grandparents have died or live far away.
- Becoming special friends to the children or grandchildren of their friends and neighbors.
- Volunteering at a day care center, residential center for children, or a Big Brother or Big Sister program.

8. Help them unload their guilt. Your parents may feel that they are somehow at fault; that you've made this choice because they were rotten parents or because you've been soured on family life. And they may perceive the decision as a way

of rebelling against them and everything they stand for. To counter this, let them know your positive reasons for remaining child-free. Tell them there's no reason to feel guilty. Of course they made some mistakes—who doesn't? But make sure they recognize that you've made the decision because it's right for you, not in reaction to them. Seek their understanding.

9. Get them to take pride in your generativity. If you tell them your positive reasons for remaining child-free, they'll be proud of you. They won't have grandchildren, but they can share, enjoy, and applaud your accomplishments. If their interests or example led you to any of your chosen commitments, point this out so they can identify more fully with your choice.

10. Realize that the relationship between your parents and your spouse may change. If your parents believe (accurately or not), that your spouse is more committed to the child-free choice, they may resent him or her and say, "If only my child had married someone more traditional. That awful son-in-law [or daughter-in-law] led my child astray." Counter by describing your active participation in the decision and giving them a chance to vent their feelings. This may smooth over the relationship.

11. Tell them—if it's true—that you value them more than ever. Whether your relationship with your parents is terrific or just mediocre their importance to you may increase after you've made your decision. More than ever, the family ties you have become a valuable resource.

12. If you have two parents, you'll have two reactions. Don't make the mistake of thinking you've talked to your *parents* if you've only talked to one. Avoid these common tactics:

- Talking to one parent only (most frequently Mom) and letting her relay the message to Dad.
- Talking to both parents, but assuming that the situation is resolved when only *one* parent has actually expressed feelings about the subject.

USING WHAT YOU'VE LEARNED ABOUT YOURSELF TO GROW

If you've made a thoughtful decision to remain child-free, you've based it, in part, on what you learned about your past, your hopes for the present and future, your definition of happiness, your own personality, and your good and bad qualities. And during the learning process, as you searched the "inner you," you may have come face to face with certain negative personal characteristics. Recognizing their existence does *not* mean that you've made the wrong decision or that they had more influence than they should have. Nor does it mean that you have more emotional problems than someone choosing parenthood. *Everyone*—parents and nonparents alike—has certain characteristics and problems he or she would like to work on.

Let's take a look at some of the problems certain child-free people may discover as a result of their inner journey:

- A need to be in control
- Perfectionism
- Unwillingness to deal with emotions
- A lack of patience with others
- Fear of being depended upon
- Fear of reliving one's own childhood, complete with feelings of helplessness, powerlessness, anxiety, and hurt
- Difficulty playing or trying new activities
- Trouble being affectionate or supportive
- Discomfort in the presence of children.

Even if you have any of the above characteristics, you don't necessarily have to do anything about them. Do they bother you, your spouse, or others close to you? Do they interfere with your enjoyment of love, work, or play? If the answer is no, accept them and live with them. If the answer is yes, you might consider:

- Reading some of the self-help books listed in the appendices
- Attending a growth workshop
- Talking to your spouse or your friends about the problem and ways to work on it
- Getting individual or group therapy.

And regardless of whether you consider these characteristics an acceptable part of your personality or a problem to be solved, keep these guidlines in mind:

1. Don't spend too much time worrying about them. You have positive reasons for remaining child-free, too. Don't forget them or forget to make the most of them.

2. Don't feel you have to cover up your problem because it fits others' stereotype of the child-free person. It's all the more reason why your choice is right for you. You have a right to be less than an ongoing live advertisement for optional parenthood!

3. Focus on the positive aspects of your discovery rather than the negative. Instead of worrying that this trait or weakness has unduly influenced your baby decision, accept it as a part of your nature and work on it. Remember Roger, the child-free man who discovered he was a perfectionist when he and his wife came in for counseling (see pages 166–7). Although he didn't change his mind about children, he began working on solving the problem. Today, he's a happier man, not only because he's child-free and living the kind of life he wants, but also because his expectations for himself and others are now within the realm of possibility.

THE CHILD-FREE PERSON—A NEW KIND OF PIONEER

Congratulations on venturing into one of the new life-styles of the twenty-first century. You're fortunate to live in the first age in which people whose talents and interests do not lie in child-rearing are able to say no to parenthood and yes to themselves. You are free to spend your time and energy on the pursuits that offer you the deepest satisfaction.

The self-awareness, risk-taking, and assertiveness you have developed during the decision-making process should stand you in good stead as you continue staking out new territories of child-free living.

ᵉᵍ 12 ᵇᵉ

Small Pleasures: Making the Most of Parenthood

Now that you've made the decision to have a baby, how are you going to live with that decision? By giving yourself some time and patience.

THREE'S COMPANY—PREPARING FOR THE BABY

1. **Don't expect to get pregnant the first night.** Many couples who struggle with the baby decision find it difficult to give up control. Often, they are the kind of people who planned everything meticulously in the past, carefully choosing their colleges, their training programs, their jobs, and their spouses. Now they unconsciously assume they can choose the baby's due date. They can't.

Moreover, once a couple have made the decision, particularly if they spent months or even years wrestling with the question, they are so excited and so eager to act on the decision immediately that more waiting becomes extraordinarily painful. It seems so ironic that after finally deciding to have a baby, the baby doesn't seem willing to be born.

If you are over thirty and haven't gotten pregnant within six months, it *is* a good idea to seek medical help. But not the first month. Your body is not a machine; you can't just program it for conception! For more information about infertility, see Chapter 9.

2. Picture yourself enjoying your choice. Close your eyes and imagine yourself and your spouse having a happy, healthy pregnancy and an easy childbirth. Now picture yourselves playing with the baby. Imagine yourselves being more in love than ever, feeling that the child has added a new dimension to your relationship. Positive imagery can serve as a self-fulfilling prophecy.

3. Prepare for parenthood.

- Take a childbirth class to make birthing a more pleasant and loving experience for everyone involved.
- Learn parenting skills. Read now; you'll be too busy later. (See the appendices for a list of useful books.) Do you know what a newborn looks like? Do you know what a three-month-old can and can't do? Is it possible to spoil a six-month-old? Find out ahead of time.
- Look for role models. If you like the way your parents raised you, analyze their behavior. What specifically did they do so well? Ask them about it. If you don't like the way they reared you, try to find other role models, couples you know personally who seem to be doing a good job with their children. Observe how they handle various situations. Ask them to describe their parenting philosophy. Parenting books can also offer alternatives to the way your parents raised you.

4. Steer clear of potential traps. Focus on aspects of the child-free life-style that appeal to you, and try to find ways of meeting some of these needs. If you crave solitude, for example, can you and your spouse spell each other so you can each have some quiet time alone? If dinner out once a week seems essential, can you cut some other corners to make it possible?

5. Work on any emotional problems that might get in the way of parenting. If you're worried or nervous about parent-

hood, seeing a counselor during pregnancy can be helpful. Here are some typical problems:

- You're absolutely terrified of parenthood even though you very much want a child.
- You realize you're expecting the baby to give meaning to your life. You're worried because you know you have to have some other meaning, too.
- You're convinced you're going to make the same parenting mistakes your parents did. This is especially serious if you were abused physically or psychologically.
- You and your spouse had a tug-of-war. The "baby person" won, but the "child-free person" gave in too easily. He or she doesn't really feel ready for parenthood yet.

6. Shoot all unrealistic expectations on sight! Don't strive to be the perfect parent. There's no such thing. A Zen concept applies here: The harder you try to be perfect, the farther away from perfection you'll fall. If you *want* a child and you're relatively mentally healthy, you *will* be a good parent, despite your faults and failings. Take comfort in the knowledge that children can survive a lot. They're more like rocks that chip than eggs that break.

Also, don't expect to create the perfect child. You cannot mold a child's personality, because he or she is already born with one. Your guidance and support, though crucial, are only part of the equation. As one mother described herself: "I am not a sculptor who molds a child from clay. I'm the gardener who tends a seed that will grow to become itself."

FINDING CREATIVITY AND JOY IN THE PARENT/CHILD RELATIONSHIP

According to some proponents of the child-free life-style, a child is at best a glaring Stop sign on the road to growth; at worst, a bundle of dynamite that shatters the road entirely. But parents who *value* children and who have, by definition, made a good baby decision, make a conscious trade-off: exchanging personal pleasure for parental pleasure—the pleasure of fostering the growth and development of another human being. And through that process, a parent can experience tremendous growth, too. In the words of Margaret Fuller: "The character and history of each child may be a new and poetic experience to the parent, if he will let it."

How Children Can Help You Grow

1. Children are "warm fuzzies" in residence. They not only receive affection; they give it, too. Hugs, kisses, and smiles can make you feel loved and important. Of course, you cannot rely on your child for love and self-esteem. But although children should not be a crutch, they can be a delightful source of pleasure. They can cheer you up on days when work doesn't go well, or when you and your spouse are at odds. It is not a reason to have a child, but it's a nice fringe benefit.

2. Children offer new perspectives. They constantly challenge the status quo by asking "Why?" In their naïveté, they can offer fresh insights and new solutions—*if* you're open to your child's sense of wonder and creativity.

3. Children teach you about yourself. It's easy to be a textbook expert on child development. But it's truly an education to watch the development of a real child. This intensive course in child psychology is especially useful if you happen to work with children and families. Having your own child forces you to refine your theories of child development, your philosophies of child-rearing, and your beliefs about human nature.

4. Children offer comic relief. They are a vivid reminder that life goes on, no matter what. When adults are absorbed in

a crisis, a child's silly giggles can provide some much-needed perspective.

5. Children force you to think about the future. They remind you that you will die some day. Even if you're good at deceiving yourself most of the time, it will occur to you, at least occasionally, that your children are going to outlive you. This realization can spur you to make some contribution; to try to ensure that the world you turn over to your progeny will be reasonably tolerable.

6. Children keep you on your toes. You have to remain flexible and open to adjust to changes in your children. You have to grow along with them.

7. Children help you develop self-discipline that you never knew you had.

   (a) In order to succeed as a disciplinarian, you have to learn self-discipline first. You have to separate your need to vent your frustration (the urge to give him a good, hard whack, for example), from your child's need to learn to obey important rules of living.

   (b) Children force you to get organized. As parents, you'll be forced to do a given amount of work in less time. It's hard to goof off when you know your children need you, or when every wasted moment raises the tab on the baby-sitter's bill. On the other hand, allow yourself some goof-off time. Everyone needs it, particularly parents.

Whether or not you'll enjoy parenthood depends largely on what *you* bring to it. If you embrace it openly and eagerly, with no unrealistic or idealistic expectations, you won't be disappointed. But if you expect it to give meaning to your life or miraculously solve your problems, you will be quite disillusioned.

Like any other life experience, parenting has its highs and lows. It is both joyous and frustrating, stimulating and draining. But as long as you base your decision to become a parent on a full awareness of both sides, you will be able to take pleasure in the pluses and cope with the minuses.

LESSONS FROM ROOM NINETEEN: HOW TO BE A MOTHER WITHOUT BEING A MARTYR

. . . I spent twelve years of my adult life working, *living my own life*. Then I married, and from the moment I became pregnant for the first time I signed myself over, so to speak, to other people. To the children. Not one moment in twelve years have I been alone, had time to myself. So now I have to learn to be myself again. That's all.

Thus speaks Susan Rawlings, middle-aged heroine of Doris Lessing's classic short story, "To Room Nineteen." The words "That's all" are ironic, because retrieving a self after so many years of denying that self is an awesome task. So awesome in fact, that Susan Rawlings can't do it. Over the years, she has not only lost her self, but also her willingness to fight for its return. Once a week, Susan breaks away from household responsibilities to spend time in a hotel room. She rents a room, not with an affair in mind, but in hopes of self-discovery. But what she finds is that when she lost her self, she also lost her ability to care. The ending: She commits suicide out of apathy rather than despair.

Although few middle-aged women resort to suicide, most, like Susan, are overwhelmed by the difficulty of finding the lost threads of their preparent existence.

However, should you become a mother you need never face such an awesome task. Not if you adamantly hold onto those threads, letting them guide you through motherhood and through your continuing growth as an adult woman. You'll never have to search desperately for your identity if you never let go of it in the first place. In this section, we're going to look at some of the ways you can assure yourself that you'll never land in Room Nineteen. You won't have to because you'll have reserved room for growth right in your very own home.

The words "mother" and "martyr" start and end with the same letters, but the similarity should end there. Regardless of whether women stay home or work part-time or full-time, they seem to fall victim to their own and to society's unrealistic expectations. As Angela Barron McBride says, "[Motherhood] is an impossible job for all women as presently defined." No mother can be held responsible for making everyone in the family happy. No mother can be expected to repress or ignore her needs in order to meet the needs of her family.

Survival Tactics

Take care of yourself, and your family will take care of itself. As Anaïs Nin said, "When you make a world tolerable for yourself, you make a world tolerable for others."

Mothers' needs don't die; they simply go underground. A frustrated mother's interactions with her husband and children are polluted by her guilt and hostility. Anger and depression are the only responses to being squelched. Whatever your family's needs are, you're entitled to fulfill your own as well.

Advice for Full-Time Mothers

1. You will need time away from the baby. Ask your husband or another relative to take the baby, hire a sitter, or exchange baby-sitting with a friend, or a local children's play group.

2. Choose one nonfamily-related goal that interests you and actively pursue it. It might be a class, an art project, a community activity, a freelance paid job—anything that you enjoy and in which you can take pride. However, it's generally best to choose something in which your progress will be visible. Although as a mother you make significant progress with your

children, it isn't tangible. Come June, you'll still be diapering the same bottom you diapered in May. So it's nice to be able to observe and measure progress in another activity.

3. Get out of the house as often as you can, with and without the baby.

4. Spend time with other grownups when you can. When you can't, use your telephone to reach out to other adults.

5. Join a mother's group or cooperative play group to give both yourself and your baby a chance for fun and friendship.

6. Seek professional help if you feel frustrated and depressed. Try talking to your husband and your friends. If that doesn't help, see a counselor.

7. Consider going back to work. If you haven't been happy at home, maybe you're just not meant to be a homebody. You might feel better if you got yourself a good job.

Advice for Working Mothers

If you work you have the advantage of getting a tangible paycheck and getting out of the house on a regular basis. But chances are you're overburdened, especially if you are a perfectionist or if your husband hasn't taken on a reasonable share of the household burdens.

1. Make a date with yourself. Set aside a block of personal time each week to do whatever you please. And don't skimp on this time because you have so much else to do. Your "for myself" time is no luxury; it's an absolutely essential form of burn-out prevention.

2. Be realistic. If your husband won't do his share, don't do it yourself. Better to let the dust pile up, than the resentment.

Advice for All Mothers

1. Don't be shocked by your feelings. Occasional urges to throw the baby out the window or to run away from home are quite common in mothers of young children. And if you do

have these feelings you're neither neurotic nor "bad." There's a big difference between fantasizing about something and actually doing it. The temptation to strike out at the baby or to run away from him is a natural psychological response to the unnatural conditions of motherhood. I say "unnatural," because it is only in postindustrial Western culture that mothers of young children have been so isolated. For most of human history, mothers have had much more contact with and support from other mothers and from their own female relatives. They have also been able to stay more involved in adult activities. The problem, then, is not you or even motherhood itself, but rather the straitjacket our society makes of motherhood.

2. Get rid of your tension. There are two necessary steps in breaking out of your frustration. The first is to reach out to caring adults—your husband, your friends, a mother's group, a professional counselor, or a parenting class. The other is to release your tension. Leave the baby in a crib or playpen, go to your room, close the door, and do whatever will make you feel better—scream, cry, pound a pillow or bam it against a wall, count to ten, take deep breaths, and so on. When the baby is napping or has gone to sleep for the night, meditate, do yoga or relaxation exercises. Leave the baby with someone else long enough to get some physical exercise. Running, swimming, bike-riding, and tennis are all great tension-releasers.

3. Express your anger and ask for changes. Let your husband know when you are angry. Explain why as specifically as possible and focus on your feelings. Don't say, "You're inconsiderate. You don't care about anybody but yourself." Instead say, "You haven't paid attention for the last three nights when I've tried to tell you how frustrated I am with the baby." And if you're not angry at him, but just want to let out your frustrations, be sure to tell him that.

Once you've talked about how you feel, discuss what you can both do about it. Make specific requests for change. Don't say, "I never have any fun and you do. I want to start having a good time for a change!" Instead say, "Will you stay with the baby on Monday nights and on Saturdays so I can paint, swim, and see my friends? I think I'll be a lot happier."

When your children are old enough, the two steps described above will work with them, too.

4. Don't do things that bore you just because they're "good for the children." As Arlene Rossen Cardozo points out, children will learn to like whatever you like. If you love the woods, put the baby in a backpack and take her hiking. If you love to dance, put on a record and go with the music. Your child will find your enthusiasm contagious. She'll be glad you care enough to share it with her. If you do things you hate, your child will notice your resentment and boredom, and it won't be a good experience for either of you.

Of course, you should not make your child into a carbon copy of yourself or discourage her interest in other things, but you must take your own interests into consideration, too. As your child gets older and develops her own interests, encourage her to pursue them on her own, with other children or other adults. You can provide the money, the materials, and the transportation required, but you don't have to provide your presence. Willing encouragement is better than unwilling participation.

5. Don't force yourself to be an earth mother. Your child needs warm hugs, but not warm bread. She won't die of malnutrition if her milk comes from a bottle instead of a breast, or if her carrots come from a can instead of the garden.

Baking, nursing, and making natural baby food are great if you do them because you want to. But if you're only doing them out of a sense of duty, you would be better off skipping them. Instead, use the time to have fun with your baby.

6. Don't let guilt get the best of you. Don't read child care books that make you feel guilty. The garbage can is the only proper place for any child care book suggesting that one false

move will land your child on the analyst's couch. Most children manage very well to survive a wide variety of parents and parenting styles. If you're reasonably happy and you respect your child's individuality, your child will probably turn out fine. A few emotional scars in the course of growing up are unavoidable, but endurable. In fact, with your guidance, a child's pain can stimulate his growth.

You do have something to feel guilty about if you're ignoring your child, yelling constantly, being cold or critical, or failing to discipline. But if you avoid such behavior your guilt is unwarranted and will only interfere with your ability to love and enjoy your child. And even if you are guilty of some of the above, all is not lost. Seek professional help right away.

Actually a little guilt can serve a useful purpose. It is a reminder that your child, like you, is a person who thrives on love and attention. In this day of valuing our own needs, we sometimes forget that children have needs, too. Not every request is a manipulation; not every parental wish can prevail over every conflicting young person's wish. Parents have a moral obligation to meet their children's basic needs. If children are viewed as deserving recipients, not as competing adversaries, we can take pride and find satisfaction in respecting them as well as ourselves.

If you're suffering from counterproductive or immobilizing guilt, try a talking cure. Other mothers and family counselors are two of the best sources of help. You need someone who can be supportive and objective. (For more advice on dealing with guilt, see page 254.)

7. Insist on retaining your personhood. Never let go of the identity questions you dealt with before becoming a mother. Always seek and make the most of whatever meaning and mission you have in life in addition to motherhood. No matter how good a mother you are, no matter how satisfying you find this role, your children are going to walk out the door later on. Don't let them take your whole reason for living with them. As Susan Rawlings knew: "Children can't be a center of life and

a reason for being. They can be a thousand things that are delightful, interesting, satisfying, but they can't be a wellspring to live from."

Work hard at finding and enjoying the other wellsprings, and you'll enjoy motherhood more than ever.

✺ 13 ✺

Grape Juice on Mommy's Briefcase, or How to Combine Motherhood and Career Without Losing Your Mind or Your Job

I don't know whether to laugh or cry when I hear one more expert say, "Women can't have it all; they can't combine career, marriage, and motherhood." Shall I laugh at the absurdity of saying we can't do what we are in fact doing? Cry at the injustice of society in general and husbands in particular for not sharing more of the burden? Swell with pride at doing the impossible, or fizzle out with exhaustion?

Nina Finkelstein, an editor of *Ms.* magazine, has some pointed comments on the problem:

> I get a little upset when women talk about having it all. Men have it all and they don't think twice about it. Instead of talking about having it all, I think we should be talking about child care . . . I'm very angry at the books that are coming out for working mothers. Where are the books for working men? Does anybody tell them what to do?

The problem, then, isn't that working mothers are doing too much—it's that everybody else isn't doing enough.

Ellen Goodman, in a brilliant article on career and motherhood, pointed out that children actually contribute to their mothers' careers because working mothers are forced to become more organized and efficient. "Working mothers take shorter coffee breaks," she wrote. However, such women may actually be defeating their own purposes. To tell the truth, I don't want to see working mothers taking shorter coffee breaks. I want to see working fathers taking shorter coffee breaks so they'll have more time for housework. I'd like to see politicians take shorter coffee breaks so they'll have time for hearings on the need for day care and supportive family services. I'd like employers to take shorter coffee breaks so they'll work on plans for flexi-time, part-time jobs with benefits, and arrangements for job sharing. And I want working mothers to take *longer* coffee breaks because they're working too hard.

Working mothers aren't the only ones who suffer from overwork; their families do, too. An overextended wife is more likely to jump down her husband's throat than to jump into bed with him. A mother who's worn out is more likely to yell like the wicked witch than to calmly read *Snow White* at bedtime. And we can't expect working mothers to take all the responsibility for social change. How can a woman write her congressman when she doesn't even have time to write a grocery list? How can she get the neighbors together to discuss day care if she hasn't even had time to meet them yet?

JUGGLING CAREER AND MOTHERHOOD

Can you combine career and motherhood? Well, you can and you can't.

1. You can if you get some form of support such as:
   - A husband who's willing to do his fair share
   - Good child care
   - Role models in the form of other working women
   - A cheering section, including your husband, your friends, and your children when they're old enough.

2. You can if you let go of perfectionistic expectations. You'll have to accept the fact that you probably won't be as outstanding a worker as a single, child-free colleague. You'll

also have to accept the fact that you won't be as available to your child as a mother who is home full-time.

3. You can if you're willing to give up most of your leisure. It is essential to give yourself at least a little leisure time each week. But many of the women who successfully combine career and motherhood do so by skimping on their social life, exercise, recreation, and goof-off time.

4. You can if you don't have high housekeeping standards. Will nothing less than spotless floors and gourmet meals be acceptable? Unless you have a housekeeper or a lot of energy, you're going to find the going rough.

5. You can if you want to badly enough. It's certainly hard to cover all the bases, but perhaps you would rather be overtired than forced to sit out the game. Some mothers who have tried both, staying home and working, strongly prefer working. They say they would rather be worn out from doing too much than depressed from not doing enough satisfying work. Similarly, many women who are already committed to their work decide to have children anyway because, even though they know they'll be overloaded, they think it will be worth it.

Journalist Letty Cottin Pogrebin expressed this succinctly when her daughter asked her on a hectic day whether she regretted being a mother. Ms. Pogrebin answered: "Sometimes my life is a little too full because I have you children, but, for me, it would be much too empty if I didn't."

6. You can if you explore options. There are other options besides carrying your briefcase into the labor room and showing up at the office two hours postpartum. You can:

- Take a maternity leave of three to twelve months, then decide whether to go back to work or stay home.
- Switch to part-time, or possibly share a job with someone else. Working part-time is especially nice if your husband does it, too and you share parenting responsibilities equally.
- Take a few years off.

- Switch to consulting, private practice, freelancing, part-time teaching, or volunteer work. These activities allow you to develop professionally while devoting large blocks of time to motherhood.

7. You can if you limit the size of your family. If you both want to continue working full-time, having an only child may be your best bet, and for most two-career couples, two is the absolute limit.

8. You can combine career and motherhood more easily if you don't try to do it all at the same time. As Sherrye Henry, New York radio commentator, put it:

I personally have been able to manage motherhood and feminism and do them both justice, as they have done me. The problem that lies ahead for my daughters, though, which did not burden me, is that they may think they have to accomplish all things at once. Impossible. The time required to fire up a career will not allow quiet nurturing moments with babes; high-powered executive actions are not consonant with lullabies. The women who try to put it all into one time-frame will pay a terrific price in terms of physical and emotional punishment. Just the time deciding how to make the trade-offs will be debilitating!

One woman who decided not to try to do it all is Liz, who worked for twelve years as a fashion buyer before she married Eric and gave birth to Daniella. Liz had enjoyed her work, but she was ready for a change. She stayed home with Daniella for three years and enjoyed every minute . . . well, almost. And during this time, to keep up in her field, she attended shows and conferences and read trade magazines.

Gloria, a paralegal, is another woman who decided that a two-act play was more appealing than a two-ring circus. The same year that she realized she wanted a baby, she also realized she wanted to go to law school. But she is the kind of person who gets caught up in whatever she does and prefers to savor one experience at a time. Her solution? She's going to stay home with the baby for a couple of years and then apply to law school.

Although the difficulties of reentry should not be underestimated, intelligent, motivated women can succeed at work even if they have spent several years at home.

As you consider options open to you as a working mother, be flexible. You can't be absolutely certain which choice will be right for you. What is perfect in January may be intolerable by June. So don't paint yourself into a corner by saying, "I'd never dream of going back to work before the baby enters school," or, "I'll never stay home."

Recently a group of researchers studied how couples adapt to their first baby. They found that the happiest couples were those who spent the least amount of time on housework and/or who both worked part-time. You may want to take their findings into consideration as you and your husband struggle for solutions.

WHO'S CHANGING THE DIAPERS—PARENTS AS PARTNERS

Many women have found the solution to their problems as overburdened working mothers—in the person of their husband. Having it all is much easier if your husband is willing to assume an equal share of the household and child-care responsibilities. But even though more men are pitching in, all too many are still enjoying the pleasure of child play while avoiding the drudgery of housework. They are the ones who will be glad to bounce the baby on their knee—after *you've* fed, diapered, and bathed him.

However, it's clear that children are an important source of happiness for today's men. And, if fathers want to receive the benefits of children, they must pay the costs, too, and accept the drudgery as well as the fun. When fathers genuinely begin to share it all, women will be able to have it all without collapsing.

Guidelines for Shared Parenting

1. Don't consider your husband to be "helping" you with "your" work. After a while, according to Ellen Goodman, the grateful wife begins to: "Wonder why she should say thank you when a father took care of his children and why she should say please when a husband took care of his house."

Remember, they're his children and it's his house, too. You didn't marry a boss, you married a partner.

2. Don't divide the chore list rigidly in half. Take into consideration which tasks each of you actually likes to do, then divide up the ones neither wants. If he loves to cook and you hate it, it's silly for each of you to cook half the meals. But it is a good idea to rotate the chores you both hate, whether weekly or monthly, so neither of you is stuck with the same ones all the time. Don't get hung up on traditional stereotypes or on feminist ideals of role division either. If he wants to change the oil and you want to polish the silver, that's fine. If you focus on your personal preferences as well as on the time, energy, and unpleasantness involved in each task, you'll be well on your way to a division of labor that suits you both and minimizes the resentments. It's also important for both of you to express your frustration and anger about these issues. After all, nobody likes chores, and complaining to an understanding spouse can be a good way to relieve tension.

3. Share the power as well as the responsibility. You can't expect to shed half the load and hang onto all the control. That means both you and your husband should have an equal say in how the house is kept and how the children are cared for.

4. Share the limelight. Many women take pride and satisfaction in being "more special" to their children than Daddy is, perhaps because they haven't had the same opportunity to shine in the work world. Traditionally, home and children were their sphere and they resented any incursion on that turf. But if you want your husband to take an active role with the

kids, you can't expect to be the only "star" in your family's constellation. Be grateful that your husband has as firm a place in your children's affections as you do.

5. Give your husband the trust and respect he deserves. You should not insist that everything be done exactly your way or perfectly. Nor should you confuse a legitimate difference in standards with irresponsibility or resistance on your husband's part. Have faith in his ability to learn. If he doesn't pin the diapers tightly enough he'll learn quickly! As Nancy Press Hawley says, "Mothers who want to share parenthood often need hold their tongues."

The authors of *Beyond Sugar and Spice* suggest that one way to deal with a wife's typically superior knowledge of domestic practices is for her to serve as a consultant. In a consultant-client relationship, the consultant provides information, but the client is free to decide whether and how to act on that information. This approach may work for some couples who would otherwise become hopelessly entangled in power struggles.

6. Try to understand the obstacles that you'll face. We tend to think we're so sophisticated and liberated that we can slither out of our old sex roles as easily as a snake sheds an old skin. But we humans are more like snails than snakes. Role-changing is a slow and painful process. We have to give up hopes of instant equality and give ourselves credit for the gains that we have already made. Otherwise we'll never have the strength for the uphill climb to a nonsexist society.

Many couples who had an equal relationship before the baby revert to more traditional patterns after the baby's birth. The main reason is that children strike a deeper cord in us than careers do. Our same-sex parents are typically the role models we rely on, and typically Dad brought home the bacon and Mom cooked it. Remember, too, that when you become a parent you identify with your own same-sex parent more intensely, and you may find yourself slipping into old behavior patterns. But you can step out of these patterns if you're aware of them and if you're willing to try new ones.

(a) Have a chair dialogue with your mother/father (see page 28). To discover some of the ways you're following in your parents' footsteps, have an imaginary dialogue with your same-sex parent. Tell her in what ways you would want to parent as she did. Then focus on the ways you would like to be different. Tell her how your friends, work, or feminist beliefs have influenced you in this regard.

Suggest that your spouse try the same exercise with his same-sex parent. You might also try a variation to broaden both your perspectives: Ask him to take your role while you play your mother or father, then take his role while he plays one of his parents. Stepping into each other's shoes in this fashion can be a nonthreatening, enjoyable way to discover some of the attitudes that may be blocking a smooth transition to shared parenthood. And you'll learn a lot about each other in the process.

(b) Discuss this issue with your spouse. Your family history influences not only your expectations of yourself as a parent, but also your expectations of your spouse. Just as a man may unconsciously slip into his father's patterns, he may also expect his wife to emulate his mother's. In fact, by taking his father's role, he may even force his wife to play his mother's role.

For example, Joel's father was overly stern with Joel and his brothers, and in reaction, his mother became overly indulgent. When Joel became a father, he was so strict that his wife, also in reaction, wound up being indulgent, too.

It's also possible to misinterpret your spouse's behavior because you may react to him as if he were your opposite sex parent. When Dale let Tessie play in the backyard mud puddles, Janet was horrified. She associated Dale's lack of concern for the dirt with her stepfather's lack of concern for her. But when she realized that Tessie was having a great time and that

Dale planned to bathe her afterward and change her clothes, she was able to separate in her mind her easygoing husband from her neglectful stepfather.

The point is that we tend to forget how deeply ingrained and how complex role behavior and expectations are. Remember that your husband didn't invent sexism. Like you, he is merely a product of a sexist society. Because he's nearby, it may be tempting to put him on trial for all the ills men have perpetrated on womankind through the centuries. And it may be equally tempting to sentence him to hard labor. But he's more likely to participate enthusiastically as a partner than as a prisoner.

(c) Seek out couples who are sharing parenthood successfully and use them as role models. Ask them for help and suggestions.

7. Even if you do wind your way around the inner obstacles successfully, you will, at some point or another, come face to face with the outer ones. Be prepared.

(a) Job discrimination. Even though women make up almost half of the work force, their jobs are still considered less important than their husbands'. Why? Because money translates into power. If one spouse has to quit or shorten hours, it's usually the wife because it's more feasible to live on a man's salary. And the unfortunate result is that the wife doesn't feel she has the right to ask him to do much housework since she's not earning any money. And even if both work full-time, in many cases the husband earns more, so the wife may feel less justified in asking for help.

(b) Reactions from others. Ridicule or disapproval from friends, family, co-workers, or neighbors can be discouraging. Men worry about being thought of as henpecked or effeminate.

Father Power

Fathers are involved during conception, but somewhere along the line, during the next nine months, they seem to forget that they had an equal stake in creating the baby. And many women become so preoccupied with themselves during pregnancy that they withdraw, compounding their husband's detachment. Therefore, it's a good idea to involve your husband right from the start. Anticipate and prepare together. Share your feelings during pregnancy. Take childbirth classes together and read the books together. Spend those first two all-important hours "bonding" with the baby immediately after birth.

Many men have trouble reconciling their masculinity with their nurturant qualities, particularly if their own fathers were distant or cold. But if you involve your husband in all aspects of the pregnancy, he'll have time to become more comfortable with his nurturant side.

Researchers are beginning to discover the intensity of father-infant bonds as well as those between infants and mothers. If the mother-child relationship is still sacred, the father-child tie is no less so.

Listen to how writer David Steinberg described the joys of fatherhood, and the growth that comes from taking on a new role:

> As a man, it's easy to always be in situations that call for aggressive, rational manipulative perspectives and skills. With Dylan I move out of that more completely than I ever have before. As a result I feel myself growing in all kinds of new ways. The clear importance of these new skills in caring for Dylan helps me respect and value them as they develop.

Finding Your Own Path to Shared Parenthood

According to Nancy Press Hawley, "The 'ideal' of shared parenthood is not for everyone, and should not be seen as yet another pressure on parents to perform."

Some women seem to feel that the Feminist Bureau of Investigation is going to send Betty or Gloria over to charge that your husband resists too much and that you do not insist enough. But pressure to conform to the new stereotype of the absolutely equal couple is as counterproductive as pressure to conform to the old traditional role divisions.

- Renata, an engineer, is being pressured by her husband Leonard to have a baby. Her response: "I tell him I'm just not cut out to stay home. And I can't see leaving a baby in day care. He says he would stay home with the baby and just work part-time. But I couldn't stand his doing that. How could I respect a husband who stayed home and changed diapers? What would people say about us?"

Although many career women would jump at such an offer, Renata won't take Leonard up on it. Despite her nontraditional career choice, she has very traditional attitudes toward motherhood.

- Mary Jane, an ardent feminist, has trouble finding time to paint because of her hectic schedule as a commercial artist. She and her husband Walt are working on the baby decision. Walt has suggested that she quit her more-than-full-time job to spend half her time with the baby and the other half in her studio. She could pay for child care out of her own savings so she wouldn't have to feel she was living off her husband. But Mary Jane won't even consider it. "If I had a baby, I'd have to work full-time. I can't stand the idea of Walt's supporting me."

While Renata felt that motherhood was possible only within a traditional framework, Mary Jane felt that it was possible only within a nontraditional one. And both women are victims of their own rigid thinking. Neither can ask, "What's best for me and for us?"

The moral of these stories: try to be flexible in considering options. That way you'll have more options to consider. All couples have to find their own unique solutions to the problems of parenthood and family life.

Don't Fall for the "I Can't Afford to Work" Fallacy

Some husbands fight shared parenthood by contending that their wives don't have to work. And if their wives don't work they will naturally have the time to do all the housework and take care of the children. The typical argument put forth by many husbands sounds like this: "By the time my wife has paid for child care, clothes, taxes, and transportation, she would be earning nothing. We can't afford for her to work."

Is this argument sexist? *Absolutely!* Why assume that a working mother is any more responsible for child care than a working father? This argument fails to consider the following financial costs:

- Lower income for the wife when she does reenter the job market in a few years. She'll be penalized for losing touch with her colleagues and for having a dust-covered resumé. And she won't qualify for promotions because she hasn't been around long enough.

It also fails to take into account the potential costs of a wife's frustrations:

- Bills for professional help including needless tranquilizers and antidepressants.
- Unnecessary purchases made to cheer herself up.
- Money spent on entertainment she wouldn't be involved in if she had a job.

And let's not forget the emotional costs of not working:

- To the wife who desperately wants to work: low self-esteem, depression, anger, frustration, boredom.
- To the family: a mother who may take out her frustration by raging, criticizing, or inducing guilt.

Can a family afford to keep a woman at home if she really wants to work? I think not. Researchers have found that mothers who are frustrated raise unhappy children.

DAY CARE? WHERE?—MOTHER'S DREAM
OR NIGHTMARE?

Where would we working mothers be if not for day care? Back in the home, that's where! But as helpful as day care is, there are problems and drawbacks.

You've heard about the crisis in day care, of course—not enough quality centers. Not enough quality homes. Waiting lists. Our society and government may say we value our children, but we never put our money where our mouth is.

Despite all this, you can probably find reasonably good care in your community. But before you even begin to evaluate day care objectively, you have to come to terms with the idea of it in your own mind. Your negative feelings about day care may be as much of a problem as the scarcity of good day care itself.

Guilt

You're afraid your child will suffer emotional damage because you aren't there all the time. Study after study has shown that children of working mothers are no more unhappy or emotionally scarred than those whose mothers are in the home. But it has been demonstrated that the children of *frustrated* mothers often have emotional problems. If you would be frustrated at home, your child is much better off sharing a happy mother with the folks at the office than having a miserable mommy all to herself. But even if you've read the studies, your guilt won't magically disappear. The thought "But my mother didn't leave *me* with anybody else!" is never far from the surface.

Follow the advice about handling guilt on page 254. And do read some of the studies listed in the Chapter Notes. Although you certainly won't be able to banish all guilt, accepting it and finding ways to soothe it will free your mind to work on solving the day care puzzle.

Jealousy

You may be jealous of a day care mother or teacher before you've even made the first phone call or been given the first name. Perhaps you're worried that your child won't know who her mother is. You're afraid she'll love the substitute more. Maybe the substitute will do a better job . . . perish the thought! You want to be the most special person in your child's world. Will you earn that place if you don't spend most of your time together?

Rest assured that children save a special place in their hearts for their mothers (and fathers). There's room in their lives and affections for a mother, a father, and a day care person. Research and my own experience as both a day care worker and a day care consumer all point to the fact that children know who their parents are, right from the first month. They feel the intensity of your love, sense the familiarity of your face and body, and respond accordingly.

Anger

It's only natural to feel anger about the incredible burden of arranging care for a child any time you're not going to be around. What a switch from being child-free! Some of your anger at day care may really be anger at the injustice of being on duty around the clock. And if your husband is not participating in the child care search, your sense of resentment may intensify.

I've been struck by the number of supercompetent women who don't bat an eyelash at all kinds of complicated arrangements at work, but who feel completely incapable of finding a day care placement for one small baby. While some of these women honestly don't know where to begin, I think the real impediment may be that they don't want to.

Get help from your husband, friends, mothers' groups, or

counselors so you won't feel so alone and so you'll get a perspective on any emotional obstacles in your way.

Now you're ready to attack the day care problem itself.

Choosing the Right Kind of Day Care

There are three main sources of child care for working parents:

1. Day care mothers who care for a small number of children in their own homes
2. Special infant units of day care centers
3. Babysitters who come to your home.

Day Care Homes

Advantages:

- Your child is cared for by an experienced mother.
- Your child may receive more individual attention than in a center.
- The environment is more homelike, and the experience more nearly approximates the mother-child relationship you would have at home.
- Your child has other children to play with.

Disadvantages:

Your child may not get as much intellectual stimulation as he or she would at a center.

- The day care mother may not be as well trained as a day care teacher.

Day Care Center

Advantages:

- A program of education and stimulation. A good infant program includes indoor and outdoor activity, sensory and language activities, massage and physical exercise.

- Stability: if the day care teacher quits, you still have a placement for your child, provided, of course, that you and the baby like the new infant care employee.
- Knowledgeable teachers. Day care workers usually have a fair amount of college course work and/or training in early childhood education.

Disadvantages:

- The child may not get enough attention if the center is understaffed.
- There may be high staff turnover. Try to find out about this.
- Your child will probably have to be sent home if moderately ill, whereas a day care mother might still keep him.

In-Home Care

The main advantage of in-home care is convenience. It's wonderful not to have to transport the baby to day care, especially in a snowstorm or downpour. It's also great for the child to be in familiar, comfortable territory.

But there is a serious problem with in-home care. Often, people who are willing and available are less intelligent, sophisticated, and experienced than day care mothers or teachers. Of course, Mary Poppins types do exist, but they're almost as hard to find as they are to pay for. On the other hand, a person need not be highly sophisticated to provide a baby with a safe and loving environment. There is one other disadvantage. If an in-home caretaker quits or gets sick, you may be stuck at home for a while. It's not always easy to make new arrangements right away, and it is a good idea to have a contingency plan if you choose this type of care.

Of the three types of care, in-home care offers parents the most convenience while offering the child the least stimulation. Children generally receive more social and intellectual stimulation from both grownups and peers if they are in day care centers or day care homes.

Guidelines for Evaluation

1. Trust your feelings. Give them more weight than any objective considerations. Strong positive feelings about a person are better indicators than any intellectual assessment. The reverse is also true. If you seem to have every reason to like a person, but you have an uneasy feeling in your stomach nonetheless, back off and try somebody else. You don't have to be best friends with your child's caretaker, but if she doesn't show you any warmth, she probably won't have much for your child, either.

2. Observe the children already in the day care home or center. In a day care center, are the children moderately noisy and rambunctious? Is the place neither bedlam nor monastery but rather a happy medium? Do the children look happy? In a day care home, do the day care children and the day care mother's own children seem happy?

3. Analyze the environment from the standpoint of the child's needs. Is it safe? Is it clean? Is it attractive and interesting? Are the facilities adequate? Would you be happy spending time there if you were a child?

4. Bring your baby with you. How do the baby and the prospective caretaker interact? Is the caretaker relaxed and warm, unnervingly sweet, or chillingly distant? Bear in mind that your baby may cry because the person is a stranger and might be quite happy with her once she gets to know her. Crying doesn't necessarily bode ill and, in fact, it can be very useful to see how the woman handles your baby's crying or discomfort. Does she know how to soothe? Does she take it in stride? Does she seem to treat the baby with respect? If you are visiting day care facilities before the baby's birth, watch how the mother or teacher interacts with the children she's already taking care of, especially any babies in her charge.

5. How flexible is the caretaker? Is she willing to accept and carry out your wishes for the child's care? Is it easy to talk to her about this? If you and she have different attitudes about child-rearing, will she be adaptable enough to accept your views? Does she resort to tactics you abhor: bribery, psychological manipulation, physical punishment when it's not really necessary? Ask questions to find out how she handles tantrums, willfulness, and so on.

6. Discuss fees and hours in advance. Don't make the mistake of agreeing to a placement for your child first and then having to negotiate payment and scheduling. Will you pay by the hour, the day, or the week? When are you expected to pay, and will you pay by check or with cash? If you're fifteen minutes late, will you have to pay extra? Will you pay for holidays, for days your baby is home sick with you? Will you pay extra for food, bring food to the day care home or center, or is food included in the day care cost? Find out ahead of time, so you know what you're getting yourself into.

7. Ask for references and follow up on them. Call a few of the people and ask them what they like or don't like about this person or center. If they are no longer using this particular placement, find out why. It may be that they moved or that their child outgrew the need for the placement. But it's also possible that the placement was less than ideal, and you'll want to investigate this.

8. Talk to more than one person or center before making the final decision. If you meet a center director initially, be sure to meet the person who would actually care for your baby.

9. Try to break the baby in gradually. Spend an hour or two the first day, a few hours the second, and so on. It will give all three of you—baby, mother, and caretaker a chance to make a smooth transition.

10. Don't hesitate to start out on a trial basis. See how it goes. If you're not satisfied, begin the search process again. Don't settle for second best because you can't bear the thought of making new arrangements, or because you're convinced

you won't find anything better. If you settle, you're cheating your child and yourself, and it will be harder to deal with that guilt than to find another place.

11. Be creative. Have you considered all the possibilities? If you've heard of a good day care home or center that's full, ask the mother or director to refer you elsewhere. Would a stay-at-home relative, friend, or neighbor be willing to care for your child? Could you and your husband stagger your schedules so that hired day care wouldn't be necessary or so that a responsible high school or college student could take care of the baby for just a few hours till your husband gets home?

12. Don't assume that the arrangement that satisfies a friend will satisfy you. Because you and your child are unique, a placement that's perfect for your friend's child may be less than ideal for yours.

13. Don't allow yourself to be so discouraged by a waiting list that you don't even bother to put your child's name on it. When an opening does occur, a center may find that many children on the list are now in other satisfactory placements, and that their parents don't want to switch them. What sounds like an impossible wait could actually be over sooner than you think.

14. Keep in mind that the child's needs change as he gets older. Every child needs a mixture of nurturance and stimulation, but infants and toddlers need nurturance most of all since they get reasonable amounts of stimulation as they're held, cuddled, rocked, changed, and sung to. Older children, on the other hand, have more complicated needs, and require a wider variety of activities. They still need a nurturant care-giver, but they'll be more interested in inspecting bugs than getting hugs during the day. After all, they'll get plenty of hugs at home. As your child's needs change, a switch from a day care home to a day care center may be beneficial.

15. Share the hassles. If you're married, share the head-

aches with your husband. Either take him along or agree that the next time day care has to be arranged, it's his headache. But whether you make the arrangements jointly, or take turns, discuss your reactions to people and places visited and the pros and cons of various possibilities with each other. Brainstorm together for other possibilities. If you're not married, use a good friend or a mother's group as your sounding board.

16. Start exploring possibilities while pregnant or even before. You'll have more time and feel less pressured. And in some cases, you'll have to put your name on a waiting list for a popular program, such as a university-run infant center.

Day Care Referral Sources:

- A child care resource center, if your city has one.
- A general information and referral center. (Call information if you don't know of any.)
- A state office for children, or a welfare department's day care section.
- Word-of-mouth—ask other working parents for names.
- Local churches, synagogues, schools, and community centers.
- Family service agencies or mental health centers.
- A local day care center that doesn't take babies but which refers parents to day care homes and, in some cases, supervises these homes.
- A baby-sitting agency or a domestic employment agency.

It may help to discuss your concerns with a professional. Child care referral workers and counselors in family service agencies are particularly likely to be sensitive to your needs, and can help you both explore your own feelings and work with you on actual arrangements.

When you're feeling frazzled about the day care situation, focus on these less obvious benefits: arranging for day care can help you learn to be assertive, to make judgments about people, to make hiring decisions, and to supervise. All of these skills will prove useful at work as well and may serve to increase your overall self-confidence.

Although finding day care is never easy, it is possible. And the experience of playing with and learning from other adults and children can truly enrich your child's life.

THE REAL RELATIONSHIP BETWEEN CAREER AND MOTHERHOOD

Children are more than obstacles in their mothers' career paths. Ellen Goodman, shuddering at the question, "How do you succeed despite having a child?" describes her fantasy: ". . . I had a vision of a million small 'despites'; lying in cribs that blocked some highway to achievement, like those metal barrels on the highways. I pictured a million school-age 'despites' innocently tripping their mothers on their way to work. And it made me recoil."

Many parents discover that their children contribute in one way or another to their professional development. The benefits are obvious for anyone who works professionally with children, but there are other benefits regardless of your line of work. These most frequently include:

- New self-knowledge
- Increased creativity
- Increased efficiency
- More patience, tolerance, and flexibility.

An additional benefit, which may be the most important of all in terms of self-actualization, is a stronger commitment to your work. Ellen Goodman describes the rebirth of her dedication that accompanied the birth of her daughter: "I remember going back to my job when my own small 'despite' was an infant. Suddenly I was no longer, in some recess of my mind, working 'until' I had a child. Whatever had been tentative about my commitment became solid. If I wasn't doing this 'until,' it was time to do it better."

Of course, some women make an exclusive commitment to their child; others make unequal commitments to both. But for the women Goodman describes, the two commitments are equally strong and thoroughly intertwined.

Portrait of the Artist as a Mother

If you are an artist of any sort, you should be very cautious about becoming a mother. As Tillie Olsen and Erica Jong have both pointed out, it's not easy to nurture babies and manuscripts at the same time. And I agree. I gave birth to my second child the same year I wrote this book, and I could easily write another attesting to the difficulties! Therefore, I would urge you to:

- Read Olsen's and Jong's comments on the subject (see Chapter Notes for a list of their articles and books).
- Talk to artist mothers about their lives and work.
- Consider your support system. Will your husband take half the responsibility?
- Consider your financial situation. Can you afford the money for child care or time for a cooperative nursery group?

Even under the best of circumstances, are you prepared to put art second, at least *sometimes?* What will you do when the baby is screaming to be held while your inspiration is demanding to be captured on canvas or paper? What if you're in the middle of something you're afraid you'll lose and it's time to pick your child up at the day care center?

Some mothers do find that pregnancy and parenting inspire new energy and creativity. Others don't agree, but still feel that their children are worth the sacrifices made to their art. Unfortunately, you can't predict in advance how your art will be affected by a child, so you need to be even more cautious and more certain than others before deciding to have a child.

Coping with Guilt

Throw away the self-help guides that claim that you can get rid of guilt. They only make most people feel guilty about feeling guilty. Guilt is like a boomerang—the harder you try to get rid of it, the faster it returns. Instead of throwing it away, accept it and make peace with it. Engage in a fantasy dialogue with your guilt, like the one that follows.

"Look, I know you're going to keep on hanging around no matter what I do. But from now on, I'm taking charge around here. I can't get rid of you, but I *can* change our relationship.

"It's no surprise you're here. My mother stayed home with me until I left for college. My best friend and my sister are both home with their babies. Many of my neighbors are home with their kids, too. How can I help feeling uneasy about having someone else take care of my baby?

"Maybe you'll even do me a little good every now and then by reminding me that I have to consider the baby's needs as well as my own. And I don't mind that sort of reminder.

"But, you know, I think you ought to hang around my husband, the mayor, the governor, the President, and congressmen a little more and me a little less. I think I've already gotten the message.

"From now on, when you come to me, I'm not going to ignore you or try to fling you halfway across the world. I'm going to think about all those research studies that show that children of working mothers are okay. I'm going to call a working mother who is supportive, or just take a realistic look at how my child's needs are being met. And if anyone is pushing my guilt button—my husband, my friends, our relatives—I'm going to ask them to stop. I'm also going to think about how my childhood experiences may relate to my guilt about working. If I can't do this on my own, I'm going to see a counselor and/or join a mothers' support group.

"So you see, you can stay around, but you can't stay on my back any more."

Can Women Have It All?

Sometimes having it all seems to mean having it all heaped on your shoulders. More grape juice is spilled on Mommy's briefcase than Daddy's. Mothers have more spillover from home life into work life than men do.

But the secret to combining career and motherhood is not to be found in how-to books. Cooking in microwaves and making grocery lists on the commuter train are Band-Aid remedies for wounds that only social change can cure. Yes, we women can have it all, but in the world we live in we still have to pay a price.

~§ 14 §~

How to Make the Most of Your Decision

1. Apply what you've learned about decision-making to other decisions. Be as critical, but not as cautious about making other commitments. Because the consequences of most other major decisions are not as irrevocable, you cannot and should not spend as much time on every choice. But it is a good idea to ask yourself: Is this really best for me/us? Will we grow from this choice? Are we choosing safety over growth? Have we based the decision on an appropriate combination of logic and emotion? Have we considered all the practicalities? Does it *feel* right?

2. Build on the intimacy you've developed with your spouse while making the baby decision. If you were able to maintain an I-thou relationship, giving each other respect and understanding, even during a tug-of-war, you've got a good model for all future shared decisions. Continue to talk about and share all your feelings and thoughts with each other. These are the building blocks for a good life together regardless of the choice you've made.

3. Keep on taking risks. Your life will be more exciting and more rewarding. If you've chosen nonparenthood, you've already faced the risks of your own regrets and others' hostility. It should therefore be a little easier to take some of the other risks that child freedom allows you—a career change, a mountain-climbing expedition, whatever. If you're going to have a baby, the physical risks of childbirth and the emotional risks

postpartum are obvious, but later risks may be less so. Children tie you down to some extent, and to combat this, you need to venture out, both literally, with and without the children; and psychologically, by exploring new ways of parenting. You'll find both choices more satisfying if you don't cling to the safety of the status quo.

4. Expect success. Now that you've made your choice, assume you'll be happy until proven otherwise. Close your eyes and visualize your future. Picture your joys and your accomplishments. Imagine yourself with your spouse in old age, looking back on your life and agreeing that you made the right choice.

5. "Steal" a little from the other choice. Consider what you'll miss most by giving up the other choice, and plan ways to inject some of these goals into your life within the limits of your choice. If you're going to become a parent, but crave exotic travel, set aside money each week for a trip. Give up some other less important activities if necessary. If you decide that you will interrupt a career that's important to you, make plans for how you will stay involved in it; such as working part-time or attending professional meetings. If you're going to remain child-free, but want a warm relationship with a child, start spending time with a friend's child, a niece, a Little Brother from a social service agency, and so on.

6. Accept your ambivalence. Everyone wonders, "What would have happened if . . . ?," especially during rough times—a hectic day for a parent, a lonely one for a nonparent. We all have to sacrifice something in order to get something else. But like guilt, ambivalence only gets worse if you try to get rid of it. The decision-maker who can't stand uncertainty is forever out of breath chasing unwanted thoughts away. So it's important to accept the fact that you'll always have *some* regrets. Perhaps it will be some consolation to know that accepting ambivalence matures you and prepares you for other decisions and dilemmas.

7. Spend time with people who have made the same de-

cision. People who have made the same choice can serve as role models and provide needed emotional support. So if most of your friends have made the other choice, seek out some new friends.

8. Spend time with people who have made the opposite choice. If you've really come to terms with your decision, you should not feel threatened by spending time with people who made the other choice. You should be able to respect your friends and their right to choose differently. Even though your friendships may be based on certain shared attitudes and beliefs, you must be able to recognize and appreciate the differences, too.

Your life will be enriched if you spend time with people who are different. Parents can offer child-free couples a sort of extended family, and a chance to be with the kids without obligations. They offer child-free friends who haven't made a decision yet a built-in laboratory for testing out feelings and reactions. Child-free couples can, if they so desire, offer parents occasional relief from the burdens of child care, and a source of vicarious satisfaction through tales of their work and recreational activities.

Frequently, friends drift apart when one couple are having a baby and the other aren't. Although the people involved typically complain, "We have nothing in common any more," the real reason is that they have *too much* in common—unexpressed ambivalence. The prospective parents worry, "If they're so much like us and they're not going to have a baby, maybe we made a mistake." The child-free couple worries, "If they're so much like us and they're enjoying the baby, maybe we're wrong." And so each couple calls the other a little less often, and begins to turn to couples who are safer because they made the same choice.

This phenomenon is by no means universal. Many people maintain close relationships with friends who made the opposite choice, unfailingly respecting and supporting their friends' decision. They even enjoy knowing someone who can offer them a bird's-eye view of a different existence. But for too many other couples, their own insecurity weakens their ties to friends who made the opposite decision.

Work on this problem by discussing it openly with your friends. Take the first step by saying, "Let's talk about our feelings. Let's not drift apart. If we pick up signs of jealousy or disapproval in ourselves or each other, let's talk about it. We're both going to have regrets sometimes, and if we don't share them, maybe we'll stop sharing other things. And our relationship is too valuable to let that happen!"

It's true that some child-free couples can't stand being around children. And it's equally true that some parents feel that their child-free friends' lives aren't very meaningful. But such people are in the minority. I believe that the doubts, rather than different interests or life-styles, keep us away from those who chose the flip side of the baby decision.

9. Don't proselytize. Generally, the amount of time that people spend talking about the decision is in direct proportion to their comfort with it. This is especially true for those who are trying to persuade everyone that their decision is best not only for them but also for everyone else as well.

Do you tend to harp on your baby decision at social or family gatherings, telling everyone and anyone why *your* decision is the right one for everybody? If so, ask yourself, "Who am I *really* talking to, the person in front of me or myself?"

If the answer is yourself, then you have more homework to do on your decision.

If the answer is "the other person," have you really considered this particular person's needs and interests or are you just imposing your own? Even if you're sincerely concerned about the other person's happiness, can you be sure that *you* know what's right for him or her? If you do feel that the person hasn't considered all the issues, you can point them out tactfully and objectively. But don't set yourself up as a judge.

SHOULD YOU ANNOUNCE YOUR DECISION?

There is one advantage in telling the world—going public reinforces your decision. As people react, both positively and negatively, your commitment may solidify. You will feel bolstered by those who are enthusiastic. And you will gain more confidence in your choice when you come up with good answers for the people who criticize you.

The disadvantage of an announcement is that it can invite criticism that you may not yet be prepared to face. The solution: be selective about whom you tell.

If you're planning a baby, you may want to wait until you're pregnant before telling anybody. If you don't conceive right away, you won't have to put up with referrals to "just the right doctor," and the kind of unwanted advice that raises your anxiety level.

If you're planning to remain child-free, expect to hear a lot of negative comments. If you've discussed the decision-making process publicly, this news won't come as a surprise. But if you haven't told a soul that you're even thinking about the baby question, it's wise to be prepared for criticism, and even wiser to be selective about making the announcement.

Don't put yourself out on a limb. Unless one of you has been sterilized, you might think twice before announcing, "We'll *never* have children." You could feel foolish if you announce a birth ten years later. Although you certainly have the right to change your mind, some people don't seem to think so. And if their teasing will drive you wild, don't give them anything to tease you about. Of course, if you are quite sure you'll never have a child, this is not a consideration.

The baby decision journey is over, but a new phase of your life is just beginning! Rest assured that if you've brought self-knowledge, courage, and love to your decision, you've made a choice you can live with.

APPENDIX A

Suggested Readings—General

THE DECISION

Bardwick, Judith. *In Transition: How Feminism, Sexual Liberation and the Search for Self-Fulfillment Have Altered America.* New York: Holt, Rinehart and Winston, 1979.

Fabe, Marilyn, and Wikler, Norma. *Up Against the Clock: Career Women Speak on the Choice to Have Children.* New York: Random House, 1979.

Rivers, Caryl. "The New Anxiety of Motherhood." In *Women in a Changing World,* ed. by Uta West, pp. 141–152. New York: McGraw-Hill, 1975.

Whelan, Elizabeth. *A Baby? . . . Maybe.* New York: Bobbs-Merrill, 1975.

Wills, Garry. "What? What? Are Young Americans Afraid to Have Kids?" *Esquire,* March 1974, p. 80.

PERSONAL GROWTH

Ellis, Albert, and Harper, Robert A. *A New Guide to Rational Living.* North Hollywood, Calif.: Wilshire Book Co., 1975.

Frankl, Viktor. *The Will to Meaning.* New York: World Publishing Co., 1969.

Goodman, Ellen. *Turning Points.* Garden City, N.Y.: Doubleday, 1979.

Maslow, Abraham. *The Farther Reaches of Human Nature.* New York: Penguin, 1976.

_____. *Toward a Psychology of Being.* New York: Van Nostrand, 1968.

May, Rollo. *The Courage to Create.* New York: Bantam, 1976.

_____. *Love and Will.* New York: Dell, 1974.

————. *Man's Search for Himself*. New York: Signet, 1967.

Perls, Frederick S. *Gestalt Therapy Verbatim*. New York: Bantam, 1971.

Rogers, Carl. *On Becoming a Person*. Boston: Houghton Mifflin, 1961.

Sheehy, Gail. *Passages*. New York: Bantam, 1977.

MARRIAGE/RELATIONSHIPS

Bach, George, and Wyden, Peter. *The Intimate Enemy: How to Fight Fair in Love and Marriage*. New York: William Morrow, 1969.

Buber, Martin. *I and Thou*. New York: Charles Scribner's Sons, 1958.

Howard, Jane. *Families*. New York: Simon and Schuster, 1978.

Lasswell, Marcia, and Lobsenz, Norman M. *No-Fault Marriage*. Garden City, N.Y.: Doubleday, 1976.

CHILD-FREE CHOICE

Greene, Gael. "A Voice Against Motherhood." *Saturday Evening Post*, 26 January 1963, p. 10.

Kamien, Marcia. "We'll Never Have Kids!" *Woman's Day*, 9 January 1978, p. 8.

Kramer, Rita. "The No-Child Family." *New York Times Magazine*, 24 December 1972, p. 28.

Peck, Ellen, and Senderowitz, Judith, eds. *Pronatalism: The Myth of Mom and Apple Pie*. New York: Thomas Y. Crowell, 1974.

Rollin, Betty. "Motherhood: Who Needs It?" *Look*, 22 September 1970, pp. 15–17.

Veevers, Jean, *Childless by Choice*. Scarborough, Ontario: Butterworth's, 1980.

PREGNANCY

Bittmen, Sam, and Zalk, Sue Rosenberg. *Expectant Fathers*. New York: Hawthorn, 1978.

Lichtendorf, Susan, and Gillis, Phyllis. *The New Pregnancy*. New York: Random House, 1979.

Whelan, Elizabeth. *The Pregnancy Experience*. New York: W. W. Norton, 1978.

Wolfe, Maxine G., and Goldsmith, Margot. *Practical Pregnancy*. New York: Warner Books, 1980.

PARENTING

Boston Women's Health Book Collective. *Ourselves and Our Children.* New York: Random House, 1978.

Chess, Stella; Alexander, Thomas; and Birch, Herbert G. *Your Child Is a Person: A Psychological Approach to Parenthood Without Guilt.* New York: Penguin, 1977.

MOTHERHOOD

McBride, Angela Barron. *The Growth and Development of Mothers.* New York: Barnes and Noble, 1974.

Rich, Adrienne. *Of Woman Born.* New York: Bantam, 1977.

SHARED PARENTHOOD

Bird, Caroline. *The Two-Paycheck Marriage.* New York: Rawson, Wade, 1979.

Hall, Francine S., and Hall, Douglas T. *The Two-Career Couple.* Reading, Mass.: Addison-Wesley, 1979.

Levine, James. *Who Will Raise the Children? New Options for Fathers (and Mothers).* Philadelphia: J. B. Lippincott, 1976.

Norris, Gloria, and Miller, Jo Ann. *The Working Mother's Complete Handbook.* New York: E. P. Dutton, 1979.

Pleck, Joseph, and Sawyer, Jack. *Men and Masculinity.* Englewood Cliffs, N.J.: Prentice-Hall, 1974.

Ruddick, Sara, and Daniels, Pamela, eds. *Working It Out.* New York: Pantheon, 1977.

SPECIAL SITUATIONS

The One-Child Family

Hawke, Sharryl, and Knox, David. *One Child by Choice.* Englewood Cliffs, N.J.: Prentice-Hall, 1977.

Peck, Ellen. *The Joy of the Only Child.* New York: Delacorte, 1977.

Infertility

Menning, Barbara E. *Infertility: A Guide for the Childless Couple.* Englewood Cliffs, N.J.: Prentice-Hall, 1977.

Silber, Sherman J. *How to Get Pregnant.* New York: Charles Scribner's Sons, 1980.

Miscellaneous

Ashdown-Sharp, Patricia. *A Guide to Pregnancy and Parenthood for Women on Their Own.* New York: Random House, 1977.

Cardozo, Arlene Rossen. *Woman at Home.* New York: Jove, 1978.

McNamara, Joan. *The Adoption Advisor.* New York: Hawthorn, 1975.

Price, Jane. *You're Not Too Old to Have a Baby.* New York: Penguin, 1977.

Roosevelt, Ruth, and Lofas, Jeannette. *Living in Step.* Briarcliff Manor, N.Y.: Stein and Day, 1976 (stepparenting).

APPENDIX B

Suggested Readings—Technical

REVIEW ARTICLE

Veevers, Jean. "Voluntary Childlessness: A Review of Issues and Evidence." *Marriage and Family Review* 2 (1979): 1–26.

BIBLIOGRAPHIES

"Children as a Factor in Marital Satisfaction: A Selected Bibliography." National Alliance for Optional Parenthood (NAOP), February 1979 (annotated).
"A Decade of Voluntary Childlessness: A Bibliography." NAOP, January 1980 (partially annotated).
Both bibliographies are available from NAOP. Write or call for price information. (See Appendix C for address.) For a good introduction to the literature, read Veevers's article and "A Decade of Voluntary Childlessness."

ARTICLES AND BOOKS

Barnett, Larry D., and MacDonald, Richard H. "A Study of the Membership of the National Organization for Non-Parents." *Social Biology* 23 (1976): 297–310.
Bernard, Jessie. *The Future of Marriage.* New York: Bantam, 1972.
———. *The Future of Motherhood.* New York: Penguin, 1975.
Bram, Susan. "Through the Looking Glass: Voluntary Childlessness as a Mirror for Contemporary Changes in the Meaning of Parenthood." In *The First Child and Family Formation,* ed. by Warren B. Miller and Lucile F. Newman. Chapel Hill, N.C.: Carolina Population Center, 1978.

Campbell, Angus; Converse, Philip E.; and Rodgers, Willard L. *The Quality of American Life: Perceptions, Evaluations and Satisfactions.* New York: Russell Sage, 1976.

Cooper, Pamela E.; Cumber, Barbara; and Hartner, Robin. "Decision-Making Patterns and Post-Decision Adjustment of Childfree Husbands and Wives." *Alternative Lifestyles* 1 (1978): 71–94.

Cowan, Carolyn Pape; Cowan, Philip A.; Coie, Lynne; and Coie, John D. "Becoming a Family: The Impact of a First Child's Birth on the Couple's Relationship." In *The First Child and Family Formation.*

DeFrain, John "Androgynous Parents Tell Who They Are and What They Need." *The Family Coordinator* 28 (1979): 237–243.

Erikson, Erik. *Childhood and Society.* New York: W. W. Norton, 1963.

Feldman, Harold. "The Effects of Children on the Family." In *Family Issues of Employed Women in Europe and America,* ed. by Andree Michel. Leiden, Netherlands: E. J. Brill (1971): 107–125.

Gilligan, Carol. "In a Different Voice: Women's Conceptions of Self and of Morality." *Harvard Educational Review* 47 (1977): 481–517.

Hobbs, Daniel F., Jr. "Transition to Parenthood: A Replication and an Extension." *Journal of Marriage and Family* 30 (1968): 413–417.

Hoffman, Lois W., and Nye, F. Ivan. *Working Mothers: An Evaluative Review of the Consequences for Wife, Husband and Child.* San Francisco, Calif.: Jossey-Bass, 1974.

Hoffman, Lois W.; Thornton, Arland; and Manus, Jean Denby. "The Value of Children to Parents in the United States." *Journal of Population* 1 (1978): 91–131.

Houseknecht, Sharon K. "Childlessness and Marital Adjustment." Paper read at the American Sociological Association Meeting, San Francisco, Calif., 1978.

———. "Reference Group Support for Voluntary Childlessness: Evidence for Conformity." *Journal of Marriage and the Family* 39 (1977): 285–292.

———. "Timing of the Decision to Remain Voluntarily Childless: Evidence for Continuous Socialization." *Psychology of Women Quarterly* 4 (1979): 81–96.

Kaltreider, Nancy B., and Margolis, Alan G. "Childless by Choice: A Clinical Study." *American Journal of Psychiatry* 134 (1977): 179–182.

Kestenberg, Judith S. "On the Development of Maternal Feelings in Early Childhood." *Psychoanalytic Study of the Child* 11 (1956): 257–291.

LeMasters, E. E. "Parenthood as Crisis." *Marriage and Family Living* 19 (1957): 352–355.

Lott, Bernice. "Who Wants Children? Some Relationships Among Attitudes Toward Children, Parents, and the Liberation of Women." *American Psychologist* 28 (1973): 573–582.

Marciano, Teresa Donati. "Male Influences on Fertility: Needs for Research." *The Family Coordinator* 28 (1979): 561–568.

————. "Male Pressure in the Decision to Remain Childfree." *Alternative Lifestyles* 1 (1978): 95–112.

————. "Variant Family Forms in a World Perspective." *The Family Coordinator* 24 (1975): 407–420.

Miller, Jean Baker, and Gartrell, Nanette. "Love, Work—and Babies? Making the Decision." Paper read at the American Psychiatric Association Meeting, 9 May 1980.

Movius, Margaret. "Voluntary Childlessness—The Ultimate Liberation." *The Family Coordinator* 25 (1976): 57–63.

Polster, Erving, and Polster, Miriam. *Gestalt Therapy Integrated: Contours of Theory and Practice.* New York: Vintage, 1974.

Russell, Martha Garrett; Hey, Richard N.; Thoen, Gail A.; and Walz, Tom. "The Choice of Childlessness: A Workshop Model." *The Family Coordinator* 27 (1978): 179–183.

Shostrom, Everett L. *Actualizing Therapy.* San Diego, Calif.: EdITS, 1976.

Teicholz, Judith Guss. "Psychological Correlates of Voluntary Childlessness in Married Women." Paper read at the Eastern Psychological Association Meeting, Washington, D.C., March 1978.

Thoen, Gail Ann. "Commitment Among Voluntary Childfree Couples to a Variant Lifestyle." Ph.D. dissertation. University of Minnesota, Minneapolis. *Dissertation Abstracts*, 1977, 38: 3760.

————. *The Parenthood Option: A Manual for Professionals Helping People Decide Whether to Have Children or Remain Childfree.* Washington, D.C.: National Alliance for Optional Parenthood, 1979 (see Appendix C: Resources).

Townes, Brenda D.; Beach, Lee Roy; Campbell, Frederick L.; and Martin, Donald D. "Birth Planning Values and Decisions: The Prediction of Fertility." *Journal of Applied Social Psychology* 7 (1977): 73–88.

Veevers, Jean. "The Moral Careers of Voluntarily Childless Wives: Notes on the Defense of a Variant World View." *The Family Coordinator* 24 (1975): 473–487.

————. "The Social Meanings of Parenthood." *Psychiatry: Journal for the Study of Interpersonal Processes* 36 (1973): 291–310.

————. "Voluntarily Childless Wives: An Exploratory Study." *Sociology and Social Research* 57 (1973): 356–366.

Wyatt, Frederick. "Clinical Notes on the Motives of Reproduction." *Journal of Social Issues* 23 (1967): 29–56.

Zinker, Joseph. *Creative Process in Gestalt Therapy.* New York: Vintage, 1978.

APPENDIX C

Resources

National Alliance for Optional Parenthood (NAOP, formerly NON). The NAOP is a nonprofit organization whose goals are to educate the public about the child-free life-style and to help people make responsible decisions about parenthood. It offers many resources to the child-free person, to the couple in the throes of decision-making, and to the professionals who work with decision-makers. Many publications (some of them free), kits, and audiovisual materials are available. The National Resource Center is a goldmine of information. You may write or call the center for the name of professionals in your community who counsel or do workshops on the baby decision. Your membership entitles you to receive the newsletter and helps to further the goals of the organization.

National Alliance for Optional Parenthood
2010 Massachusetts Ave., N.W.
Washington, D.C. 20036
(202) 296-7474

OTHER ORGANIZATIONS

Family Service Association of
America
44 East 23rd St.
New York, NY 10010
(212) 674-6100

Feminist Women's Health Center
1112 Crenshaw Blvd.
Los Angeles, CA 90019
(213) 936-6293
The Feminist Center provides self-help materials by mail. Referral to women's health clinics and mothers' groups throughout the country.

National Foundation of the
March of Dimes
Genetic Counseling Centers
1275 Mamaroneck Ave.
White Plains, NY 10605
(914) 428-7100
Refers to genetic counseling and amniocentesis nationwide.

American Fertility Society
Suite 101
1608 Thirteenth Ave., South
Birmingham, AL 32505
(205) 933-7222

Planned Parenthood
810 Seventh Ave.
New York, NY 10019
(212) 541-7800

La Leche League International
9616 Minneapolis Ave.
Franklin Park, IL 60131
(312) 455-7730

American Association for
  Marriage and Family Therapy
924 West 9th St.
Upland, CA 91786
(714) 981-0888
  Can refer you to a marriage
and family counselor in your
community.

Resolve
Box 474
Belmont, MA 02178
(617) 484-2424
  National organization for couples with fertility problems. Call or write for address of your local chapter.

Association for Voluntary
  Sterilization
708 Third Ave.
New York, NY 10017
(212) 986-3880
  Can refer you to clinics and private practitioners in your area.

FILMS

NAOP (see p. 269)

Parents Magazine Films, Inc.
685 Third Ave.
New York, NY 10017
(212) 878-8700

"The Parenthood Option: A Manual for Professionals Helping People Decide Whether to Have Children or Remain Childfree." Available from NAOP, it describes a number of films and ways they can be used in workshops.

SCALES

"Commitment to Childfree Living Scale." Available from:
  Gail Thoen

The Childfree Option
2513 Zenith Ave., North
Minneapolis, MN 55422
(612) 373-5264
(612) 588-6170

"Comprehensive Parenthood Questionnaire." Available from:
Tim Wernette
354 South Grande
Tucson AZ 85705
(602) 884-4293

"Optional Parenthood Questionnaire." Available from NAOP, along with a clinician's manual with information on scoring and interpreting.

Although all three of the above scales enable clients/workshop participants to take stock of their leanings, they are not alike. Because it goes into the most detail, the Optional Parenthood Questionnaire is recommended for those who do in-depth counseling or who do research on the baby decision. The Thoen and Wernette questionnaires are easier to use and are recommended for workshop leaders and for couples working on the decision on their own.

Write to the above addresses for further information, including the current prices.

APPENDIX D

A Guide for Counselors and Workshop Leaders: Helping People Make the Right Decision

This section is for therapists, counselors, and teachers who counsel people on the baby decision. It offers suggestions for conducting sessions and workshops.

Before we look at any techniques, we have to take a look at the person administering them.

1. Start with yourself. Have you already made your decision, and if so, how? Do you have any regrets? How do your feelings about your own choice affect your feelings about other people's choices?

If you are in the process of deciding yourself, it's possible that your own anxieties or leanings will affect your clients/participants. Have you taken this into consideration?

If you are young and/or single, and your own decision is a long way off, will you be able to empathize with other people's dilemmas?

Actually, whether you are undecided, in the process of deciding, or already a parent or a nonparent, you can still do a good job as counselor or workshop leader *if:*

(a) You are open-minded enough to accept both choices.

(b) You are honest with your clients about your own choice and your feelings about it.

(c) You present yourself not as a salesperson but as a consumer information specialist. Your job isn't to sell anybody a pregnancy or a vasectomy. It's to provide a rundown on the advantages and disadvantages of each choice, *always* in the context of the individual's and couple's needs. And, of course, you must always allow the client to make the decision.

If you have trouble with these issues but are nevertheless interested in professional work involving the baby decision, consult with a supervisor or colleague.

2. Get more information. If you think all child-free people are immature and neurotic, you need to do a lot of homework before you do any counseling. Join NAOP to get more information about the child-free life-style. Read some of the journal articles and professional books listed in the technical bibliography in this book (Appendix B). If you believe single parenthood is almost always a poor choice, read up on the subject.

3. Talk to your colleagues.
   (a) Talk to other baby decision counselors and workshop leaders. They'll be able to give you useful tips and recommend books they've found helpful, techniques they like to use, and so on.
   (b) Let your colleagues know that you're interested in baby decision counseling and/or workshops. If they don't counsel on this topic, they'll be glad to know that you do. If they do, they might give you referrals if they have waiting lists, or they might be interested in teaming up with you to do a workshop, conduct research, or write an article. You may even want to plan a conference on this topic or a workshop for professionals on how to counsel and do workshops on this decision. Write NAOP for names of other nearby professionals who share your interest.
   (c) Find out about the work your colleagues across the country are doing on the baby decision. Keep up with new research on the child-free option and on parenthood so that you will be able to apply the latest findings to your work. (See Appendix B.)

Individual Counseling

Have your clients read *The Baby Decision* on their own and do some of the exercises between sessions. That way, they will be able to pinpoint some of their problem areas in advance.

1. Start by telling the client or couple about your openness to both options (if you can't do this sincerely, please don't counsel people on the decision). If you've made a decision yourself, tell them briefly how you made it and what it is. Obviously you should not spend the therapy session discussing your own troubles or exploring

your feelings, but a few general statements will help the client(s) feel more at home with you. Personal statements show that you are a real human being who has also made this crucial decision. (Or who will have to make it at some point.) If your clients are worried about your impartiality, encourage them to discuss their doubts.

2. Work with the *couple*, not just with the more verbal spouse. Actively encourage the less verbal person to express his or her feelings. Ask *each* spouse how he or she perceives their decision-making style as a couple. Find out if one spouse is twisting the other's arm about the decision or about coming for counseling.

3. Work with the present. Find out why the baby decision is such a problem now; what's going on in the client's present life; whether the biological alarm clock is going off; whether one spouse or a set of parents is getting pushy; whether the pressures are realistic. For example, if the woman is thirty-eight, she does have to decide quickly. But if she's twenty-seven, what accounts for her sense of pressure?

4. Work with the past. Even if you don't like the psychoanalytic model and generally believe in dealing with the present, I think you're going to discover that people's feelings about parenthood have a lot to do with their past. A person collects more information on family life from the experience of growing up in one particular family than from any other source. The exercises in Chapter 3 are effective tools for exploring the impact of the past on the decision-making process.

Whether one's feelings about one's parents are mostly negative, mostly positive, or quite ambivalent, they have a profound effect on one's choices. However, this does not mean that people who choose parenthood had happy childhoods or that those who choose non-parenthood did not. A person whose childhood was rough may choose to parent in spite of this, fervently hoping to do a better job than his parents. He may even unconsciously hope for the vicarious satisfaction of parenting his child as he wishes *he* had been parented. A person whose childhood was happy may have warm feelings of connectedness with her family of origin but still choose not to parent. Her excellent start in life may have contributed to her creativity and commitment to various pursuits that meet her needs better than parenting would. A good childhood can be the foundation upon which such a person develops the necessary independence and confidence to make an unconventional decision.

5. Find out about significant others. What decisions have the clients' close friends, siblings, colleagues, and role models made? How does this influence the couple?

6. Find out about the couple's commitment to feminism. Are

the clients involved with feminism, and if so, how does their involvement affect their conflict about parenthood or their resolution of the conflict? If the partners presently define themselves as equals, how well will they be able to maintain this balance if they have a baby?

7. Explore prejudices. Encourage the couple to carefully consider all the options. If a couple is leaning toward parenthood, have they really given serious thought to the child-free option? Perhaps they would be happier without children, but have simply accepted pronatalist views at face value.

If the couple is thinking of remaining child-free, have they really thought about whether they want to forgo parenthood entirely or just parenthood as their parents experienced it? Have they considered shared parenthood and various combinations of career and parenthood? If they do reject parenthood they must do so because it absolutely doesn't suit them, not because they have distorted or mistaken attitudes about what parenthood should or does mean.

8. Find out about the marriage. Is the couple worried about how a child would affect their relationship? If so, find out specifically what their anxieties are. Are the partners dependent on each other? Are they prepared to share each other with a child, or will two parents and one child all compete for what seems like a limited amount of attention?

9. Consider the pathology. Are there "wrong" reasons involved? If so, try to discuss them tactfully. The way the clients react to your questions—responsibly, childishly, defensively, or openly—will also help both you and them assess their "right" reasons.

10. Consider growth. What are the growth needs of the individuals and of the couple? Will children help or hinder them?

11. Is the couple locked into a tug-of-war over this issue? First, see Chapter 9 for an overview of this problem. If the couple are considering divorce, encourage them to consider all possible options within the marriage first. Make sure the baby issue is the *real* issue of the divorce and not just a convenient shorthand or a cover-up for issues that are more painful, harder to talk about, or even unknown.

If the couple divorce, each will probably need some individual help in coming to terms with this. You may refer one or both to a colleague if you don't think it's appropriate to continue seeing both individually.

12. Refer the clients to a workshop if you're doing one or hear of one. A workshop will provide them with general information so that your sessions can be devoted to personal issues.

Planning a Workshop

Allow approximately ten to twenty hours for a workshop. You might set up two eight-hour sessions or five two-hour sessions. The five-week format is sometimes preferable because it gives people more time to think and reflect individually and together, and to do exercises at home. It increases the likelihood that they will actually go through the various stages of decision-making while the help of the workshop leader and participants is still available.

If you do choose the two-day format, I would recommend running it on two consecutive Saturdays rather than on a Saturday and a Sunday of the same weekend. A week of digesting is better than no digesting at all.

In your workshop schedule, you will want to include:

- A personal introduction, as well as brief introductions from all the participants, including a brief statement of what they hope to get out of the workshop.
- An overview of the five-step decision-making process.
- An assessment of everyone's starting point. The exercises in Chapter 3 would accomplish this purpose. You may want to supplement them with one of the scales in Appendix C: Resources.
- A combination of informal presentation, actual exercises, and lots of discussion of participants' feelings about their dilemma and about their reactions to specific exercises.
- A closing statement from each participant summarizing what he or she got out of the workshop.
- An evaluation from the group, either oral or written (preferably both), to find out what people liked and what they didn't like about the workshop. Ask for suggestions for improvement.
- Consider arranging for some kind of a follow-up, either a reunion, a newsletter, or if preferred, private communication to find out what people eventually decided. Refer people to counseling if the follow-up reveals unfinished business the couple can't seem to resolve.

Suggestions for the workshop

1. Share your own choice, your beliefs, and your respect for both options.

2. Help members feel comfortable while participating:

- Allow participants to sit out an exercise or two. Sometimes a group member has been dragged in by a spouse or is just plain shy. In such a case, forced participation in a seemingly scary exercise will only make matters worse.

- Let group members teach each other. Encourage the group to brainstorm. You might ask people to call out the stereotypes that come to mind when they think of parenthood and of the child-free choice. Write them all down on a blackboard or flip chart. This is a way of telling participants they all have something to contribute. And it's a much easier way to get started in the group than telling too much too soon about one's personal dilemma. A group could also brainstorm on new ways to share parenting and combining it with career and personal development. They can put their heads together to make a list of ways child-free persons can be creative and/or involved with children while retaining their freedom.
- Limit the size of your group. A range of eight to twenty is preferable (counting couples as two).
- In general, group participants will participate more fully, and be more relaxed if some exercises are done in smaller groups. Be flexible and creative in breaking down groups. A rule of thumb is that the more personal and potentially threatening the exercise, the more necessary it is to break the group down. You might do low-threat exercises such as Knapsack or Epitaph with the larger group, medium-threat exercises such as Going Home Again or Fifty-fifty in a group of four to eight, and the highly personal Gestalt dialogue or dream journals in spouse dyads.

  Many of these exercises are done in silent fantasy followed by discussion in the subgroup. Others such as Family Sculpture and the Gestalt dialogues are first performed in front of the subgroup and then discussed by that group. It is helpful to all the participants to have a round-robin with the entire group to share, if they choose to do so, whatever insights they've gained from the smaller group exercises.
- Tell your participants that this is a teaching situation, not a therapy session. As tactfully as possible (and this may need to be done quietly during a break), refer anyone who seems to have psychological problems that can't be dealt with in the workshop format to a therapist. If you happen to be a therapist, resist the temptation to focus too intensely on one person's or one couples' emotions. You want to expose *everyone* to the relevant information and issues. That means getting *everyone* in on the action.

Some preparation tips

Consider querying your participants in advance. Gail Thoen, who does baby decision workshops at the University of Minnesota, questions her participants once they've enrolled in the workshop. She asks them to tell her exactly what they want to get from the experience. That way, even before the first session, she is already prepared to meet the needs of her participants.

Consider recommending some readings in advance. You might ask participants to read *The Baby Decision* before the first session so that the workshop won't have to start from scratch, but can get right down to the nitty-gritty.

Ideas for workshop publicity

- Local TV and radio stations might interview you on a talk show.
- Local newspapers may be willing to do an article about your workshop.
- Get into public service slots on the radio if you are doing the workshop for a social service agency.
- You might contact NAOP for publicity ideas, since NAOP members have been interviewed on talk shows and by newspapers throughout the country.
- Consider buying advertising space in a local paper if you can't get a free ad.
- To facilitate publicity, consider doing a workshop under the aegis of a social service agency such as Planned Parenthood, a Family Service Agency, or a YWCA.
- Send announcements to:

  - Planned Parenthood
  - Community Mental Health Centers
  - Family Service Agencies
  - Private practitioners, especially if their caseload includes many of your potential participants—child-free persons who are college-educated professionals between the ages of twenty-five and forty
  - Women's Centers
  - Universities. You might send separate announcements to the College Counseling Center and the departments of psychology, psychiatry, social work, sociology, home economics, and education. (Don't overlook universities in nearby communities if they're within a reasonable commuting distance.)
  - Gynecologists who have a high proportion of your target clientele.

You can also put announcements on bulletin boards at these schools. Also put announcements on bulletin boards of stores, churches, temples, and community centers in college neighborhoods and neighborhoods with a high concentration of your target clientele.

Call up people you think would be most likely to refer participants. Even if you sent out a flyer, if they work in an agency, you can't be sure they've seen it. Even if they have, a brief telephone conversation may pique their interest more than a flyer.

APPENDIX E

My Own Baby Decision

I was nineteen and working as a camp counselor in Michigan when the idea of remaining child-free first occurred to me. On a cool summer night when my eleven-year-old charges were finally asleep, I basked in the silence and asked myself, "Do I *really* want to be a mother some day?" I had come to realize that my least favorite part of the day was the time I spent with my campers, while my favorite part was the time I spent reading—alone. I wondered if I was unfit to be a mother because I preferred quiet study to rowdy kids. Perhaps motherhood and I were not compatible.

A year later I met my husband-to-be, and as we began to consider marriage, it quickly became clear that the baby question would have to be resolved *before* the marriage question. Although the idea of children had some appeal, I wasn't prepared to sacrifice my career or my precious solitude, and I was seriously considering remaining child-free. Rocco, on the other hand, was eagerly looking forward to fatherhood. One of the oldest of six children, a member of a warm, vivacious extended family, Rocco considered children and happiness inextricably linked.

We agreed not to marry if we couldn't reach a mutually acceptable decision. It wouldn't be fair for Rocco to have to give up fatherhood or for me to submit to motherhood only to please him.

Since I was ambivalent rather than committed to the child-free choice, I set about to resolve that ambivalence, ever aware of the danger that I might foolishly give up my freedom in order not to give up Rocco. Over a year passed before our eventual engagement. During that time the women's movement was picking up momentum, and both social science research and feminist literature reassured me that women could combine careers and motherhood. I also worked in a day care center where I had a chance not only to enjoy being with young children, but also to meet their parents—flesh-and-blood role models of successful two-career families. These parents were enthusiastic about their children despite the frustrations and sacrifices involved in two-career family life. Rocco and I also discussed his commitment to child care and the crucial role he could play in preserving my career and my quiet time. The upshot was that I reached a point where I truly looked forward to becoming a mother.

We waited five years after marrying before having our first child. We wanted to enjoy more freedom, finish our education, and establish our relationship. In the five years between our wedding and Marcella's conception we earned two graduate degrees, lived in Brazil and Mexico, and traveled in Europe. We enjoyed lots of friends and activities, some shared, others apart.

We're now in our early thirties and we have two daughters, ages 4 and 1½, whom we enjoy immensely. Certainly there are days of overwork punctuated by temper tantrums when we envy our child-free friends. But overall we're pleased with our decision.

I'm happy to say I've managed to build and develop my career as a psychotherapist and even start a new one as a writer, and enjoy reasonable amounts of solitude as well. All of this has been possible because of Rocco's firm commitment to fathering his daughters and to making motherhood enjoyable for me.

I'm not sorry I waited these five years and questioned motherhood as carefully as I did. Not only did I learn about myself, my marriage, and my intense commitment to both career and motherhood, but I also learned a great deal that has contributed to my happiness as a mother. Rather than ignoring my child-free side, I used it as an ally. By talking with Rocco about the needs I thought motherhood would thwart we were able to begin working out acceptable solutions even before we married.

Had I married a different man I think I could have remained child-free and lived a happy life. I would have missed something by not having a child, but I would also have enjoyed many experiences that motherhood precludes.

CHAPTER NOTES

CHAPTER ONE

Page 6. See Abraham Maslow, *Toward a Psychology of Being,* D. Van Nostrand, Princeton, New Jersey, 1968, pp. 21–59.

Page 11. See Rollo May, *The Courage to Create,* Bantam, New York, 1976, pp. 125, 127.

CHAPTER TWO

Page 14. See *Publishers Weekly,* April 9, 1979.

CHAPTER THREE

Page 37. See Ellen Moers, *Literary Women,* Doubleday, Garden City, New York, 1977, 138–151. The quote from *Frankenstein* is on p. 142 of *Literary Women.*

Page 46. See "Wondering If Children Are Necessary," by Lance Morrow, *Time* Magazine, March 5, 1979, p. 47. For Betty Rollin's article, "Motherhood—Who Needs It?" see *Look* Magazine, September 22, 1970, pp. 15–17.

Page 56. The family sculpting technique was developed by family therapist Peggy Papp, who teaches at the Philadelphia Child Guidance ᑤ·nter and the Ackerman Family Institute in New York City. It is ᴎsed in family therapy to enable each family member to demonstrate ˙˙ ᵐn view of his family.

CHAPTER FOUR

Page 61. See Murray Bowen, *Family Therapy in Clinical Practice,* Jason Aronson, New York, 1978.

Page 65. See Mel Roman and Patricia Raley, *The Indelible Family,* Rawson, Wade, New York, 1980, pp. 5, 48.

Page 65. Nancy Kaltreider and Alan Margolis found that child-free women had had poor relationships with their mothers. See "Childless by Choice: A Clinical Study," *American Journal of Psychiatry,* February, 1977.

The idea that child-free persons may be acting out their parents' unconscious wishes was expressed by psychiatrist E. James Anthony in Rita Kramer, "The No-Child Family," *The New York Times Magazine,* December 24, 1972.

One study finding no differences in the childhood/parenting experiences of parents and child-free persons is Harold Feldman's "Three Perspectives on Parents and Childless Couples." Unpublished article, 1978. The work of Teicholz and of Campbell, Converse and Rodgers (see Suggested Reading—Technical, Appendix B), finding no differences in the mental health of parents and child-free persons, also suggests that child-free persons' childhoods were not significantly different from parents'.

Page 69. See Marilyn Fabe and Norma Wikler, *Up Against the Clock,* Random House, New York, 1979, p. 194.

Page 81. See Sharon Houseknecht, "Reference Group Support for Voluntary Childlessness: Evidence for Conformity," in *Journal of Marriage and the Family,* vol. 39, May 1977.

Page 83. Manuel Smith was the first to describe what he calls "fogging" and I call "dodging" in *When I Say No I Feel Guilty,* Bantam, New York, 1975.

Page 84. "Why Does It Matter to You?" is adapted from the Negative Inquiry technique described by Manuel Smith in *When I Say No I Feel Guilty* (see above), pp. 120–132.

CHAPTER FIVE

Page 94. The $100,000 estimate was mentioned by Caroline Bird in *The Two-Paycheck Marriage,* Pocket Books, New York, 1979, p. 198.

Page 106. Emerson's statement is quoted in *The International Thesaurus of Quotations,* compiled by Rhoda Thomas Tripp, T. Y. Crowell, New York, 1970, p. 107.

CHAPTER SIX

Page 108. The Sherrye Henry quote is from a personal communication, December 5, 1979.

Page 109. See Betty Friedan, "Feminism Takes a New Turn," *New York Times Magazine,* November 18, 1979.

The conference mentioned was entitled "The National Assembly on the Future of the Family," and was convened by the N.O.W. Legal Defense and Education Fund.

Page 111. The Carol Nadelson quote is from a personal communication, December 12, 1979.

Page 112. Nina Finkelstein is quoted from a personal communication, December 12, 1979.

Page 112. See Betty Friedan, "The Second Stage," *Redbook,* January, 1980.

Page 113. See the Boston Women's Health Book Collective's two books: *Our Bodies, Ourselves,* Simon and Schuster, New York, 1976; and *Ourselves and Our Children,* Random House, New York, 1978.

Regarding lifelines to new mothers, the next best thing to a mothers' group is Angela Barron McBride's *The Growth and Development of Mothers,* Barnes and Noble, New York, 1973. This wonderful book has lifted dozens of my clients out of guilt and depression.

Page 114. See Alice Abarbanel, "Redefining Motherhood," in *The Future of the Family,* edited by Louise Kapp Howe, Simon and Schuster, New York, 1972, p. 359.

Page 114. Regarding reading feminist literature while tied down with young children, see Alice Abarbanel, above, also Angela Barron McBride, *Living With Contradictions: A Married Feminist,* Harper and Row, New York, 1977.

Page 115. The generativity concept is from Erik Erikson, *Identity, Youth and Crisis,* W. W. Norton, New York, pp. 138–139.

Page 116. See Adrienne Rich, *Of Woman Born,* Bantam, New York, 1977, p. 256.

Page 117. See Wendy Coppedge Sanford's introduction to *Ourselves and Our Children* (see above) pp. 11, 14.

Page 118. Jean Baker Miller is quoted from a personal communication, February 23, 1980.

Erica Jong is quoted from a personal communication, January 16, 1980.

Page 119. See Charlotte Perkins Gilman, *Herland.* Pantheon, New York, 1979. Also see "The Yellow Wallpaper" in *The Charlotte Perkins Gilman Reader,* Pantheon, New York, 1980.

CHAPTER SEVEN

Page 127. See Gail Sheehy, *Passages,* Bantam, New York, 1977.

Page 128. See Robert Jay Lifton regarding the importance of facing death in order to live fully, *Boundaries,* Random House, New York, 1969. The quote on natural immortality is from page 23.

See also Ernest Becker, *The Denial of Death,* The Free Press, New York, 1973.

Page 129. See Martin Buber, *Hasidism and Modern Man,* Harper Torchbooks, New York, 1958, pp. 139–140.

Page 130. See Abraham Maslow, *The Farther Reaches of Human Nature,* Penguin, New York, 1971. The Jonah complex is defined on p. 34 and explained on the following pages.

Page 133. See Erich Fromm, *Escape from Freedom,* Avon, New York, 1965.

Pages 136–137. See Jane Howard, *Families,* New York, Simon and Schuster, 1978. She described the intensity of ties in "chosen" families on pp. 237–241. She lists the characteristics of successful families on pp. 241–245.

Page 140. The first four points about happiness are documented in *The Quality of American Life: Perceptions, Evaluations and Satisfactions* by Angus Campbell, Philip A. Converse, and Willard L. Rodgers, Russell Sage Foundation, New York, 1976. Also Harold Feldman, "The Effects of Children on the Family" in Andrée Michel, ed., *Family Issues of Employed Women in Europe and America,* E. J. Brill, Leiden, The Netherlands, 1971. Researchers interested in further documentation should refer to Suggested Reading, Technical, Appendix B.

Page 140. The nationwide study of parents' beliefs that children had contributed to their marital satisfaction can be found in Anthony Pietropinto and Jacqueline Simenauer, *Husbands and Wives, a National Survey of Marriage,* Times Books, New York, 1979, p. 198.

Page 140. The apparent relationship between marital happiness and successfully controlled fertility is described by Harold T. Christensen in "Children in the Family: Relationship of Number and Spacing to Marital Success," *Journal of Marriage and Family,* Vol. 30, May, 1968. See also Andrée Michel, and François L. Feyrabend, "Real Number of Children and Conjugal Interaction in French Urban Families," *Journal of Marriage and the Family,* Vol. 31, May 1969.

Chapter Eight

Some interesting research has been done on couples who conflict on the baby decision. See Pamela E. Cooper, Barbara Cumber, and Robin Hartner, "Decision-making Patterns and Post-decision Adjustment of Child-free Husbands and Wives," *Alternative Lifestyles,* Vol. 1, February, 1978.

See also Teresa Donati Marciano, "Male Pressure in the Decision to Remain Child-free," *Alternative Lifestyles,* Vol. 1, February, 1978 and, by the same author, "Male Influence on Fertility: Needs for Research," *The Family Coordinator,* October, 1979.

Page 145. The Clark Moustakas quote is from his book *Creative Life,* D. Van Nostrand, New York, 1977, p. 42.

Page 145. See Martin Buber, *I and Thou,* translated by Ronald Gregor Smith, Charles Scribner's Sons, New York, 1958.

CHAPTER NINE

Page 169. See Gail Sheehy, *Passages,* Bantam, New York, 1977, pp. 340–341.

Page 223. According to Victor Berman, M.D. and Salee Berman, RN, there is a 1% chance of miscarriage after amniocentesis, which may accidentally puncture the placenta, umbilical cord, or fetus. See their article, "Who Runs a Higher Risk? A Consultation About Childbearing After 30," in *The Pregnancy After 30 Workbook,* edited by Gail Sforza Brewer, Rodale, Emmaus, Pa., 1978, p. 17.

The limits of amniocentesis' predictive powers is documented by Jane Price in *You're Not Too Old to Have a Baby,* New York, Penguin, 1977, p. 69. See also Pamela Daniels and Kathy Weingarten, "A New Look at the Medical Risks in Late Childbearing," *Women and Health,* Vol. 4, Spring 1979, p. 30.

Page 171. For more information on the influence of prolonged contraceptive use on later fertility, see Daniels and Weingarten (above) pp. 19–20 and Price (above) pp. 56–58.

For documentation of the fertility problems that may result from venereal disease or abortion, see Daniels and Weingarten, pp. 18, 20–21, and Price, p. 58.

Page 172. Albert Decker's suggestion of fertility check-ups for couples delaying parenthood may be found in Jane Price (above), pp. 58–59.

Page 172. Sherwin Kaufman's statement can be found in Jane Price, p. 59.

Page 186. See Toni Ihara and Ralph Warner, "Making Illegitimacy Legitimate," April, 1979.

Page 188. See Sharryl Hawke and David Knox, *One Child by Choice,* Prentice Hall, Englewood Cliffs, New Jersey, 1977.

Page 188. See *Margaret Mead, Some Personal Views,* edited by Rhoda Metraux, Walker and Company, New York, 1979, pp. 65–66, and *Passages,* p. 340.

Page 190. The Mama and Papa bird quote is from Sharryl Hawke and David Knox, "The One-Child Family: A New Life-Style," *The Family Coordinator,* July 1978, p. 217.

Page 193. The recommendation that potential stepfamilies get premarital counseling comes from Ruth Roosevelt and Jeannette Lofas, *Living in Step,* Stein and Day, Briarcliff Manor, New York, 1976, p. 27.

CHAPTER ELEVEN

Page 210. Increased enjoyment of sexual relations following sterilization has been reported by Betty Gonzales, "Psychosexual Aftermath of Voluntary Sterilization," *Advances in Planned Parenthood,* Vol. 14, 1980.

The Gonzales study also reports child-free women's new burst of creativity and commitment after sterilization.

Pages 210–211. Research studies about child-free persons getting sterilized in their twenties include George C. Denniston, "The Effect of Vasectomy on Child-free Men," paper presented at the International Family Planning Association, Beverly Hills, CA, October, 1976, available from NAOP.

See also Nancy B. Kaltreider and Alan B. Margolis, "Childless by Choice: A Clinical Study," *American Journal of Psychiatry,* Vol. 134, February 1977.

The Betty Rollin quote is from personal communication, December 10, 1979.

Page 211. The Carol Nadelson quote is from a personal communication, December 12, 1980.

Page 211. See Erik Erikson, *Identity, Youth, and Crisis,* W.W. Norton, New York, 1968, pp. 138–139.

Page 212. Maxine Ravech is quoted from my interview with her on February 28, 1980.

CHAPTER TWELVE

Page 222. The mother describing herself as a gardener was quoted by Letty Cottin Pogrebin in "Motherhood!" *Ms,* May 1973.

Page 223. Margaret Fuller is quoted from *Summer on the Lakes* in *The International Thesaurus of Quotations,* compiled by Rhoda Thomas Tripp, T. Y. Crowell, New York, 1970, p. 454.

Page 225. See Doris Lessing, "To Room Nineteen" in *Women and Fiction,* edited by Susan Cahill, New American Library, 1975, p. 204.

Page 226. See Angela Barron McBride, *The Growth and Development of Mothers*, Barnes and Noble, New York, 1973, p. 141.

Page 226. Nin is quoted from *The Book of Quotes*, compiled by Barbara Rowes, E. P. Dutton, New York, 1979.

Page 229. See Arlene Rossen Cardozo, *Woman At Home*, Harcourt, Brace, Jovanovich, New York, 1976, p. 125.

Page 230. Susan Rawlings' insight is from Doris Lessing, "To Room Nineteen," in *Women and Fiction* (above) pp. 198–199.

CHAPTER THIRTEEN

Page 232. Nina Finkelstein is quoted from a personal communication, December 12, 1979.

Pages 232–233. See Ellen Goodman, "Crossing the Great 'Despite,' " *Boston Globe*, April 10, 1979.

Page 234. See Letty Cottin Pogrebin, "Motherhood!" *Ms*, May 1973.

Page 235. Sherrye Henry is quoted from a personal communication, December 5, 1979.

Page 236. The research on couple adjustment to their first child is from Carolyn Pape Cowan, "How a Couple Become a Family," *Redbook*, September 1978. Social scientists and psychotherapists will want to read the more technical report of the research project: Carolyn Pape Cowan, Philip A. Cowan, Lynne Coie, and John D. Coie, "Becoming a Family: The Impact of a First Child's Birth on the Couple's Relationship," in *The First Child and Family Formation*, Warren B. Miller and Lucile F. Newman, editors, Carolina Population Center, Chapel Hill, North Carolina, 1978.

Pages 236–237. The pleasure men are finding in fatherhood is reported in "Choices Today's Men Must Make," *Boston Globe*, October 21, 1979; in Gail Sheehy, "Introducing the Postponing Generation," *Esquire*, October 1979, and James Levine, *Who Will Raise the Children?* J. B. Lippincott, Philadelphia, 1976.

See Ellen Goodman, "Being a Grateful Wife Means Always Having to Ask," *Boston Globe*, December 11, 1979.

Page 238. See Nancy Press Hawley, "Sharing Parenthood," in *Ourselves and Our Children*, Random House, New York, 1978, p. 139.

The wife-as-domestic-consultant idea is from Caryl Rivers, Rosalind Barnett, and Grace Baruch, *Beyond Sugar and Spice*, G. P. Putnam, 1979, pp. 41–42.

Page 241. Exciting new research about the intensity of fathers' and babies' attachments to each other are reported in Martin Greenberg and Norman Morris, "Engrossment: The Newborn's Impact Upon the Father," *American Journal of Orthopsychiatry*, Vol. 44, July 1974 and in Milton Kotelchuck, "The Infant's Relationship to the Father: Experimental Evidence," in *The Role of the Father in Child Development,* ed. Michael E. Lamb, Wiley, New York, 1978.

Page 241. See David Steinberg, "Redefining Fatherhood: Notes After Six Months," in *The Future of the Family,* edited by Louise Kapp Howe, Simon and Schuster, New York, 1972, p. 377.

Nancy Press Hawley is quoted from "Sharing Parenthood" in *Ourselves and Our Children,* The Boston Women's Health Book Collective, Random House, New York, p. 130.

Page 244. For studies reporting no ill effects on children in full-time day care, see Lois Wladis Hoffman and Francis Ivan Nye, "Working Mothers: An Evaluative Review of the Consequences for Wife, Husband and Child." Jossey-Bass, San Francisco, 1974.

See also Mary C. Howell, "Effects of Maternal Employment on the Child," *Pediatrics,* Vol. 52, September 1973, and also by Howell, "Employed Mothers and Their Families," *Pediatrics,* Vol. 52, August 1973, and A. E. Siegal and M. B. Hass, "The Working Mother: A Review of Research," *Child Development,* 1963.

Page 252. See Ellen Goodman, "Crossing the Great 'Despite,'" *Boston Globe,* April 10, 1979.

Page 253. See Erica Jong, "Creativity versus Generativity, the Unexamined Lie" in *The New Republic,* January 13, 1979 and Tillie Olsen, *Silences,* Delacorte, New York, 1978.

APPENDIX D

Page 279. See Gail Thoen, "The Parenthood Option: A Manual for Professionals Helping People Decide Whether to Have Children or Remain Child-free." NAOP, Washington, 1979. This manual has many helpful suggestions for workshop planning.

INDEX